Negotiating relief and freedom

Manchester University Press

STUDIES IN IMPERIALISM

When the 'Studies in Imperialism' series was founded by Professor John M. MacKenzie more than thirty years ago, emphasis was laid upon the conviction that 'imperialism as a cultural phenomenon had as significant an effect on the dominant as on the subordinate societies'. With well over a hundred titles now published, this remains the prime concern of the series. Cross-disciplinary work has indeed appeared covering the full spectrum of cultural phenomena, as well as examining aspects of gender and sex, frontiers and law, science and the environment, language and literature, migration and patriotic societies, and much else. Moreover, the series has always wished to present comparative work on European and American imperialism, and particularly welcomes the submission of books in these areas. The fascination with imperialism, in all its aspects, shows no sign of abating, and this series will continue to lead the way in encouraging the widest possible range of studies in the field. 'Studies in Imperialism' is fully organic in its development, always seeking to be at the cutting edge, responding to the latest interests of scholars and the needs of this ever-expanding area of scholarship.

General editors:
Andrew Thompson, Professor of Global and Imperial History at Nuffield College, Oxford
Alan Lester, Professor of Historical Geography at University of Sussex and LaTrobe University

Founding editor:
Emeritus Professor John M. MacKenzie

Robert Bickers, University of Bristol
Christopher L. Brown, Columbia University
Pratik Chakrabarti, University of Houston
Elizabeth Elbourne, McGill University
Bronwen Everill, University of Cambridge
Kate Fullagar, Australian Catholic University
Chandrika Kaul, University of St Andrews
Dane Kennedy, George Washington University
Shino Konishi, Australian Catholic University
Philippa Levine, University of Texas at Austin
Kirsten McKenzie, University of Sydney
Tinashe Nyamunda, University of Pretoria
Dexnell Peters, University of the West Indies
Sujit Sivasundaram, University of Cambridge
Angela Wanhalla, University of Otago
Stuart Ward, University of Copenhagen

To buy or to find out more about the books currently available in this series, please go to: https://manchesteruniversitypress.co.uk/series/studies-in-imperialism/

Negotiating relief and freedom

Responses to disaster in the British Caribbean, 1812–1907

Oscar Webber

MANCHESTER UNIVERSITY PRESS

Copyright © Oscar Webber 2023

The right of Oscar Webber to be identified as the author of this work has been asserted in accordance with the Copyright, Designs and Patents Act 1988.

Published by Manchester University Press
Oxford Road, Manchester M13 9PL

www.manchesteruniversitypress.co.uk

British Library Cataloguing-in-Publication Data
A catalogue record for this book is available from the British Library

ISBN   978 1 5261 6039 3   hardback
ISBN   978 1 5261 9486 2   paperback

First published 2023
Paperback published 2026

The publisher has no responsibility for the persistence or accuracy of URLs for any external or third-party internet websites referred to in this book, and does not guarantee that any content on such websites is, or will remain, accurate or appropriate.

EU authorised representative for GPSR:
Easy Access System Europe – Mustamäe tee 50,
10621 Tallinn, Estonia
gpsr.requests@easproject.com

Typeset
by New Best-set Typesetters Ltd

Contents

Acknowledgements	*page* vi
List of abbreviations	viii
Introduction	1
1 Disaster and providence	18
2 Passing visitors	42
3 'Aid' in the absence of freedom	74
4 'Freedom', decline and fear	99
5 Practical sympathy	137
Conclusion	172
Bibliography	180
Index	191

Acknowledgements

First and foremost, this book is dedicated to Brenda Webber who made my pursuit of postgraduate education possible.

No project of this size is ever a solely individual endeavour and from its very inception, I have received help and guidance in putting this book together and in conducting the research it is based on. I must thank my partner Josephina Worrall who has, and continues to patiently read, edit and proofread just about everything I have written. In this respect, I must also thank Hannah Wilmore for a fruitful writing exchange in which she also read many early drafts of this book's chapters, providing useful and thoughtful feedback at every stage. There are also many colleagues at the various institutions I have worked and studied at who must be thanked. At the London School of Economics, early drafts of chapters, and later the full manuscript were read by Tom Ellis and Imaobong Umoren who provided much thoughtful feedback and encouragement. I want to also thank the staff and community at the Centre for Latin American and Caribbean Studies (CLACS) where I was a Fellow in 2022. The fellowship was integral to completing the final pieces of research for the project but also to providing me with the space and time to finish the manuscript. I am grateful to those who attended our seminars and listened to my presentation of the work and gave their invaluable feedback. The research for this book was partly conducted with assistance from Anya Anim-Addo and Malcolm Chase for whose help I am grateful. Malcolm spent much time encouraging me to believe more in my own abilities as a scholar. Were he still with us, he would probably be resistant to being mentioned here, feeling it unnecessary and in some taking away from my achievements; nonetheless, Malcolm was an important mentor in my life, and I did not feel he could go unmentioned. I also must thank Adrian Rotheray and Franco Picco who, for the best part of ten years, provided their house, countless meals and an array of baked goods that have powered me through lengthy sessions in The National

Archives all the way from my first undergraduate research project through to this book. Finally, I want to thank my parents for inspiring in me a love of both history and ecology that has blended together into a passion for environmental history.

Abbreviations

HoC – House of Commons
PP – Parliamentary Papers
TNA – The National Archives
WIC – West India Committee
WIR – West India Regiment

Introduction

When the sun set on the island of Barbados on 10 August 1831, the weather had already begun to portend an eventful night. From five o'clock onwards the horizon was said to resemble an 'impenetrable body' of 'dismal blackness'.[1] As the night progressed there was a moment of calm as rising winds cleared the sky. However, at midnight, when the sky was sundered by lightning, and thunder reverberated throughout Bridgetown, the island's capital, that calm was revealed to be a momentary pause. At two o'clock in the morning, the storm reached its apex, as a hurricane passed over the island. When the morning sun finally broke through the clouds at ten o'clock the following morning, an eyewitness remarked that the 'whole face of the country was laid waste'.[2] The strength of the hurricane that passed over the island that night was such that it was said to have shaken the very foundations of the island, with some residents reportedly experiencing an earthquake simultaneous to the storm. Regardless of the veracity of these reports, in just eight hours, an estimated 1,787 people were killed and the capital and property throughout the island were demolished.

For those who survived the night, however, their hardships were far from over. The hurricane had not only destroyed shelters of all descriptions throughout the island, but had ripped both sugarcane and subsistence crops from the ground. Surviving crops soon began to rot in the deluge of rain and mud that followed the storm. Starvation and exposure threatened to increase the number of casualties. And yet, despite the desperation and the losses felt across the spectrum of Barbadian society, mutual aid and cooperation were not forthcoming. In fact, if anything, the hurricane and its aftermath sharpened the already colossal racial divides of Barbadian society. The island, like the majority of British colonies in the early nineteenth-century Caribbean, was an island on which a white minority exercised a near totalising grip over the lives of an African-Caribbean population enslaved to provide plantation labour. The hurricane of 1831, coming as it did when the island's white minority felt attacked by a resurgent abolitionist movement back in Britain and threatened by an enslaved population increasingly agitating for their freedom, provoked a violent and regressive response from the island's authorities. As the enslaved population began migrating from the plantations to the island's capital in search of food and shelter, the island's governor and its planter-dominated assembly, fearing a challenge to their authority, rewrote existing laws to harshen the punishments for 'looting' and 'vagrancy'. To police the enslaved population and enforce these punishments, an armed militia was dispatched around the island. In the aftermath of the disaster, planters and colonial officials worked primarily, not to ameliorate suffering, but in the flux created by disaster, to restore a racialised 'order' in which they sat at the top, while the African-Caribbean population were fixed at the bottom, in the position of labourer.

Though informed both by planters' ever-present fear of a rebellion by the enslaved population and, more broadly, of contemporary political developments in Britain, the colonial response to the hurricane of 1831 was not a unique aberration. Instead, it stands as broadly representative of a pattern of disaster response that was exhibited in the region throughout the period 1812–1907 transcending the end of formalised, coerced labour in 1838.

Disasters suspended normality and in doing so created the circumstances for a complex set of formal and informal negotiations as the white minority strove towards returning it. With the physical manifestations of their power destroyed – plantations, barracks and later police stations – they sought to curtail movement and narrow the already narrow aperture of permissible conduct for the enslaved. When slavery ended, much like the apprenticeship system that followed, disaster saw whites use coercion, violence and threats to again find ways to control and limit the legal freedom of the African-Caribbean population. However, they were caught in a bind: the material realities of disaster meant that they could not simply oppress their way back to normality. To return the enslaved, later the so-called 'labouring classes', back to work they needed food, shelter and medical aid. Thus a careful, informal negotiation took place between these groups as whites balanced reasserting their authority against the reality of disasters, their aftermath and the anger which they might provoke.

Once their concerns about 'order' were allayed, the white elites of the Caribbean still did not entirely have a free hand; they themselves were frequently caught in much more protracted, formal negotiations with Parliament about financial aid, where they had to balance their desires to be made whole again against a Parliament reticent to sink money into colonies that over the nineteenth century were popularly perceived as having entered a terminal decline.

These negotiations, despite the unique insights they offer us onto life in the nineteenth-century Caribbean have received little sustained examination.

This book rectifies that and, in doing so, provides a new perspective on a period in which the region, on the face of it, went through fundamental changes not just in the organisation of labour and in its relationship with Britain. As we will see, however, disasters often forced a temporary but significant lapse in those small areas in which social progress had been made.

More broadly, this book seeks to develop an understanding of how Britain responded to disaster in its Empire. There have been excoriating examinations of Britain's actions during the Irish famine and successive famines in India.[3] But historians of the British Empire more broadly have tended to neglect the study of disaster response because, arguably, it has long been viewed reductively as a neutral process in which the suffering are fed, the dead are buried, and homes are rebuilt. By contrast, reflecting insights provided by scholars of more contemporary disasters, this book shows the extent to which disaster response is an inherently political act. Whose suffering is addressed, who lives, who dies, and whose losses are made whole again are all decisions those responding to disaster have to make, and they cannot make them free of prejudice. In this light, the book uncovers the environmental, racial and social prejudices that informed the decisions of those responding to disaster on the islands of the British Caribbean.

As a result, in this book there is an effort to differentiate between disaster response and disaster relief. I have used disaster response to refer to the broad range of actions white elites and the colonial state pursued after disasters. Disaster relief refers specifically to acts in which relief, of a kind, was provided. I made this choice of phrasing because to frame the book solely around relief felt both limiting and anachronistic. It felt limiting because much of the way in which white elites and the state responded to disasters cannot be conceived as part of a process of relief. Though genuine relief activities, such as the distribution of provisions and clothing did take place, British responses were also often directly antagonistic towards the African-Caribbean population. Relief, when it was provided, was a negotiated process and often occurred simultaneously with violence and coercion perpetrated by colonial officers and plantation owners who sought the restoration of 'order'.

I also felt that framing the book solely around 'disaster relief' felt somewhat anachronistic because today the phrase is generally used to describe the actions of modern states and non-governmental organisations. Both these entities typically provide relief on the basis of codified principles and have set responses for different types of disasters. Given this, I felt using the phrase 'disaster relief' to describe all the actions undertaken by the British risked giving the erroneous impression that they had a formal, codified approach to providing relief. In fact, what this book shows is that despite near annual disasters, British responses to them, though they followed certain patterns, were for the most part ad-hoc. Governors and their subordinates received little, if any, formal guidance on how to respond to the different hazards of the Caribbean. For me, early into my research in this area, this quickly raised the question why, if disasters occurred with frequency, did the British engage in little planning for them? I argue that, at its broadest level, the answer lies with the primary motivations underpinning the colonial project in the region.

Throughout its existence, the expansion of the British Empire was driven by many factors. One of them stands out clearly from the inception of the imperial project: colonisation was driven in large part by a desire to enrich England as it was then, and later Britain. An insatiable hunger for valuable raw materials, the drawing up of unequal trade agreements and the securing of monopolies were all hallmarks of British colonisation in the seventeenth, eighteenth and early nineteenth centuries, and reflect the fact that men set out from Britain to increase their own wealth and, by extension, Britain's wealth. I would argue, nowhere more clearly did these desires shape the pattern of colonisation than in the British Caribbean colonies.

The jungles of many of the Caribbean islands were the first to fall in this quest for wealth. Beginning with St Kitts in 1623 and then Barbados in 1627, British colonisers began intensive deforestation of the Caribbean islands, clearing ground not just for subsistence agriculture but also to explore the possibilities for growing exotic export crops in the tropical climate. On Barbados, for example, there followed experiments with growing tobacco and cotton, but these failed; Barbadian tobacco, in particular, was poorly regarded compared to competitors from the American colonies.[4] In the 1640s, following a period of technological exchange with Dutch colonists in Pernambuco (now situated in modern-day Brazil), sugarcane emerged as the most promising crop for the developing plantations. With Barbados acting as a part model for the rest of the British colonies in the region, sugar monocultures were planted with rapidity.

Intensive monoculture came with an enormous environmental and human cost. The Caribbean islands began a rapid transformation that would end with them effectively becoming large factories focused almost entirely on producing crops for export. Once jungle had been cut back and land burnt and levelled, the advantages of the Caribbean's fertile soils and year-round heat were unlocked, providing all the necessary ingredients for those seeking to make a profit from sugar, coffee and other commodities. However, the region's environment, as much as it presented opportunity, also presented serious dangers and thus obstacles to the extraction of wealth. Diseases such as yellow fever decimated the Irish prisoners of war, indentured servants and transported vagrants initially sent to work these new plantations.

Searching for a steady supply of 'disposable' labour the British, taking inspiration from both the Dutch in Brazil and the Portuguese experiments in plantation agriculture off the coast of Africa, turned to the enslavement of Africans to provide the labour to work the plantations.

As the model of trafficking African people across the Atlantic to the Caribbean was adopted wholesale to expand the plantations, many whites in the Caribbean islands made immense fortunes. The fact remained, however, that the Caribbean was still a dangerous environment for both British and African people, and money offered little protection from disease or the impacts of natural hazards such as hurricanes, earthquakes and volcanic eruptions.

Disease presented risk for both people of African descent and British people in the Caribbean, but the burden of mortality primarily fell on the enslaved, who were often forced to work themselves to death or suffered appalling nutrition and/or a range of injuries that made them more vulnerable to all of the above. By contrast, whites were able to afford some medical care – rudimentary though it was – and otherwise convalesce or simply return to Britain.

The natural hazards of the region presented unique risks not only to individual lives but also to the very foundations of British colonialism in the region. Hurricanes, earthquakes and volcanic eruptions destroyed the plantation buildings, the barracks and the government buildings, which were all seen by the British as intrinsic not just to the extraction of wealth but to the survival of their control. These buildings were essential tools in the arsenal that whites – always in the minority – used to exert their control. They were pillars of the regimes of spatial and temporal discipline instituted by slavery and, later, after emancipation, wage labour. Disasters disrupted these regimes and they drove African-Caribbeans from the plantations, halting labour and production. Thus, even with the end of coerced labour in 1838, the temporary suspension of labour and production still occasioned great anxiety in the white minority. Under the guise of both making African-Caribbean people 'fit' for freedom and protecting their own interests, whites still saw it as their place to dominate and control their lives.

Investigating responses to disasters triggered by the natural phenomena of the Caribbean is valuable but also distinct from the excellent work that has been done on disease in the region. Hurricanes, earthquakes and volcanic eruptions exposed different tensions from outbreaks of disease because the scale of the physical destruction they wrought nearly always necessitated the need for external help. Here, disasters of the kind considered in this book give us new insights into the relationship between the Caribbean colonies and Britain, and how it changed over the course of the long nineteenth century. Negotiations between planters, colonial officials and Parliament reveal just how the Caribbean declined in importance to the Empire as slavery ended and the plantation model faltered.

Studying these disasters and the negotiations around relief also gives us insights into how domestic ideas about the state's role in providing welfare – something that went through its own transformation in the nineteenth century – were transmitted to and then mutated in its colonies. Providing food, shelter and, at times, financial relief was necessary to restore profit-making industry, but it chafed against dominant elite ideas, embodied in Parliament, the Colonial Office and thus the officials it despatched, about reining in the state's role in the provision of welfare. This conflict was further intensified by the fact that the Caribbean's commonly envisioned role within the imperial design was solely as a net contributor to Britain's coffers. For a nation that frequently debated the distinction between the 'deserving' and the 'underserving' poor these concerns were further complicated by race; by virtue of the demographic trends Britain had created, relief was often needed en masse for African-Caribbean people. All of this conflicted not just with Britain's contemporary racial politics, but also with a tradition of punitive and conditional relief that had long been at the heart of the British state approach to domestic welfare.

From the formalising of the workhouse system in 1723 through to the New Poor Law Amendment of 1834 and beyond, the British state approach to welfare was one that stressed an individual's capacity to work as the key determiner of their eligibility for relief. Historians who have investigated British famine relief in Ireland and India have shown that in the nineteenth century this principle was not only deployed to the colonies but intensified during times of need. In both countries, public works programmes were set up to force starving individuals to labour to earn food. Yet, in contrast to famines, the acute hazards of the Caribbean nearly always destroyed the central sites of labour. The British could not send the enslaved and later labouring class elsewhere; forced to improvise, white elites made food and materials for shelter contingent on the African-Caribbean population working to reconstruct the buildings that facilitated their oppression. Disasters thus not only broaden our understanding of how these colonies functioned in crisis and the latitude afforded to white elites, but also serve as an important reminder that the injustices and prejudices of slavery persisted long into the era of emancipation.

The temporal boundaries of this study were defined both in respect to the existing research in this area, the scale and timing of the disasters themselves, and the resultant archival traces they left. The earliest disaster examined in this book is the eruption of La Soufrière on St Vincent in 1812.

This starting point was chosen because Matthew Mulcahy, in his book, *Hurricanes and Society in the British Caribbean, 1624–1783*, has already expertly surveyed disasters in the seventeenth and eighteenth centuries ending with a study of the so-called 'Great Hurricane' of 1780. Now, between 1780 and 1812, the British Caribbean certainly faced hurricanes and other natural hazards, but the impacts do not seem to have been large enough to have left any significant traces in the archives and thus studying them provides little insight into British responses to disaster. Consequently, the eruption of 1812, unprecedented (for British colonists) in its scale, sparked a great flurry of communication across the Atlantic and occasioned many eyewitness accounts. The last disasters considered in this book are the 1902 eruption of La Soufrière and the 1907 Jamaican Earthquake. They both prevent the book from being neatly framed as a study of the nineteenth century, but their inclusion felt essential because British responses to these events highlight its declining power and influence in the region, something which in many ways represents a conclusion to the themes examined throughout the book. British colonies, of course, suffered disasters after 1907 – the category-five hurricane that hit Belize in 1931 was the next severe one – but the outbreak of the First World War and the depression that followed inaugurated a new era in the Caribbean, one not entirely separate from that which went before, but one that had distinct political and social constellations outside of the scope of this book.

The period 1812–1907 presents a fascinating study because it is the period in which the Caribbean, both in the organisation of labour and in the balance of colonial power, went through fundamental change. From its outset, slavery had always been contested by the enslaved, but after the ending of the transatlantic slave trade in 1807 and with full emancipation seeming – to planters in particular – all but inevitable by the late 1820s, the stage was set for the next major conflict between these two groups. As soon as emancipation was even an outside possibility, planters and colonial officials began to express anxiety over how they might control and retain the labour of African-Caribbean people on the plantations. Cut off from a supply of labour they had once inhumanely treated as inexhaustible, white elites also became preoccupied with trying to stabilise and intervene in the reproduction of the African-Caribbean population. By the end of the nineteenth century, new approaches to welfare did emerge. They were significantly developed, but not entirely divorced from their antecedents. Ultimately, legal freedom created great antagonism between the African-Caribbean people attempting to exercise it and the white elites desperate to carry on the patterns of exploitation that had enriched them before emancipation.

This period was also one of significant scientific and political change. Telegraph cables were first laid between the islands of the British Caribbean during 1870–1872, followed by connections to the mainland Americas.[5] Communication with Europe was later possible, albeit indirectly, by the 1880s. These developments enabled comparatively rapid communication with London and, by extension, global print media about, amongst other things, disasters. Their impacts and the responses that followed quickly became events of international interest, placing British actions under a new level of scrutiny.

Significant developments also arrived in the form of America's expansion into the region following the ending of the Spanish War in 1898. America brought a zeal for technology that saw it acquire the Panama Canal Company and expand telegraphic links. Partly as a result of this, it also had a major effect on the geopolitics of the region, with its businesses acting as major poles in the migratory patterns of labourers. This growing influence came, as some British officials saw it, at the expense of British power and prestige. Their resultant sense of unease would go on to have significant implications for how they responded to disaster and how they sought to retain the goodwill of some Caribbean people.

This book can also be differentiated from much of the existing research in this area through its interdisciplinary approach. Some work has begun in this area with a similar approach such as Phillip D. Morgan's *Sea and Land: An Environmental History of the Caribbean* published in 2022.[6] The edited collection includes a chapter by Matthew Mulcahy and Stuart Schwartz specifically on 'natural disasters' in the Caribbean up to 1850. By virtue of its temporal framing, it comprises a survey of disasters and does not contain the granular detail on disaster response that occupies much of this book. Moreover, the chapter takes a broader survey of colonies, including those outside of the British Caribbean and includes a wider range of disasters. That said, it is a welcome contribution to this area of investigation, but this book still has a clear contribution to make to this very much emergent area of research. It situates the study of disaster responses within an examination of the relationship between the British and the Caribbean environment. It does this, I argue, because the way in which the British conceptualised the Caribbean and its role within the Empire deeply informed their responses to disasters. Colonists saw the region as being good for nothing but the growing and exporting of agricultural produce. A range of social and organisational practices arose as a product of this narrow view and, in turn, they had a role in creating a limited disaster response whose primary goal was to uphold racial hierarchy and quickly rebuild extractive industry.

In line with ideas emergent throughout the frontiers of the Empire, the British saw the Caribbean environment as a 'wilderness' that they had a

Introduction 9

duty to 'improve' through cultivation. This unremitting desire for cultivation and, by extension, profit undermined the self-sufficiency of the colonies rendering them more vulnerable to environmental hazards. It also often dictated the size and scope of the financial aid Parliament was willing to provide. Understanding the relationship between the British and the Caribbean environment is essential to understanding the full range of factors informing the British responses to disaster.

A critical approach to disaster

This linkage between disaster response and the broader relationship the British had with the Caribbean's environment is very much informed by the scholarship that emerged from the early 2000s onwards from the discipline of Disaster Risk Reduction studies. Scholars in this area have tended to argue for a critical approach to disaster. At the most basic level, this means going beyond the traditional treatment of disasters as static backdrops to human activities. Typically, historians have considered disasters' destructive power as shapers of history but have largely written about them as events that act upon humans who are simply in the wrong place at the wrong time. This one-directional rendering of disaster reflects the fact that traditionally historians have tended to regard disasters as entirely natural events and have consequently left the human role in creating disaster underexamined.

In the 1960s and 1970s, a number of historians began to examine the reciprocal relationship between humans and their environment more closely. Within this field, some, such as Donald Worster in his ground-breaking study of the 1930s American Dust Bowl, began to elucidate the human role in creating disaster.[7] Worster argued that the Dust Bowl was not simply the product of declining rainfall, but rather the result of declining rainfall on an area that humans had over-farmed and deforested. In 1981, Amartya Sen published *Poverty and Famines*, where, in a similarly path-breaking manner, he argued that famines were not simply natural events but rather the products of human failures to respond adequately to drought.[8]

In more recent years, events such as Hurricane Katrina and the scholarship that has followed (a topic to which I will return) have made the link between human driven historical processes and the scale and often, uneven impact of natural hazards. In this scholarship, it is argued that disasters should be seen not as inherently natural but rather as the product of an interaction between hazards such as hurricanes, floods and earthquakes and human-created conditions. In this formulation, it is those conditions that are seen to be the key determinant of whether the impact of the natural hazard actually induces a disaster; a flood alone is not a disaster but when humans choose to build on a floodplain the stage for one is set. Firmly in agreement with this critical approach, this book not only incorporates this literature and its insights but also its technical terminology. In particular, it makes frequent use of 'vulnerability' and 'resilience'.

Vulnerability lacks a fixed definition, as different scholars have included different factors within its scope. For example, the United Nations define vulnerability as:

> Vulnerability is the potential for loss (human, physical, economic, natural, or social) due to a hazardous event. It is the characteristics and circumstances of a community, system or asset that make it susceptible to the damaging effects of a hazard.[9]

This definition is useful in that it accounts for the ways in which human-created conditions can exacerbate loss. However, this book is not just an exploration of the immediate effects of the impact of hazards; it is also concerned with the factors shaping disaster response and implementation of that response over time. In their foundational work on disaster study, *At Risk*, Blaike et al. define vulnerability as:

> The characteristics of a person or group and their situation that influence their capacity to anticipate, cope with, resist and *recover from the impact of a natural hazard*.[10]

This is more useful because, as emphasised here, it accounts for the temporal aspects of disaster response and recovery. As this book shows, the way in which Caribbean society was structured played a crucial role in lengthening the worst effects of both natural hazards and recovery.

While vulnerability is concerned with the ways in which societies are rendered more exposed to loss and less able to quickly recover, many societies do still manage to recover and rebuild in the wake of disasters; this is where the concept of resilience comes in. Resilience, in some ways the inverse of vulnerability, describes not only how well a society can withstand hazard impacts, but also how it adapts and changes in response. Resilience can cover a plethora of adaptations, from changing building materials to enhance their resistance against seismic shocks, to creating mutually beneficial social structures than encourage cooperation in rebuilding. To put this terminology into practice, we can return to the earlier example of a flood. Even with the obvious vulnerabilities associated with building on a floodplain, a flood in this situation does not have to become a disaster, as a well prepared and resilient society plans ahead for such events and can mitigate disaster.

We must also understand the ways in which human actions during disaster response can worsen the impacts of hazards. In 1976, Tangshan in China was hit by an earthquake that measured 7.6 on the Richter scale and reportedly resulted in the deaths of at least 240,000 people. Chairman Mao had always stressed the value of self-reliance and argued that foreign assistance would undermine Chinese dignity, and so the disaster response was one shaped by the slogan 'resist the earthquake and rescue ourselves'. The example of Tangshan also presents us with a clear example of the unique role the historian can play in the study of disaster; the Chinese state's response to the earthquake was indelibly shaped by the country's socio-political history, which the historian is well situated to contextualise. Along with other scholars such as Greg Bankoff, I would argue the historian's role in the study of disaster and response does not end there, however.[11] Historians can play a significant role in helping us to understand the historical processes that render certain people or societies more, or less, vulnerable and resilient to disaster.

Hurricane Katrina presents perhaps the clearest example of how historical processes can create both disaster and unequal distribution of impacts. When it hit the Gulf Coast of Louisiana in 2005, Katrina caused a severe storm surge that cracked flood protection levees in the city of New Orleans in fifty-three places, flooding large swathes of the city, killing 1,836 people and leaving thousands stranded without the basic necessities for life. Overwhelmingly, the people worst affected by the storm were the city's African-American population. But this was no coincidence, as the African-American population lived predominantly in the lowest lying areas of the city, which were the most vulnerable to flooding.

The reason why they overwhelmingly lived in this area can be explained, in large part, through the legacy of segregation in the city. African-Americans were segregated to that area of the city because it is where the cheapest, lowest-quality housing was located – housing in which the middle-class whites did not want to live in. The reason why that housing was so cheap is because it was known that this area of the city was vulnerable to flooding. In 1965, a storm surge following Hurricane Betsy breached levees in lower New Orleans, with the Lower Ninth Ward, where fifty-seven people were killed, experiencing some of the worst flooding. In 2005, this still predominantly African-American neighbourhood experienced some of the greatest devastation of any neighbourhood in the city, due to a series of what Carlton Waterhouse called 'failed plans and planned failures'.[12] In the case of Katrina and the population of the Lower Ninth Ward, their vulnerability was created over time, through a long history of racial injustice. Going beyond the idea of disasters as 'natural' and subsequently bringing out the role of historical processes in enhancing vulnerability is not only an integral part of campaigning for environmental justice but also offers a better chance of mitigating hazard impacts in the future.

The scope of the book

The first chapter of this book is divided into two halves. The first half looks at how British colonial society evolved in the Caribbean, from a number of settler colonies with tenuous footholds on a scattering of islands into one of the main wealth producers of the British Empire by the middle of the eighteenth century. It looks at how the plantations and slave labour came to be the central pillars around which these colonies were organised. The second half of the chapter looks at how in the seventeenth and eighteenth centuries this emergent and deeply unequal society encountered disaster. Specifically, it considers at how these threats were conceived of and prepared for by colonists and enslaved who already faced a multiplicity of other deadly hazards.

The second half of the chapter, by comparing British responses to the Jamaican earthquake of 1692 and the 'Great Hurricane' of 1780, argues that even though they were geographically separated from the European enlightenment, those in control of the Caribbean, connected as it was to the Empire, began to see its hazards less providentially and more scientifically, albeit a lot more slowly than those in Europe. Where prayer had been the primary response to what were considered visitations of God's wrath, disasters, interrupting trade and conflict as they regularly did, increasingly became seen as events in which individuals and, on occasion, the state, could intervene and mitigate.

The second chapter of this book explores the impact British colonialism had on the Caribbean environment. It argues that both the model of intensive plantation agriculture and the haphazard urban settlements that came to characterise British Caribbean society rendered the islands more vulnerable to the acute hazards considered in this book. It shows that these vulnerabilities – deforestation, the lack of self-sufficiency and the fragile inadequate construction of most Caribbean property, to name but a few – are not something historians can just observe with hindsight, but were readily raised by those who visited and lived in the Caribbean. Consequently, this chapter explores why these apparent vulnerabilities were never addressed and the societies engineered with so little resilience. It argues that, broadly speaking, because the British never saw the region as a place for permanent, developed white settlement they never deemed it worthwhile to invest the time, effort and capital there to build resilience.

Having established the social and organisational practices of the British Caribbean as well as having explored how colonists related to its environment, the third chapter of this book explores how these factors intersected with conceptions of race and the perceived 'natural' order of colonial society to fundamentally shape British responses to disaster in the era of slavery. It argues that, above all, the British response to disaster prioritised the restoration of the region's racial hierarchy and its extractive industry. To achieve this, colonial officials resorted to coercion and tactics informed by Britain's approach to domestic poor relief, and on occasion they also resorted to violence. The chapter also shows that, in the post-abolition era when planters felt increasingly caught between African-Caribbeans fighting for their freedom and hostile politics in Britain, more than ever they sought to use disaster as a crisis they could exploit to shore up the crumbling certainties of Caribbean life.

The fourth chapter looks at how British responses to disaster adapted to the post-emancipation era and at the unprecedented change that this brought with it. It argues that responses to disaster still retained their overwhelming focus on the restoration of order and productive industry, but shows that, if anything, the racial rhetoric deployed in this process displayed a marked intensification from the era of slavery. Crises created moments in which African-Caribbean people could truly test the boundaries of their freedom, and white elites, smarting from the loss of power occasioned by emancipation, were more concerned than ever about controlling and policing those limits. Simultaneously, as the nineteenth century progressed, it reflected a growing colonial preoccupation with managing the growth of the African-Caribbean population. The language and methods of British domestic poor relief were increasingly deployed in the Caribbean, both shaping and, crucially, limiting the distribution of relief.

The final chapter examines the long-term aspects of British responses to disaster. Specifically, it examines the relationship that planters and the colonial officials in the Caribbean had with the Colonial Office and Parliament. Notoriously indebted and working to increasingly shrinking margins as the nineteenth century progressed, Parliament was the primary port of call for planters looking to secure financial aid to rebuild disaster-stricken colonies. Yet, as this chapter shows, securing aid was never straightforward. Parliament was reticent to spend large sums of money on island colonies that over the course of the nineteenth century appeared to be diminishing not just in profitability but in their general importance to the Empire at large. By examining transatlantic correspondence and parliamentary debates, this chapter shows that those same perceptions of the Caribbean environment outlined in the first chapter, and the racial conceptions of order integral to the British responses outlined in the third and fourth chapters, played a large role in shaping and ultimately circumscribing the financial aid provided by Parliament. As the century came to its end, this chapter shows that Britain's declining influence in the Caribbean, along with increased media scrutiny, brought the geopolitics of disaster and the optics of British responses into a new harsh light.

Sources

Chapters 1 and 2 draw heavily on contemporary travel writing and natural histories of the Caribbean. Writing in these genres is often highly descriptive of people and places and thus provides unparalleled insight into how different groups related to the region's environment. What is particularly interesting is that these sources provide a window onto a kind of conflict of representation about the Caribbean and its environment. Those invested in the plantation economy often wrote in praise of the way cultivation had transformed the environment of the region, a genre of writing David Lambert has dubbed the 'plantation pastoral'. In his 1833 poem 'Barbados', Barbadian planter Matthew James Chapman wrote: 'Each trim plantation like a garden shines – Here waves the cane, there creep the nurturing vines.'[13]

By contrast, outside travellers to the region often remarked on its excessive cultivation, a critique that increased markedly with the emergence of the European romantic aesthetic that favoured an idealised vision of rugged uncultivated wildernesses. In 1835, Robert Madden, a traveller to the island that Chapman describes so idyllically wrote:

> I could see no beauty in this island. If rivers, mountains, and forests are necessary ingredients in the composition of a beautiful landscape, Barbadian scenery has no claim to picturesque attractions.[14]

Where Chapman saw the land as a verdant, cultivated garden, Madden saw an island stripped of its beauty by that very same cultivation.

Chapters 3, 4 and 5 are primarily based on Colonial Office records held at The National Archives in London and augmented by Hansard records of British parliamentary debates, Caribbean and international newspapers and, where possible, first-hand accounts from those who endured these events. Many of these records paint vivid and detailed pictures of these disasters, not just because they were shocking and traumatic events, but often because the planters and colonial officials writing them felt that providing such detailed accounts ensured them a greater chance of claiming financial aid from Parliament. It must be noted that they often exaggerated their accounts to give those back in London the impression that without generous and wide-ranging financial relief the very survival of the respective colony hung in the balance. Nonetheless, despite the exaggerations, these sources in concert with Hansard records, which provide the other side of the debate, provide us with some of the only records of these events.

There are, of course, drawbacks to these sources. The first and foremost of these is that they primarily comprise communications written by the white elites of the Caribbean and then responded to by white Colonial Office secretaries, Members of Parliament and other invested parties back in Britain. This obviously indelibly shapes the rhetoric of these sources and the perspectives they offer. It also complicates a study of this kind, because there are very few different perspectives to counterbalance them with. As Saidya Hartman once put it, the encounter with the archive of slavery is almost always an 'encounter with nothing', and that rings true in the records which detail the disasters examined in this book;[15] there are almost no surviving account of these events written by the African-Caribbean population. This absence could be for a number of reasons: education and literacy were denied to them for much of the nineteenth century due to fears that education would undermine white control; their accounts may not have been deemed worthy of being archived; or they may simply not have chosen to preserve their memories of these events in text.

The idea that memory and history is something conveyed solely through the written and printed word is a distinctly Western epistemological tradition. To this day, memory in the Caribbean continues to be passed down and preserved in varied non-textual forms such as folk songs, dances and stories. It is also worth considering that given that African-Caribbean people often suffered the greatest impact from disasters and endured the longest recovery from them, the very traumatic and disruptive nature of the disasters may have precluded this population from recording their experiences.

That said, just because the voices of the colonised are rarely present in these records, I think we should resist overcorrecting and avoid often well-meaning but ultimately ahistorical attempts to bestow 'agency'. We cannot accurately know how the African-Caribbean population felt about these events or how they felt about British responses to them. The least we can do, then, as Hartman encourages us to, is highlight the silences and the erasures in the archival record where they exist. In practice, this means being clear, particularly when examining actions taken against the subaltern or behaviour attributed to them, that there are no records detailing their experience that would allow us to counterbalance colonial observations.

Despite their obvious shortcomings, sources written by officials and planters do have worth, not least because in this case they largely comprise the only records of these events. To best use them, my approach is to read these sources, which consist largely of letters, reports and newspapers written by colonial officials and planters, both along and against the grain. It would be easy to form a ready-made conclusion that in a slaveholding society, disaster responses were always violent and antagonistic; these sources do reveal that there were complex nuances to British responses to disaster within which genuine relief giving did take place. However, reading against the grain means maintaining an awareness of the positionality of their authors. Colonial sources are interwoven with the multiplicity of observations and views inseparable from the crude racist worldview that underpinned the project of empire. For example, as Ranajit Guha observed, these documents often contain rhetorical 'sleights of hand', where petty crimes are reclassified as political subversion or, as is often the case in the sources used for this book, where the act of surviving and/or scavenging for food, provisions and material shelter is recast as 'looting'.[16] Highlighting these sleights of hand does not mean simply deciding when one thinks something does or does not constitute looting (to carry on that example), but rather by trying, as far as possible, to give a full picture of these events so that we might contextualise these classifications; so-called looting often took place in the context of widespread food shortages and in response to punitive action from colonial authorities that refused to distribute aid when it was needed.

The communications between the various Caribbean colonies and the Colonial Office that form the bulk of the material drawn on for this book evince a complex relationship in which governors, officials and planters are simultaneously postured to present themselves as capable of managing chaos and disruption while seeking to emphasise their losses in the hope of encouraging financial aid. By critically exploring these descriptive and at times emotive accounts of disaster this book expands our understanding not just of the British Caribbean in the long nineteenth century but also our understanding of British responses to disaster. It strips back modern, mainstream assumptions that historic disasters were moments in which 'atomized communities put divisions aside and pull[ed] together', and shows that in the British Caribbean, responses to disaster were fractured, violent and deeply informed by environmental, political and racial divisions.[17]

Notes

1 Editor of *The West Indian, Account of the Fatal Hurricane by Which Barbados Suffered in August 1831* (Barbados: Printed for Samuel Hyde, 1831), p. 33.
2 Ibid., p. 47.
3 See, for example, Mike Davis, *Late Victorian Holocausts: El Nino, Famines and the Making of the Third World* (London: Verso, 2000).
4 Franklin C. Knight, *Working the Diaspora: The Impact of African Labor on the Anglo-American World, 1650–1850* (New York: New York University Press, 2012), pp. 68–69.
5 Ken Beauchamp, *A History of Telegraphy* (London: The Institute of Engineering and Technology), pp. 157–158.
6 Stuart B. Schwartz and Matthew Mulcahy, 'Natural Disasters in the Caribbean to 1850', in *Sea and Land: An Environmental History of the Caribbean*, ed. by Phillip D. Morgan (Oxford: Oxford University Press, 2022), pp. 187–252.
7 Donald Worster, *Dust Bowl: The Southern Plains in the 1930s* (Oxford: Oxford University Press, 1979).

8 Amartya Sen, *Poverty and Famines: An Essay on Entitlement and Deprivation* (Oxford: Oxford University Press, 1981).
9 United Nations International Strategy for Disaster Reduction, *UNISDR Terminology on Disaster Risk Reduction* (Geneva, 2009), p. 30.
10 Piers Blaikie et al., *At Risk: Natural Hazards, People's Vulnerability and Disasters* (London: Routledge, 2003), p. 11. Emphasis added.
11 Greg Bankoff, 'Time is of the Essence: Disasters, Vulnerability and History', *International Journal of Mass Emergencies and Disasters*, 22:3 (2004), pp. 23–42.
12 Carlton Waterhouse, 'Failed Plans and Planned Failures: The Lower Ninth Ward, Hurricane Katrina and the Continuing Story of Environmental Injustice', in *Hurricane Katrina: America's Unnatural Disaster*, ed. by Jeremy I. Levitt and Matthew C. Whitaker (Lincoln, NE: University of Nebraska Press, 2009), pp. 156–182.
13 David Lambert, *White Creole Culture, Politics and Identity during the Age of Abolition* (Cambridge: Cambridge University Press, 2010), p. 180.
14 Richard Robert Madden, *A Twelvemonth's Residence in the West Indies, during the Transition from Slavery to Apprenticeship; with Incidental Notice of the State of Society, Prospects, and Natural Resources of Jamaica and Other Islands* (Philadelphia: Carey, Lea and Blanchard, 1835), p. 35.
15 Saidiya Hartman, *Lose Your Mother: A Journey Along the Atlantic Slave Route* (New York: Farrar, Straus and Giroux, 2007), p. 19.
16 Ann Laura Stoler, *Along the Archival Grain: Epistemic Anxieties and Colonial Common Sense* (Princeton, NJ: Princeton University Press, 2010), p. 42.
17 Naomi Klein, *Shock Doctrine: The Rise of Disaster* Capitalism (New York: Metropolitan Books, 2008), p. 413.

1

Disaster and providence

Disasters in the nineteenth-century British Caribbean took place in the context of the biggest change to ever sweep through the colonies. In 1807 the slave trade was abolished, and in 1833 enslaved people were emancipated – though, with the exception of Antigua, the majority would have to wait until 1838 and the ending of the apprenticeship system for true legal freedom. The end of coerced labour threatened the collapse of the central pillar upon which the entire British Caribbean enterprise had been built. Early seventeenth-century experiments with indentured British labour and Irish prisoners of war had not facilitated the dynamic expansion that many planters had been hungry for. The growth of the plantations, the monopolisation of land and the accumulation of vast fortunes had only been possible through the total exploitation of African people.

The put-upon planters, as they saw themselves, were hit by another hammer blow in 1846 when, as free trade became an increasingly popular concept within political circles, import duties on sugar from British colonies were equalised. The British Caribbean colonies had long enjoyed reduced import duties, which enabled their comparatively expensive sugar to remain competitive but, in 1846, the region's planters found themselves unprotected from global competition and, initially, without recourse to a coerced labour force.

British ardour for the Caribbean's place at the heart of Empire waned over the nineteenth century; there was little imagination or enthusiasm for the wholescale reimagining of the region's purpose within the Empire. By the end of the nineteenth century, Britain, with its attention on Europe, India and Africa appeared – though not without tension – to give way to America as the hegemon of the region. Over the century, the waning of Britain's interest in the Caribbean profoundly shaped its responses to disaster in the region, but it was not the only factor shaping them.

To best understand the long nineteenth century, we also need to understand what went before it. British colonists and enslaved people had been contending with the natural hazards of the Caribbean for centuries. The disaster responses of the long nineteenth century cannot be divorced from this history, which this chapter explores, paying particular attention to the evolution in how hazards and their impacts were understood over this period. States took time in seeing disasters as something to be responded to.

As Vincent Brown has so powerfully demonstrated, from the outset of Europe colonisation efforts in the region, death – and in particular death caused by the environment – stalked all in the Caribbean.[1] The English settlement of St Christopher in 1623, followed by the settlement of Barbados between 1625 and 1627, and then Montserrat, Antigua and Nevis in 1628 marked the first exposures of British colonists, their servants, and trafficked Africans to an alien and often unforgiving environment.

Equatorial heat fatally exhausted, mosquitos spread fever, and hurricanes and earthquakes frustrated colonists' attempts to gain a permanent foothold. Volcanic eruptions were also a powerful cause of death that colonists would later have to contend with, but by virtue of the length of tectonic cycles, they were a rare occurrence and even then, only experienced in the British Caribbean on the island of St Vincent. Despite the ample and frequently fatal risks, driven by a heady mixture of the opportunity to transcend their societal status and a sense of divine purpose, English colonists persevered. They only succeeded in the task of imposing themselves on the region, however, with the use of slave labour.

Replanting crops uprooted by hurricanes, and rebuilding structures collapsed in winds and earthquakes became a regular part of life for those indentured or enslaved in the Caribbean. Initially, the settlers had to respond to these occurrences almost entirely without external help.[2] The distance from England was not only physically prohibitive of rapid assistance but it also constrained aid because the early seventeenth century was still a time when most people's conception of charity and care had not yet extended to include the neighbouring parish.

Such was the distance that England did not provide much ongoing support to settle the colonies. Larry Gragg notes that colonists in Barbados could not even get England to send them the tools to help clear and settle the island.[3] The English people who had initially settled the Caribbean had done so as part of private ventures and chartered companies desirous of land and fortune. As a result, early settlement of the region was fractious and characterised by chaos and lawlessness; while some were attracted by the opportunities the Caribbean offered, it had a limited attraction for most English people and this, for the most part, put the region beyond their concerns. After 1653, when Oliver Cromwell began personally directing an effort to entirely remove the Spanish from the Caribbean, the English state became increasingly directly involved with colonisation, something which only increased when, under the Navigation Acts, England began requiring all colonial imports and exports to travel exclusively in English ships. Though these laws were not enacted without contention, they set in motion a process that increasingly brought the Caribbean colonies closer in the English imagination.

When thinking about the history of how disasters have been understood, two things might come to mind. Firstly, disasters were once solely conceived as the literal acts of the gods – the direct manifestation of a deity's wrath, most often a punishment for wayward worshippers. Secondly, it is also often posited that, at least in Europe, the intellectual enlightenment of the eighteenth century kick-started an erosion of these superstitions and saw them gradually replaced them with a 'scientific' understanding of hazards and their origins.

Reality is obviously never quite this neat: the transition from a providential understanding of hazards to a scientific one was not quick or evenly spread. What is more, our understanding of how these ideas travelled and were transmitted from metropole to colony is incomplete. In the case of the British Caribbean, we see that while over the eighteenth century, planters and colonial officials turned from providential explanations for disaster and focused their attention to negotiating practical responses to these events, the intertwining of providence and disaster remained a central part of their public-facing responses well beyond the 'enlightenment' and into the nineteenth century.

Over the course of the seventeenth century, as colonists moved past their experiments with cotton and tobacco and found success exploiting slave labour to grow sugar, the colonies became an increasingly important appendage of empire. As trade grew, so too did consumption of Caribbean products; Britons became gradually accustomed to sugar, coffee and cocoa. When it came to disasters, the growing importance of the Caribbean meant that colonists did begin receiving more charitable aid from other Britons and by the nineteenth century could reasonably expect some assistance from Parliament. However, this was a slow and halting process, involving not only increased state oversight of the colonies and closer trade ties, but also that crucial transition from a providential understanding of hazards to a scientific one. Two disasters in particular, the Jamaican earthquake of 1692 and the 'Great Hurricane' of 1780 are events that help us clarify the changing nature of disaster response over the seventeenth and eighteenth centuries and contextualise how disasters were understood at the beginning of the nineteenth century.

The Jamaican earthquake of 1692

Jamaica was captured from the Spanish by the English in 1655. As Matthew Mulcahy points out, early on, the island had earned a reputation somewhat as a sanctuary because it was considered outside of the reach of hurricanes. In the early years of British settlement, while the colonies in the Leeward Islands were notoriously battered by repeated hurricanes, Jamaica remained relatively unscathed. This is not to say Jamaica was not regarded as a dangerous place – its early settlers were devastated by disease – but nonetheless, for the relative lack of hurricane impacts, Jamaica, and its capital Port Royal with its deep, sheltered harbour, came to be valued as a strategic hub both for trade and for the berthing of military and pirate vessels. Though their encounters with hurricanes were initially limited, the inhabitants had familiarity with small earthquakes and tremors. In 1687, an earthquake, said to have lasted a minute, cracked the edifices of many houses, and caused disruption throughout Port Royal, but it was not until 1692 that assumptions regarding the island's safety were truly shattered.[4] On 7 June that year, Port Royal was struck by an earthquake so severe that portions of the capital were literally swallowed by the sea.

When they had taken the island from the Spanish, the English, obviously desirous of protecting their new acquisition, decided to build a fort on a narrow sandbar that extended out from the mainland. The sandbar, which separated the large natural harbour from the Caribbean Sea, created a chokepoint that would allow even a limited force to effectively defend the island. Fort Cromwell, as the fort was named, was joined quickly and haphazardly, by warehouses, houses and inns, all densely packed on to the sandbar.[5] In a period of intense conflict and piracy in the Caribbean Sea, merchants, the military and pirates alike came to enjoy the protective advantages presented by the protected harbour but, with this mix of visitors, Port Royal, as the town became known, also quickly gained a lurid reputation. Trades, both legal and illegal, proliferated and piracy boomed, even after successive governors had sought to limit activities. Visiting in 1687, English traveller Edward Ward described it in biblically damming terms; Port Royal was, he said, the 'very Sodom of the Universe'.[6]

Though the sandbar may have been a relatively strong place for protecting the island from a naval force, it was immensely vulnerable to disaster. It is estimated that by 1692, there were perhaps 6,500 inhabitants living in Port Royal, all crammed into multi-tiered buildings of stone and brick but built, ultimately, on a foundation of nothing but sand.[7] On 7 June 1692, shortly before noon, Port Royal was shaken by a devastating earthquake. There are several first-hand accounts of the event, amongst which perhaps the most illustrative are those compiled by noted naturalist Hans Sloane for the journal of the Royal Society, *Philosophical Transactions*. The rapidity with which the damage occurred is one of the most striking aspects of these accounts. Within two minutes the quake was said to have shaken down and drowned 'nine tenths of ... Port Royal'.[8] The danger persisted after the initial quake, however. One eyewitness account collected by Sloane comes from a man who lost his entire family in the quake, with the exception of his son who, even then, was nearly drowned by a surge from the sea that caused waves to rise 'six foot above the surface'.[9]

The presence of God and providential descriptions of the earthquake's effects are woven throughout nearly all these accounts of the disaster. The aforementioned man's son was spared because, in his words, because he had 'God to save [him]'. Similarly, in the hours that followed the main tremor he prayed to God to 'divert those heavy judgements (aftershocks) which still threaten us'.[10] These biblically inflected accounts are not surprising: providence was the primary means through which the English people of the seventeenth century understood the forces of nature and, when it came to a disaster on this scale, the way they sought to make sense of the loss. With hindsight, what explains the severity of this disaster is the fact that the earthquake, acting as it did on the narrow sandbar, appears to have induced a state of liquefaction in the very ground on which Port Royal was built. To first-hand observers, however, it appeared as if the very ground opened up and swallowed buildings and people alike.

One account collected by Sloane described 'the sand in the street [rising] like the waves of the sea; lifting up all persons that stood upon it, and immediately dropping [them] down into pits; and at the same instant a flood of water breaking in'.[11] The earthquake claimed approximately 2,000 lives and a further 2,000 to 3,000 were lost in the conditions afterward from fever and 'want of warm lodgings'.[12] Despite these near total losses of life and property, at every point, the authors of these accounts stressed their thanks to God that the earthquake had not been worse.

It would not be until 10 August 1692 that those in England heard of the earthquake. Almost all of the public printed discussions of the event that followed were centred around providential understandings of the event. Many also sought to instrumentalise the event as a warning. Samuel Doolittle, an English preacher, connected the 1692 earthquake to one experienced by the English in September of that year, preaching that 'they of Jamaica were greater Sinners than we in England'; 'He Visited them in a terrible manner indeed. His Anger was hot, it burnt like Coals of Fire; his Arm was strong and threw down all before him'.[13] Implicit in his sermon was the suggestion that God had a capacity for judgement that the people of England, with their recent experience of a tremor, had not come close to experiencing. In that sense, it was a clear lesson to his audience that England should avoid the degeneracy of the notorious Port Royal. Like many sermons on disaster in the early modern world, Doolittle sought to use the disaster as a means to bring the wayward back into the fold.

Doolittle's sermon was just one of many providential explanations of the earthquake that proliferated throughout England. The scale of the disaster, combined with Port Royal's reputation, made it irresistible for many preachers. It formed the perfect lesson for those seeking to emphasise the need for renewed and constant piety. What is interesting, in the context of disaster response, however, is the effect that this primarily providential understanding of the earthquake had in shaping and, ultimately, circumscribing the response and relief provided to Jamaica.

As disasters were understood as a physical manifestation of God's will, the words of some preachers suggest that they considered an intervention a subversion of God's will. The suffering of those affected was understood by some to be a necessary part of bringing them back into the fold. Speaking in 1693 as part of an anniversary fast commemorating the 1692 quake, William Corbin, a preacher in Jamaica, impressed upon his audience that the only true means for recovering from the disaster and preventing future calamities was a 'speedy and hearty repentance and amendment'.[14] Not all agreed with this analysis, however, and in August of 1693, Parliament and Queen Mary II were moved to respond to the Jamaican calls for aid. What stands out, however, is the limited form the eventual relief would take; aid mostly went directly to military defence and not those still suffering. It serves to illustrate not just the limited way in which disaster was conceived at this point but also the relatively peripheral role Jamaica still occupied in the Empire.

The first documented petition for aid was drafted by men aboard the *Richard and Sarah* on 20 June 1692. It not only established the need for relief and military support but also asserted the colonists' right to select their own leader until a replacement could be drafted in from England:

> We beg therefore for relief and defence. Till we can fortify we shall want five men-of-war, or five hundred soldiers, and arms and ammunition. Pray also let a Governor be sent us of care and charity equal to our needs, and let us point out that a tolerable choice may be made from ourselves till the office grow again to be fit reward for greater persons.[15]

The petition is vaguely worded and does not contain any of the extensive and detailed estimates of financial losses that would come to define those written by planters in the eighteenth and nineteenth centuries. We do not know England's initial response to this petition, but it gained prominence because it most probably came to the attention of William Beeston. Beeston was a member of the Jamaican assembly and had been appointed Lieutenant Governor, but was in England in 1692. Already planning to return to Jamaica, he requested from Parliament not only the tools to begin the rebuilding effort but also two regiments of foot.

In a move that would reflect the basis of successful relief negotiations for centuries, Beeston, clearly understanding how to persuade Parliament to provide aid, stressed to them that, above all, he would strive to limit Crown expenditure. He proposed that while men in the requested companies have their passage across the Atlantic paid for, their pay would end upon their arrival in Jamaica, only to be resumed if they participated in the rebuilding efforts. Moreover, his proposals centred not on the welfare of the Jamaican colonists but rather on the need for ships, troops, small arms and ammunition to defend the island in its weakened state.[16] This line of argument was clearly persuasive, as the Crown concurred and sent at least six ships to defend the island against possible French attack.[17]

We know that in Jamaica, that there was a little more done for the colonists. The island's council did allot £250 from the colony's funds for the poor of Port Royal and Kingston.[18] For those with greater means, however, it recommended that the rebuilding of Port Royal's fortifications should be done, not with its collective funds, but rather at the expense of individuals.[19] As for the £250, the Calendar of State Papers does not provide us with the detail of how that money was distributed, though it is perhaps safe to say that this financial relief or the provision it bought probably did not reach the island's enslaved population. In late September 1692, the island's council, in seeking to underscore the severity of the situation on the island, were briefing that the colonists were 'brought so low that we are not strong enough to secure ourselves against the slaves.'[20] If they were worried about securing themselves from a potential attack it does not seem likely the exclusively white council would be sharing the limited relief that had been allotted. As shown in later chapters, with local government dominated by planters anxious about their losses, financial aid for the poor rarely reached them.

Jamaica's recovery was slow but did spur long-term change. The island's colonists came to recognise the risk they had exposed themselves to from building the capital on the sandbar and this prompted a new inland site for the capital. In this respect, the council reacted quickly; in early August 1692 they both approved moving the capital and selected the existing settlement of Kingston on the other side of the harbour as the new site. In a spirit that would be unevenly revived in the following centuries, the new development was also conceived in the spirit of a 'conscious effort at improvement'.[21] In effect, the council attempted to better adapt the new capital to the environment, setting forth a gridded plan for Kingston with wider streets to enable air flow and including some aspects of the architecture of the Spanish buildings that remained and had survived the earthquake.

Julie Matlock convincingly makes the argument that the earthquake also had a profound impact on the shape of the Jamaican economy going forward.[22] Until the earthquake, Jamaica had operated a dual economy based on equal parts piracy and plantations. The destruction of Port Royal effectively ended piracy in Jamaica and cemented the power of the large plantation owners, who had the capital to weather the short-term downturn from the earthquake. It was not only in Jamaica that the disaster spurred change, however. Providential and moralising accounts of the disaster and its origins proliferated but some coverage of the disaster also reflects a subtle shift toward a more scientifically orientated discussion of disasters and their origins, which was beginning to emerge across the Atlantic.

At the broadest level, we can see this shift reflected in the very fact that the Hans Sloane collected and published accounts of the earthquake in the journal *Philosophical Transactions*. It indicates that there was a growing audience for accounts of disaster and suggests an emergent inquisitiveness toward the origins of natural phenomena. Within the accounts that Sloane collected was one written by a gentleman in Jamaica who, though not present during the earthquake, pontificated about the origins of the earthquake which he guessed may have lain deep in the earth.[23]

Over the course of the eighteenth century, people both free and enslaved would continue to experience suffering at the hands of the region's natural hazards. Repeated exposure appears to have driven to key trends. Firstly, as generations of colonists gained more experience in the Caribbean environment, some, and not just European intellectuals, turned from entirely providential explanations for disaster to ones increasingly based on their own observations. Secondly, as the region assumed importance within the Empire through the wealth the slave plantations brought in, disaster response took on more importance. By the middle of the eighteenth century, some Caribbean planters had amassed large fortunes and had relocated back to Britain and began taking up seats in Parliament. There they lobbied for their interests as part of what became known as the so-called 'West Indian interest'.

Changes in how Caribbean colonists saw hazards were also reflective of wider trends in the increasingly interconnected eighteenth-century Anglo-Atlantic world. Cynthia Kierner has shown that with the growing importance and expansion of shipping, the resultant rise in shipwrecks prompted new attempts to study and map weather patterns. Newspapers and journals targeting an increasingly literate merchant class emerged to help feed their desire to find ways to try and protect their profits from the vagaries of nature.[24]

In respect of these trends, the eighteenth century saw Britain increase its receptiveness to the pleas of its colonists stricken by disasters throughout its Empire, though direct financial aid did not always follow. Even the Caribbean, with its recognised importance to Britain's Atlantic designs, did not always receive the help its colonists requested. Matthew Mulcahy has shown that through the seventeenth and the first half of the eighteenth century, colonists had to rely in part on private networks of aid and donations.[25] Petitions from suffering colonists alone were not usually enough to motivate the provision of aid. Often it took the convergence of political and economic factors larger than the islands themselves to motivate a relief effort.

The so-called 'Great Hurricane' of 1780, the deadliest disaster witnessed in the Caribbean since the Jamaican earthquake, provides the clearest example of the efforts colonists had to go through to successfully procure financial relief from Parliament, and gives us a snapshot of the extent to which disaster had developed into a negotiated process since 1692. Moreover, it shows the waning importance of providential explanations of disaster.

The 'Great Hurricane' of 1780

October of 1780 brought the most devastating disasters seen in the British Caribbean since the earthquake of 1692. Indeed, for one survivor of the hurricane, planter William Beckford, the earthquake of 1692 still occupied a prominent place in his imagination as he reflected on the events of 1780 in his book, *A Descriptive Account of the Island of Jamaica*. If anything, he appears to lament that the hurricane damage would only leave a temporary mark and not the permanent reminder left by the ruins of Port Royal. For Beckford, the ruins formed a record of destruction that 'still [taught] the infidel to believe'.[26] Jamaica was struck first on 3 October and then the Lesser Antilles, particularly Barbados, Dominica and St Vincent, were struck a week later on 10 October. The hurricanes claimed between 20,000 and 22,000 lives and the financial losses in parts of Jamaica were estimated at £678,571, while Barbados suffered around £1,000,000 of damage.[27]

The private correspondence Parliament received from the affected areas is marked by its pragmatism. It spoke of the hurricane, its damage and the long list of patriotic, strategic and other reasons that meant Parliament should provide relief. In particular, the petition sent by Barbados stated that the once-flourishing colony's fortune had been slowly reversed by a series of calamities with 'natural causes', and then any hopes of a recovery from these were obliterated by the hurricane.[28] Though the petition did end by noting that it has 'pleased Divine Providence lately to visit the British West-India Islands', the use of 'natural' causes is notable.[29] It stands to reason that if planters were to say they were deserving of the disaster because of sin they would be less likely to receive aid. Instead, the planters understood the need to paint themselves in as human a light as possible, innocent sufferers of a calamity, which as one petition put it, no 'human prudence could not provide'.[30]

By virtue of the growth of the settlements, populations and regularity of post since 1692, Parliament received far greater numbers of petitions and communications than it had then. No doubt, this is also reflective of Parliament's growing power and centrality to the emerging British state. Over the eighteenth century, it had increasingly provided slim financial aid following a number of disasters (chiefly following storms but also fires) in the Thirteen Colonies.

The relief eventually agreed upon by Parliament in January 1781 exceeded any offer of relief it had made previously. It allotted £120,000 for Jamaica and Barbados, with £80,000 for Barbados – considered worse hit – and £40,000 for Jamaica.[31] It is immediately striking that money agreed upon by Parliament was so much significantly smaller than planters' own estimated losses. This is in part reflective of the basic nature of Britain's colonial arrangements. The Caribbean colonies were envisioned as tributaries to enrich Britain, not to be a drain on its coffers.

This was the arrangement that, in part, drove the Thirteen Colonies to independence, but Caribbean planters tolerated it because they maintained much closer ties to Britain than their American counterparts did to America. Even if born in the Caribbean they often left as soon as the opportunity presented itself. Living in Britain had advantages; typically, they invested their plantation wealth in land, allowing them to become MPs and thus obtain the representation which those in the Thirteen Colonies felt was denied to them.[32]

Nonetheless, even with the influence they exerted collectively as the 'West India Interest' in Parliament, they did not have the strength to get Parliament to compensate the losses of them and others in the Caribbean. This, in part, reflects the fact that Parliament as a whole and, more specifically those MPs not connected to the Caribbean, were distrustful of the estimated losses provided by the planters. Indeed, as shown in chapter 5, this mistrust was a repeated theme throughout much of the communications exchanged between Britain and the Caribbean following disaster in the nineteenth century.

While the amount provided by Parliament in 1781 may appear comparatively paltry, it was, as Mulcahy points out, significant that Britain provided such a sum at all. The explanation for this response, argues Mulcahy, lies in the geopolitical situation, not just in regard to the Caribbean but also the Thirteen Colonies. In the years immediately preceding 1780, some Caribbean planters had, despite the close connections of their community as a whole to Britain, become discontented with their country's Caribbean policy. During the Seven Years War, the region had become a site of global conflict and then again during the American War of Independence, something which only intensified when France and Spain joined the conflict. Planters railed against what they saw as a lack of adequate military protection for the colonies. At times relations became so strained that factions of planters emerged who even went so far as to publicly express their support for the Americans in their actions against Britain.[33] It is in the context of these tensions that, as Mulcahy puts it, the provision of some relief to Jamaica and Barbados after the hurricane of 1780 'made good political sense'.[34]

It still remains that the relief agreed on in 1781 was limited, falling far short of the estimates supplied by planters, despite both the unprecedented damage caused by the hurricanes and the political context. In this respect, 1780 would maintain trends cemented in the eighteenth century and that would continue well into the nineteenth. Relief was something that had to be negotiated between a trifecta of parties: planters, colonial officials and Parliament – and it was never wholly driven by humanitarian concerns. It had to be petitioned for, and petitioners had to justify their claims. In 1780, as they would continue to do following subsequent disasters, they did this by buttressing their estimated losses with a reference to several key themes: the Caribbean's importance to Britain, the humanity of the situation, and the fate that might await whites if racial 'order' were not re-established.

In 1780, Prime Minister Lord North gives us a clear window onto not only the negotiations around financial relief, but also the distrust with which some viewed the planter class. North explained that such was the scale of the losses that the planters, while entitled to some assistance from the parent state, should not expect a 'total indemnification for their losses'.[35] In his justification for this position he implicitly revealed not only where he felt the limits of state intervention lay but also where the Caribbean lay in his priorities. He argued that the damage caused by the hurricane was a private hardship and that in any case Britain may well be next to suffer it an unexpected hardship and, were it to make the planters whole, it may well be unable to provide for itself in that eventuality. Unlikely as that was, North was clearly resistant to the entire enterprise and was looking for reasons to limit Britain's expenditure. He further suggested that the financial relief that was to be sent should be targeted to the poor classes and that relief for the wealthier classes should be limited, as their estimates were unrealistic, and Parliament had no evidence on which to judge them.

Exposing how little control Parliament had on the distribution of financial relief once they had voted on it, much of the relief intended by North for the poor ended up in the hands of planters. As discussed in chapters 3 and 4, planters continued to control much of the distribution of relief through the long nineteenth century. What marks a crucial change, however, is that in that period their actions were mediated through the new eras inaugurated by the Act for the Abolition of the Slave Trade in 1807 and the Slavery Abolition Act in 1833. The former act curtailed the ability of planters to readily replace their slaves, and the latter act intensified their fears of a total loss of control of the Caribbean colonies.

More than was ever the case in the eighteenth century and earlier, the long nineteenth century added a new party to the previously tripartite negotiation of relief: African-Caribbean people. Though it would not be until the twentieth century that they were permitted to formally participate in shaping the contours of disaster response, the long nineteenth century saw their informal participation through protest, complaint and compassion impose a set of considerations on the planters, colonial officials and Parliament that they had paid little attention to before.

It should be noted that Parliament's decision in 1781 to provide relief was not entirely informed by geopolitical concerns. As already discussed, the Caribbean colonies had, over the course of the eighteenth century, become increasingly important to Britain, not just in terms of the wealth they generated and the personal fortunes they cemented but also in terms of the commodities they provided to Britain.

As many scholars have noted, by the mid-eighteenth century, sugar, coffee and cocoa were increasingly regarded as dietary essentials for Britain's middling and upper classes. Alongside the connections fostered by commodities, there was the aforementioned expanding print sphere that, by providing these same classes with detailed accounts of disasters and suffering, drove an unprecedented amount of charitable relief to the affected colonies in 1780.

By that year, Britons had, arguably, never felt closer to the Caribbean colonies. The hurricanes occurred simultaneously to the British campaign against the Continental Army. In that moment, the Caribbean colonies were Britain's most valuable Atlantic possessions. It would not be until the beginning of the twentieth century that the British Caribbean would see such a suffusion of charitable relief again and even then, a large proportion of that aid, as shown in chapter 4, arrived from a number of global donors outside of Britain, reflecting further change in the nature of public giving.

By 1780, as providential explanations waned, disasters were something that – unlike in 1692 – Britain and its public appear to have felt it were worth responding to. This was not a change solely explicable through a focus on Britain and the Caribbean. One European event in particular not only advanced 'scientific' explanations of disaster but also inaugurated a culture of aid-giving that had significant impacts on Britain.

The Lisbon earthquake of 1755

The Lisbon earthquake of 1755 not only acted as a catalyst for further scientific inquiry into the causes of earthquakes and disasters more broadly, but created a flashpoint in which providential and scientific explanations, and those advancing them, came into conflict. While we cannot simply say that the event resulted in the triumph of scientific explanations of disasters, it certainly played a role, at least for the intelligentsia of the European enlightenment, in the turn away from wholly providential explanations of disaster.

The earthquake which occurred on 1 November 1755 was one of the strongest ever recorded to have affected Europe. Estimated at somewhere between 8.0 and 9.0 on the Richter scale, it utterly devastated the Portuguese capital. Given that 1 November was All Saints' Day, many of the capital's population were inside its numerous churches and when the tremor began, the tightly packed citizens fell prey to tons of falling masonry. Casualties only increased when those who were not killed in the initial shock attempted to flee the city across the river Tagus where they were met with waves that quickly overwhelmed their small crafts. Such was the power of the tremor that tsunamis also rippled out across the Atlantic, even reaching the Caribbean.[36]

The immense and almost incomprehensible destruction was widely and rapidly reported across Europe and had lasting effects on the minds of some who read about it. An eight-year-old Johann Wolfgang von Goethe received news of the event and later in life recorded the profound effect it had had on him:

> God, the Creator and Sustainer of heaven and earth, whom the First Article of Faith had portrayed as so wise and merciful, had allowed the just to suffer the same fate as the unjust, thus in no way proving to be fatherly.[37]

But, of the noted enlightenment thinkers, it was Voltaire who wrote perhaps the most striking rejoinder to those who sought to interpret the event as providential in origin. In *On the Lisbon Disaster*, Voltaire railed against what he saw as complacent deists, writing:

> To that appalling spectacle of woe,
> Will ye reply: 'You do but illustrate
> The iron laws that chain the will of God'?
> Say ye, o'er that yet quivering mass of flesh:
> 'God is avenged: the wage of sin is death'?
> What crime, what sin, had those young hearts conceived
> That lie, bleeding and torn, on mother's breast?
> Did fallen Lisbon deeper drink of vice
> Than London, Paris, or sunlit Madrid?[38]

The reflections of Goethe and the writings of Voltaire are but a sample of the material written in response to the 1755 earthquake. In the following year, Immanuel Kant wrote three pioneering essays exploring the origins of the earthquake concluding, ultimately, that the movement of the seafloor must have played a crucial role in the event.[39] The writings of these three individuals, so closely associated with the European enlightenment, underscore the point that 1755 spurred a point of inflection in Europe. It must be said that the earthquake was certainly also, for many thousands of Christians and adherents of other religions, firmly interpreted as a providential event. No one schema of explanation can be said to have won out but, not by coincidence I think, along with the emergence of an increasing audience for scientific explanations, so too from 1755 emerge new types of centralised disaster response.

The number of casualties in Lisbon was immense, modern estimates of the death toll placing it at around 40,000, but the scale of the suffering brought the church and state into conflict from the outset.[40] The clergy was accused of inflating the death toll, and the Marquis of Pombal, chief minister to King Joseph I, ordered his own report into the casualties and the damage.[41] This initial conflict set the tone in many ways for Pombal's response. Described by Van Bavel et al. as the personification of enlightenment 'godlessness', Pombal used the earthquake as the moment not just to reform the construction of Lisbon – rebuilding it in accordance with new, scientifically informed building codes – but also the Portuguese state.[42] The scale of the disaster, combined with new diplomatic allegiances, motivated the British monarch, George II, to provide £100,000 of assistance in addition to three warships for the protection of the capital.[43] This relief was not entirely altruistic, as British merchants in Lisbon had lost a great deal in the earthquake and they were given priority when the relief was distributed but beyond that, Britain wanted to aid its ally against Spain. In this sense, the relief was tied up in political 'game playing' but nonetheless such largesse was unprecedented, particularly to a foreign power at a time when disaster response was considered primarily the purview of local authorities.[44]

Viewed on a linear trajectory, the search for scientific explanations of the earthquake and the interventionist, centralised state response to the disaster represented one of the significant leaps forward in the understanding of and response to disaster. Indeed, Deborah Coen shows that 1755 continued to be a touchstone well into the nineteenth century:

> In the nineteenth century, the Lisbon earthquake became a cultural shorthand for initiation into a sceptical, rational, and self-consciously modern search for natural causes. In an age fond of likening human history to a progression from infancy to maturity, Lisbon figured as the coming of age of the European mind.[45]

Developments in the Caribbean

While the British response to the hurricanes of 1780 reflects in some respects eighteenth-century developments in the thinking around disasters, it is striking that many of the accounts, petitions and letters reporting disasters that reached Britain from the Caribbean in the nineteenth century still contained strong providential themes. There seems to have been a significant lag between the transformation alluded to by Coen and developments in the Caribbean. At the beginning of the nineteenth century, this is perhaps because slavery and the question of abolition had already made the region into a metaphorical battlefield riven by religious fault lines. For many, there was a clear link between slavery, divine wrath and Caribbean disasters. Preacher William Agutter, in a sermon which he later published and sent to noted abolitionist Granville Sharpe, wrote that the loss of America and disasters in the Caribbean were the direct results of the continued existence of slavery against God's wishes:

> The Western Empire is gone from us, never to return; it is given to another more righteous than we; who consecrated the sword of resistance by declaring for the universal abolition of slavery. The West India islands have been visited with most tremendous hurricanes and earthquakes; by these, the cruel traders have been deprived of all their unrighteous gain or have been involved with it in one common grave. Verily, there is a reward for the righteous and for the wicked: doubtless there is a God who judgeth the earth.[46]

Perhaps an even more famous drawing of this link comes to us through abolitionist William Cowper's poem, *The Negro's Complaint*, where in the fifth stanza he writes:

> Hark! He answers!
> Wild tornadoes Strewing yonder sea with wrecks,
> Wasting towns, plantations, meadows,
> Are the voice with which he speaks.
> He, foreseeing what vexations
> Afric's sons should undergo,
> Fixed their tyrants' habitations
> Where his whirlwinds answer 'No.'[47]

Agutter and Cowper were noted abolitionists and, of course, pro-slavery campaigners readily contested their interpretation of disasters, especially as the debate around abolition reached its climax. In Parliament, George Hibbert, one of the most prominent pro-slavery MPs rebutted abolitionist Samuel Whitbread MP, who had made the same links as Agutter and Cowper:

> The hon. member has intimated a conjecture, that the crimes attendant upon the Slave Trade in the West Indies have provoked the judgments of God, and that the hurricanes to which those climates are subject are the signals of his vengeance. Sir, these [sic] is much moral and physical evil in the world, but it is a bold and rash attempt in any mortal to impute that evil as a judgment of Providence upon the heads on which it may chance to fall ... I am better

acquainted with the history of Jamaica than with that of any other island in the West Indies. Jamaica has been for 20 years free from hurricanes, that period no way marked by a forbearance as to the purchase or labour of slaves ... the era in which the slave trade was authorized and encouraged by the British legislature was one of distinguished prosperity in that country, one in which she became the envy of the world.[48]

Agutter's sermon, Cowper's poem and Hibbert's intervention do not represent a sincere debate on the nature and origins of the natural phenomena that frequently afflicted Britain's Caribbean colonies. While in part representative of the elevated rhetoric surrounding the abolition debate, it shows that at the beginning of the nineteenth century providential explanations of disaster had not entirely slipped from conversation around the Caribbean and its hazards.

On the ground, over the course of the nineteenth century, providential explanations of disaster did wain, but interestingly providential language remained woven through both private colonial communications and public announcements. One could take a shallow reading of the persistence of providence that sees it more as a rhetorical device and a call back to religious tropes of using crisis to promote a renewal of faith; there certainly were occasions where this was the case.

When the volcano La Soufrière erupted on St Vincent on 30 April 1812, Barbados, though not directly affected by the worst aspects of the volcano's destructive forces, experienced a loss of sunlight because of the volume of ejecta in the air. The situation was described in the *Caledonian Mercury* thus:

> To describe the feelings that pervaded the community during this awful period, is impossible – it is far easier to be conceived; many considered it as an infliction of that Almighty wrath, which was denounced against the Israelites of old, as we are informed in Holy writ: 'The Lord shall make the rain of the land powder and dust; from Heaven shall it come down upon thee, until thou be destroyed ... and thou shalt grope at noon day, as the blind gropeth in darkness'. 'It was, in short, a scene that can never be obliterated from the memory; and it may at least have some good effect, that of strengthening the believer in his ideas of Omnipotence, as well as producing in the mind of the disbeliever (should there unhappily be one among us) a conviction of the error of his ways'.[49]

The account published in the *Mercury* drew a clear link with the sin of non-belief and, like William Corbin after the Jamaican earthquake of 1692, expressed a clear hope that the disaster would bring wavering disbelievers back into the fold. In other cases, when planters did make reference to God and providence in private correspondence, these appear as literary affectations, ways to frame the seriousness of an event and to highlight the randomness of disasters and thus elicit sympathy from Parliament. Planters from St Vincent sent a petition to London that spoke of a 'severe visitation of divine providence' before going into far greater detail on the conditions of the island and their losses.[50]

The question remains then, why this language is still in vogue in public-facing reporting of Caribbean disasters, particularly in light of changing understandings of disaster in Europe. The most obvious answer is that the Caribbean colonies were just that: colonies. They were not the metropole, whereas Lisbon was the seat of the Portuguese Government and empire. Its importance as a capital and the importance of the people who lived there far eclipsed the Caribbean colonies. The Caribbean, particularly as the number of planters who choose to live in Britain grew, was distant from the finer points of enlightenment thinking. The earthquake of 1755 brought the questions around the nature of providence to the fore also because of who it affected – primarily Europeans in contrast to the Caribbean colonies, where owing to the demography attendant on slavery, disasters primarily affected African-Caribbean people who were considered racially inferior. Thus disasters in the Caribbean did not elicit the same emotive and searching response in the rulers of the region as those in mainland Europe did.

I argue there is more at play here, however. I believe we can see it as representative of a key theme running through British responses to disaster: hierarchy. Religious and providential language was often used as a powerful rhetorical tool to remind and impress upon the non-white population their place within Caribbean society, and the deference with which they should behave in moments of crisis.

The link between and religion and control is clear when one contrasts private and public communications. For example, after the 1831 hurricane hit Barbados, St Vincent and several of the Leeward Islands, the private correspondence exchanged between white elites and London talks of the melancholy nature of the event but makes no mention of God and providence. By contrast, the public-facing coverage, as expressed in local newspapers and the proclamations issued by the authorities both implicitly and explicitly referred to providence and judgement. Sir James Lyon, the Governor of Barbados, opened a public proclamation on the events with the remark 'it having pleased Almighty God to afflict this colony with a most awful and destructive hurricane'.[51] The *Royal St Vincent Gazette* recorded the hurricane as the 'most awful and destructive visitations of Providence ever experienced in this island'.[52] The *St Lucia Gazette* drew perhaps the most explicit link when reporting on the 'dreadful consequences of our recent and no doubt justly merited, though severe manifestation of the dire displeasure of the All Just Disposer of Events'.[53] Similarly, in 1834, when a hurricane hit Dominica, it was described as an 'awful phenomena [sic]' in private correspondence and an 'awful visitation of Providence' in the governor's public proclamation.[54]

These framings of disaster would have had a powerful effect because we know that, at least for some in the Caribbean, religion and disasters remained deeply connected in the nineteenth century. Lady Maria Nugent wrote an extensive diary of her experiences in the Caribbean when she travelled there as the wife of George Nugent, who was appointed Lieutenant Governor and Commander-in-Chief in 1801. Lady Nugent's diary gives us many interesting insights about life in Jamaica from atop its racial hierarchy but, in the context of this book, what is particularly interesting is that she shows the commonplace position which disaster and religion occupied in everyday life. On 17 August 1801 Nugent writes of a 'short, sharp earthquake' experienced across Jamaica. She records no serious damage as a result. Yet, five days later, when she visits a church on the island, she finds 'all the world staring, and the church crowded to excess. – A prayer against earthquakes, in which I joined most heartily.'[55] Though she does not describe the exact composition of the congregation, it is clear that the small earthquake left an impression. I would argue that there can be little doubt that those offering their prayers following the minor earthquake were conscious of wanting to prevent a far more dangerous one. The year 1692, as it was for Beckford writing his *Descriptive Account of Jamaica*, must have been present in their thoughts. Indeed, Nugent's diary suggests that, at least for high society in Jamaica, disasters were never far from people's minds; she recounts that one evening the 'conversation fell upon hurricanes, when many frightful stories were told'.[56] Similarly, on a visit to Savannah-La-Mar whilst her husband was inspecting a development to protect the harbour, Nugent encountered a man who gave her a full and evocative account of the hurricane of 1780, noting where the 'sea had rushed in, and carried all before it, and then retreated, bearing away with it to the deep many houses with their hapless inhabitants, almost in a moment'.[57]

The planter class had done much to resist both the practising of indigenous African religions and later, with the growth of Christian missionary activity, religious 'education'. At the most basic level, planters recognised religion and religious education as a threat to their authority; planters were keen to present themselves to enslaved people as the ultimate authority with sole control over life and death, but religion in its most basic form gave enslaved people a sense of something greater and a framework of morality that transcended the bounds of the planter and their plantation. Yet, disasters appear to see planters actively promote a religious, providential understanding of disaster.

Like William Corbin in 1692, the white elites of the nineteenth century were seeking to bring the wayward back and thus within their preferred societal conventions. Religious understandings of disaster could be instrumentalised to provoke fear, stymie demands for change and promote the value of labour. We can see this play out in even the earliest accounts of encounters between Englishmen and hurricanes. Writing in 1609 after being shipwrecked in Bermuda, William Strachey tells us that a belief that the wreck had been caused by God motivated those who survived to work collectively in an unprecedented manner: 'whether it were the fear of death in so great a storm or that it pleased God to be gracious unto us', never had the men on the ship 'in all their lifetimes' worked so many hours to survive.[58]

We know that the proclamation written by Sir James Lyon in Barbados after the hurricane of 1831, quoted above, was read out to enslaved people. In another account of the hurricane, not read as public proclamation, the link between religion and order was made explicit; the author singled out the island's Moravian community for praise after the hurricane because they had 'long impress[ed] on [the] minds [of the enslaved] the duty they owe to those who are in authority over them'.[59]

The link between disaster, religion and control is made even clearer by the fact that it existed beyond the page. Just as Corbin's sermon to the Jamaican people on the anniversary of the earthquake of 1692 was held on a day of fast, so too did Sir James Lyon in Barbados call for a day of 'humiliation and fast' after the 1831 hurricane. In a second public proclamation, Lyon called for the day to show respect to God and thank his mercy that the storm only persisted for two days.[60]

Days of humiliation and fast had been part of the fabric of British life throughout the seventeenth and eighteenth centuries. Typically, they were instituted by the church and figures of authority during times of war, famine and other environmental calamity.[61] Their use had waned over the eighteenth century, and by the nineteenth century – but for a day of fast called following an outbreak of cholera in 1832 and one in 1865 in response to bovine disease and cholera – were solely reserved for times of war and royal occasions. That they were used far more commonly in the Caribbean reflected not just the desire for control but a wider trend throughout the Empire to use them as a means to instil authority and tie together the community when it frayed. In religiously divided eighteenth-century Canada, the Church of England sought observance of days of fast and humiliation with 'threats of God's wrath and indignation for non-observance'.[62]

In 1835, the Governor of Antigua, Evan Macgregor, issued a public proclamation to appoint a day for 'humiliation and thanksgiving' and called 'on this most solemn occasion, to ... all orders of society, to consider the duties they owe to one another'.[63] Toward the end of the proclamation Macgregor wrote directly to the African-Caribbean population, stressing to them that as slavery had been ended in 1833, God had sent them a memorable warning of their duties to the community.[64] It is clear that the reflex to call these fast-days reflected elite unease about the potential for disorder on the islands.

Eight years later, after another earthquake, the then governor, Charles Fitzroy, deemed it his 'first' duty to declare a day of humiliation and prayer.[65] The written proclamation issued in the colonial newspaper called on 'all members of [the] community to perform with humility and cheerfulness the duties they owe to their God and to their neighbours'.[66] On Montserrat, also affected by the same earthquake, the call was softer; the president of the island's government, Edward Baynes, called not for a day of fast and humiliation but rather one of 'general thanksgiving', to thank God for his protection. Nonetheless, he did order all colonial officers to observe it and set the expectation that all of her majesty's subjects do the same.[67]

Even when officials did not call for days of fast and humiliation the link between providence and order remained. On Tobago, following a hurricane in 1847, the governor, Laurence Graeme, published a public proclamation noting that it had 'pleased the Almighty, in his great wisdom, to visit the island with the calamity of a hurricane' but called for all Tobagonians to work towards the restoration of the island and promised to punish anyone caught taking advantage of the situation.[68]

This desire to instrumentalise religion as a means to restore order is one of the central continuities of British Caribbean society, even as, first the slave trade ended and then coerced labour ended in 1838. By the end of the nineteenth century and into the early twentieth century, however, the language of providence appears to have retreated entirely from both public and private communications, as did the practice of issuing public proclamations. That said, as chapter 4 explores, the desire to restore order as envisioned by white elites remained a fundamental pillar of British responses to disaster.

Though they were clearly willing to use religion as tool to restore 'order', that it was largely absent from private communications reminds us that the British responding to disasters did not see them primarily as acts of God. Response and relief had to be negotiated and mediated through a number of imperial concerns, but the long nineteenth century saw Britain respond to Caribbean disasters and provide relief far more consistently than it ever had, a significant development from the primarily military response in 1692, for example. This change, however striking, did not represent an entirely humanitarian turn. What is demonstrated throughout this book is that responses were not primarily driven by a need to help those suffering in the Caribbean, but rather a pragmatic assessment of what was needed to restart productive industry. Where relief was provided it was often highly conditional and punitive. This limited and often circumscribed relief was a product of many factors. One of these, which has, as of yet, been given little attention is the relationship between the planter class and the Caribbean environment.

Notes

1. Vincent Brown, *The Reaper's Garden: Death and Power in the World of Atlantic Slavery* (Cambridge, MA: Harvard University Press, 2008).
2. For accounts of early English settlers in the Caribbean see Natalie A. Zacek, *Settler Society in the English Leeward Islands, 1670–1776* (Cambridge: Cambridge University Press, 2010); Matthew Mulcahy, *Hurricanes and Society in the British Greater Caribbean, 1624–1783* (Baltimore, MD: Johns Hopkins University Press, 2006); Larry Gragg, *'Englishmen Transplanted': The English Colonization of Barbados 1627–1660* (Oxford, New York: Oxford University Press, 2003).
3. Larry Gragg, *'Englishmen Transplanted'*, p. 18.
4. Hans Sloane, 'A Letter from Hans Sloane, M.D. and S.R.S. with Several Accounts of the Earthquakes in Peru October the 20th 1687. And at Jamaica, February 19th. 1687/8 and June the 7th. 1692', *Philosophical Transactions*, 209 (1694), pp. 81–82.
5. For the most comprehensive history of Port Royal see Michael Pawson and David Buisseret, *Port Royal, Jamaica* (Jamaica: The University of the West Indies Press, 2000).
6. Edward Ward, *A Trip to Jamaica: With a True Character of the People and Island* (London, 1698), p. 16.
7. Michael Pawson and David Buisseret, *Port Royal, Jamaica*, p. 134.
8. Hans Sloane, 'A letter from Hans Sloane', p. 83.
9. Ibid.
10. Ibid.
11. Ibid., p. 85.
12. Ibid., p. 83.
13. Samuel Doolittle, *A Sermon Preached upon the Late Earthquake, Which Happen'd in London, And Other Places On the Eighth of September, 1692* (London: Printed by J.R. for J. Salusbury, at the Rising-Sun near the Royal Exchange in Cornhill, 1692).
14. William Corbin, *A Sermon Preached at Kings Town in Jamaica Upon the 7th of June, Being the Anniversary Fast for That Dreadful Earth-Quake Which Happened There in the Year 1692* (New York: William Bradford, 1703), p. 2.
15. The President and Council of Jamaica to Lords of Trade and Plantations, 20 June 1692, *Calendar of State Papers Colonial, America and West Indies*, xiii, 1689–92, ed. by J.W. Fortescue (London: Eyre and Spottiswoode, 1901), British History Online. Accessed 27 July 2022, https://bit.ly/3acKAGp.
16. Colonel Beeston's proposals as to Jamaica, 19 August 1692, *Calendar of State Papers Colonial, America and West Indies*.

17 *Journal of Lords of Trade and Plantations*, 2 September 1692, *Calendar of State Papers Colonial, America and West Indies*; The Queen to the President and Council of Jamaica, 7 September 1692, *Calendar of State Papers Colonial, America and West Indies*.
18 At this point Kingston was the smaller settlement, not yet the capital but had also been partially affected by the earthquake.
19 Minutes of Council of Jamaica, 23 September 1692, *Calendar of State Papers Colonial, America and West Indies*.
20 Julie Yates Matlock, 'The Process of Colonial Adaptation: English Responses to the 1692 Earthquake at Port Royal' (unpublished Master's thesis, Eastern Kentucky University, 2012), pp. 47–48.
21 Ibid., p. 33.
22 Ibid.
23 Ibid., p. 99.
24 Cynthia Kierner, *Inventing Disaster: The Culture of Calamity from the Jamestown Colony to the Johnstown Flood* (Chapel Hill, NC: University of North Carolina Press, 2019), p. 69–98.
25 Matthew Mulcahy, *Hurricanes and Society*, pp. 141–164.
26 William Beckford, *A Descriptive Account of the Island of Jamaica: With remarks upon the Cultivation of the Sugar-Cane, throughout the different Seasons of the Year, and chiefly considered in Picturesque Point of View; Also Observations and Reflections upon what would probably be the Consequences of an Abolition of the Slave-Trade, and of the Emancipation of the Slaves*, Vol. 1 (London: T. and J. Egerton, 1790), p. 136.
27 Matthew Mulcahy, *Hurricanes and Society*, p. 165.
28 Hansard, HoC Deb. vol. 1, 23 January 1781, p. 242.
29 Ibid., p. 244.
30 HoC Deb. vol. 1, 23 January 1781, p. 242.
31 Matthew Mulcahy, *Hurricanes and Society*, p. 168.
32 For further insight and comparisons between America and Caribbean elites see Andrew Jackson O'Shaughnessy, *An Empire Divided: The American Revolution and the British Caribbean* (Philadelphia, PA: University of Pennsylvania Press, 2000).
33 Matthew Mulcahy, *Hurricanes and Society*, p. 172.
34 Ibid., p. 173.
35 HoC Deb. vol. 1, 23 January 1781, pp. 256–257.
36 Valérie Clouard, Jean Roger and Emmanuel Moizan, 'Tsunami Deposits in Martinique Related to the 1755 Lisbon Earthquake', *Natural Hazards and Earth System Sciences Discussions*, 2017, pp. 1–13.
37 Peter Boerner, *Goethe* (London: Haus Publishing, 2005), p. 9.
38 Voltaire, *Toleration and Other Essays*, trans. by Joseph McCabe (New York: The Knickerbocker Press, 1912), pp. 255–263.
39 Immanuel Kant, *Kant: Natural Science* (Cambridge: Cambridge University Press, 2012), pp. 327–373.
40 Mark Molesky, *The Gulf of Fire: The Destruction of Lisbon, or Apocalypse in the Age of Science and Reason* (New York: Knopf, 2015), 17.218. Epub edition.

41 Bas van Bavel et al., *Disasters and History: The Vulnerability and Resilience of Past Societies* (Cambridge: Cambridge University Press, 2020), p. 28.
42 Ibid.
43 *The Parliamentary History of England, from the Earliest Period to the year 1803*, xv (London: T.C. Hansard, 1831), pp. 543–544.
44 John Hannigan, *Disasters Without Borders: The International Politics of Natural Disasters* (Cambridge: Polity Press, 2012), p. 98.
45 Deborah R. Coen, *The Earthquake Observers: Disaster Science from Lisbon to Richter* (Chicago, IL: University of Chicago Press, 2012), p. 107.
46 William Agutter, *The Abolition of the Slave Trade Considered in a Religious Point of View. A Sermon Preached before the Corporation of the City of Oxford, at St. Martin's Church, On Sunday, February 3, 1788* (Printed for J.F. and C. Rivington, St. Paul's Church-yard; and G. Philips, George-yard, Lombard Street., 1788), p. 26.
47 William Cowper, *Poetical Works of William Cowper*, Vol. I (Boston, London: Little, Brown & Company, John W. Parker and Son, 1854), pp. 242–244.
48 George Hibbert's family owned a number of plantations in Jamaica. He also co-led the West India Dock Company and the Society for West India Merchants. For more information on Hibbert see Catherine Hall, *Legacies of British Slave-Ownership* (Cambridge: Cambridge University Press, 2014); HoC, Deb 16 March 1807, vol. 9, columns 114–140.
49 *Caledonian Mercury*, 'Phenomena at Barbados', 20 June 1812.
50 PP (1812–13), HoC [182], St Vincent. Report from committee on petition of persons interested in estates in the island of St Vincent, p. 11, Memorial of several merchants in London, on behalf of several proprietors of Estates in the Charaib county, in the island of St Vincent.
51 TNA, CO 28/107, Despatches from Sir James Lyon, Governor of Barbados, Proclamation issued 15 August 1831.
52 *Royal St Vincent Gazette*, 12 August 1831.
53 *St Lucia Gazette*, 17 August 1831.
54 Copies of Communications received by His Majesty's Government, relating to the Hurricane at Dominica, 1 June, 1835, p. 7.
55 Maria Nugent, *Lady Nugent's Journal of Her Residence in Jamaica from 1801 to 1805*, ed. by Philip Wright (Kingston: The University of the West Indies Press, 2002), p. 17.
56 Ibid., p. 78.
57 Ibid., p. 92.
58 Cynthia Keirner, *Inventing Disaster*, p. 24.
59 Editor of *The West Indian*, *Account of the Fatal Hurricane by Which Barbados Suffered in August 1831* (Barbados: Printed for Samuel Hyde, 1831), p. 109.
60 TNA CO 28/107, Despatches from Sir James Lyon, Governor of Barbados, Proclamation issued 15 August 1831.
61 Alasdair Raffe, 'Nature's Scourges: The Natural World and Special Prayers, Fasts and Thanksgivings, 1541–1866', *Studies in Church History*, 46 (2010), pp. 237–247.

62 Joseph Hardwick and Philip Williamson, 'Special Worship in the British Empire: From the Seventeenth to the Twentieth Centuries', *Studies in Church History*, 54 (2018), p. 264.
63 TNA, CO 7/74 (Antigua & Montserrat) Correspondence, Original – Secretary of State: Despatches, Macgregor, Proclamation issued by Sir Evan Macgregor, 20 August 1835.
64 Ibid.
65 TNA, CO 7/74, Fitzroy to Stanley, 10 February 1843.
66 Ibid.
67 TNA, CO 7/74, Proclamation issued by Edward Baynes, 10 February 1843.
68 Laurence Graeme, 'A proclamation', 16 October 1847, in *Tobago Hurricane* of 1847: Papers relative to the Hurricane in Tobago Presented to Both Houses of Parliament by Command of Her Majesty Queen Victoria, on April 11, 1848. Historical Documents of Trinidad and Tobago No. 3 (Port of Spain: Government Printer, 1966).

2

Passing visitors

In his book *The English in the West Indies*, which he wrote toward the end of the nineteenth century, James Froude reflected upon the centuries of British occupation of the Caribbean. He concluded that the 'English have built those islands as if we were but passing visitors, wanting only tenements to be occupied for a short time'.[1] Froude was not only a passionate believer in the British imperial project but had a white supremacist racial politics that was controversial for its explicitness, even in the nineteenth century.[2] In this context, his melancholia for underdeveloped Caribbean colonies was no doubt reflective of his disagreements with abolition and the loss of white control it represented. Nonetheless, Froude succinctly characterised the nature of British colonialism in the Caribbean. In North America, English colonists settled and dispossessed indigenous lands with the intent of making themselves a permanent home. In the Caribbean, they may have started with that goal, but that desire quickly evaporated. Unlike in America, land was limited and quickly monopolised. Opportunities for white settlers dried up quickly over the course of the seventeenth century, and without easily obtainable land, any lustre the region had as a land of opportunity disappeared.

Over the eighteenth century the white relationship with the Caribbean was, at the elite end of the scale, characterised by absenteeism. Planters would return to Britain, often obtaining land, titles, and as a result of which – unlike the Americans – political representation. At the lower end of the scale of wealth, the plantations left absented by their owners were usually managed by middle-class English and Scottish men looking for opportunities denied to them by the aristocracy back home. When they made money, they often returned back to Britain to spend and invest it. Across the spectrum of the white population throughout the Caribbean colonies there was a shared desire, above all, to maintain their Britishness and their connections with Britain. This gave birth, at least on the face of it, to the strong racial bifurcation of Caribbean society but also a mindset that saw the region as primarily a site for extraction and not development.

Exploring the relationship between British colonists and the Caribbean colonies is fundamental to fully understanding British responses to disaster in the Caribbean. Its influence over the process of disaster response is clearly seen in two ways. To borrow Walter Rodney's term, it led to the 'underdevelopment' of the region. The building and maintenance of the infrastructure and institutions of oppression necessary to extract labour from enslaved people were prioritised above all. For British visitors, the accoutrements of the modern life to which they were accustomed were hard to find. In the long term this meant that, with little emphasis on settlement and focus firmly on production, Britain effectively locked its colonies into a form of agricultural stasis centred around the plantation and varying monocultures of sugar, coffee and fruit crops.

What has been discussed in less detail, however, is how the extractive focus at the heart of the British Caribbean project and the toll it took on the environment not only made colonies more vulnerable to disaster but also shaped the number of hazards they had to respond to. For example, food shortages commonly followed hurricanes because sugar dominated arable land, and for planters often on the other side of the Atlantic, stockpiling food or preparing other contingencies rarely entered into their narrow, profit-focused thinking. Food shortages were but one of the epiphenomenal hazards that disasters frequently triggered but they stand as a prime example of how the extractive relationship British elites had with the Caribbean shaped the experience of disasters.

This extractive relationship was defined by the engine at the heart of the British Caribbean project: the plantation. As a mode of production, it quickly assumed the position of the productive core of the colonies. With centuries of investment into land, equipment and the coercive labour that drove it, for the wealthy British it effectively became a metonym for the Caribbean colonies; it was all they could conceive of them as being.

Plantations, by their nature as a purely commercial form of agriculture, profoundly shaped life in the Caribbean colonies. One cannot feed a society wholly through plantations – intensive monocultures do not provide the range of nutrients needed to support human life – thus plantations prefigured an export focus to the economies of the Caribbean. Furthermore, monocultures on the scale necessary to make investment in plantations profitable are not possible, with constant labour used to curb natural checks on single plant dominance. On their own, plants struggle to overcome the limits to their expansion imposed by competition for soil nutrients and the consumption patterns of animals. Establishing a plantation thus requires the radical simplification of the surrounding flora and fauna and then a constant expenditure of energy to maintain it.

The sugar plantation, though central to Caribbean history, did not originate in the region. Sugar plantations existed throughout the Arab world, particularly in Persia where sugar was grown in vast quantities for a burgeoning market in India. They were gradually introduced to Europe as it came into contact with the Arab world through conflict and trade. Caribbean plantations were distinct from their earlier progenitors, however. They represented an unprecedented refining and intensification of the model.

In the fifteenth and sixteenth centuries, the Spanish and the Portuguese had experimented with plantations off the Atlantic coast of Africa. The English, inspired by these successes, had also tried their hand with similar projects in Ireland, clearing and enclosing land and extracting labour from the native people through violence and coercion. In these places the blueprint of 'new world' settlement was unknowingly sketched out. When Europeans began conquering and then colonising the Caribbean and the Americas, enticed by the vast swathes of land and year-round warmth, they began vociferously imposing their established blueprint with the forced labour of both indigenous people and enslaved Africans. The process set in motion an unprecedented change to the region's environment, which would ultimately intensify and harshen disasters and lengthen the recovery process.

Deforestation

When the first English colonisers arrived in the Caribbean, the prospects for agriculture as they understood it must have looked bleak. Landing on Caribbean islands, they were greeted by deep, seemingly impenetrable jungle often extending down to the shoreline. Quickly, however, as had been done in England for centuries, they began a process of mass deforestation, clearing space for agriculture and using the timber for constructing buildings and repairing ships.

It has long been established that widespread deforestation quickly gives rise to soil erosion and thus depletion of soil nutrients. In the contemporary world, it is one of the defining ways in which the global south still suffers the environmental legacy of colonialism. Without tree roots to bind the soil, it often washes and blows away in the face of even light rain and winds.

Soil erosion was endemic throughout the British Caribbean, and it had a significant effect on the capacity of the region's soil. What English colonists did not know was that the soils of the Caribbean were already comparatively nutrient poor. They are now understood to be comparatively more dependent on nutrient recycling from trees and other flora and fauna which fed the soil over the course of their lifespan.[3] In this respect, from the outset, the political economy of the British colonies was entirely at odds with its environment. Planters, both hungry for wealth and notoriously indebted, were driven to expand their plantations to all arable land, and to plant and harvest at a relentless pace that severely taxed this delicate ecosystem. In all, the export-driven economies of the British Caribbean and the rapid depreciation of natural resources created an almost ironic situation in which, despite the energies directed to soil, hunger and fatal landslides only rose in frequency. Nowhere was this cruel irony clearer than on the island of Barbados, which endured the most extreme environmental transformation and set out a model for the rest of British Caribbean colonisation.

When the English first discovered the island in 1623 and when they began settling it from 1625 onwards, it was almost entirely covered in thick jungle. In the space of just fifty years, however, so total had deforestation been that the island had become almost entirely reliant on imported timber to continue building residences and infrastructure. By the eighteenth century, the island in effect resembled a single 'vast sugar plantation'.[4] This denuding of the island also quickly began to have more than just an aesthetic affect. Visitors to the island, particularly those previously unfamiliar with the Caribbean, were struck by the prevalence of soil erosion. Welsh naturalist and clergyman Griffith Hughes moved to Barbados in 1736 and over the following years wrote a natural history of the island, which he published in 1750. Amongst many insightful observations he notes that around the plantations there were 'barren, rocky gullies runaway land, waste land, worn out, not fertile'.[5] By the nineteenth century, the cumulative effects of this erosion were clear. Richard Madden, who visited the island in the early 1830s, tells us that were it not for the use of a variety of seaweed called 'varek' as fertiliser, there would be no growth at all on the island. He also notes that Barbadian planters, distressed by the lack of soil fertility, had even resorted to trying to ship in soil from the considerably less deforested colony Dutch Guiana to try and revive Barbados' soil.[6]

Madden tells us that this problem was not confined to Barbados. As he puts it, on both Barbados and Jamaica, 'the far greater quantity of land that is in use is worn out', and, hinting at the fact that a key cause of this is the planters and their narrow focus, he goes on to write: 'too much has been taken out of it, and too little care expended on it'.[7] Like Griffiths, Madden, was struck by the extent of soil erosion, though he wrongly identified its proximate cause as its primary cause:

> In countries between the tropics, [rain falls] with such violence as to tear up the soil, and wash away all that is rich and valuable in it. In fact, the ports and harbours of the West Indies are the depositaries, to no small extent, of that soil which formerly constituted the riches of these countries.[8]

In light of Griffiths' and Madden's observations, it is clear that the plantation had a transformative effect on the environment of the Caribbean. What is particularly interesting is the way in which the region's hazards interacted with this altered environment.

The plantation and its role in creating epiphenomenal hazards

As the longer quotation from Madden already suggests, in periods of extreme weather, heavy rains, winds and, on occasions, the tremors of earthquakes could create devastating landslides. These landslides rendered the colonies more vulnerable by increasing loss of life and property, and prolonging recovery. It was not just deforestation affecting soil cohesion either. Hughes noted that where sugarcane was planted closely, the soil 'often [ran] away' and when there was heavy rain it moved with 'violence' and came 'tumbling down'.[9] Indicating that on Barbados the problem had by no means lessened over time, explorer Robert Schomburgk, writing in the nineteenth century, noted the frequency with which significant landslips occurred during periods of heavy rain.[10] Like Madden before her, American traveller Nancy Prince also observed that in Jamaica, heavy rains frequently carried away whole sections of earth and trees.[11]

That Griffiths, Madden, Schomburgk and Prince all saw fit to inform their readers of the landslides tells us something of the impression they left on those who observed them. They were clearly regarded as a notable feature of life in the Caribbean. Indeed, an American traveller to Jamaica, Robert Baird, not only had knowledge of them but remarked that their notoriety extended beyond the island's shores despite never having observed one on the island.[12] It is true that these authors' observations are limited to Barbados and Jamaica, but with the same pattern of deforestation and intense monoculture being mirrored around the British Caribbean, it does not feel too much of stretch to imagine that other colonies were experiencing similar issues. It just happened that Barbados and Jamaica were two of the most frequently visited and thus written about islands.

Another commonality of these authors is that they write of landslides as being triggered by periods of 'heavy rain'. I am inclined to think that they are talking of just inclement weather, and not specifically hurricanes because eyewitness accounts tell us that the consequences were far more severe when hurricanes did arrive. In 1815, Jamaica was struck by a hurricane, and the landslides it triggered were so severe that victims recorded whole plantation buildings being swept away, threatening to bury their inhabitants. So large was the amount of ground which gave way, that local rivers filled with soil.[13] Through this example, we can already begin to see the way in which the plantation, alongside the ecologically destructive processes associated with its creation and maintenance, promoted epiphenomenal hazards that increased its vulnerability. Indeed, an eyewitness testimony recorded in 1815 noted that the most significant movements of soil occurred on the plantations themselves.[14] Nowhere is this link more clearly expressed, however, than in the wake of the Barbadian hurricane of 10 August 1831.

As already indicated, the hurricane was immensely destructive, hitting Barbados and St Vincent with a force that some contemporaries considered the most powerful since colonisation began. Of the many disasters considered in this book, for the historian, 1831 stands out because – unlike other disasters, where one has to build a picture of events from colonial records, clipped quotes in newspapers and fragmented accounts sometimes written long after danger had passed – an anonymous author, presumed to be the editor of the Barbadian paper *The West Indian* left an extensive and singularly detailed account of the hurricane.

Immediately striking from this account is the effect that the hurricane and the rain and wind it carried with it had on Barbados' ecology. On the morning after the hurricane, the author of the account, having climbed the tower of St Mary's Church in Bridgetown, the colony's capital, looked out on the island and saw that 'no sign of vegetation was apparent' and that the very 'surface of the ground appeared as if fire had ran [sic] through the land'.[15] The strength of the hurricane is suggested by the severity of the destruction of property. From the bell tower, the island's plantation houses were only visible because the white stone of their ruins glinted in the sun.

Other eyewitness accounts the author collected from around the island recount having seen, much like in Jamaica in 1815, huge chasms opening up in the ground around the plantations, large enough to swallow livestock whole.[16] The endemic deforestation on Barbados also meant that the people fleeing collapsing buildings throughout the night of 10 August had no natural forest to shelter in. Exposed in the open, many were killed by flying debris such as roofing slates. Over the course of the night and the early hours of the following morning, over 1,787 Barbadians, primarily the enslaved, lost their lives to the hurricane.[17] In 1831, deforestation played a role not just in worsening the outcomes for people and property; landslides around the island also blocked roads and delayed recovery. Through comparative analysis we can isolate the role it played even further.

In September 1834, the island of Dominica was hit by a hurricane. It was less heavily populated and, crucially, less intensively planted than Barbados. As had been the case in 1831, the hurricane was of such a strength that the full spectrum of buildings in Dominica, be they timber huts, or multilevel stone buildings, were destroyed, and the waves arising from the storm surges it caused submerged entire villages.[18] The hurricane was also preceded by extremely heavy rains, and the day of its impact brought further rains still, swelling the island's rivers. Yet, despite the level of rain and winds the island was subjected to, unlike in Barbados or Jamaica in 1815, there are no reports of landslides or severe subsidence.[19]

The answer to this striking difference lies in the fact that Dominica was a 'second phase' settlement, settled in 1763 and sugar, though planted, never achieved dominance on the island; coffee instead was the island's central commodity.[20] As a result both of the later period of its settlement and of its more mixed agricultural production, the island was never subjected to the same level of deforestation as Barbados or Jamaica. In the early nineteenth century, Dominica was described as having many patches of 'uncultivated woodland' or, as one British visitor put it in more extreme terms, parts of the island were in 'a state of absolute wilderness'.[21] Some trees would have been felled to clear the ground for planting, but the very nature of the coffee plant means that it mitigates some of the worst effects of deforestation. The coffee plant has roots that can extend up to three metres below the soil not only binding the ground in a way that sugar does not but also making the crop more resilient to hurricanes in particular.[22] This is borne out in the fact that much of Dominica's coffee crop was said to have survived the storm.[23] The island's soil was considerably more fertile than any others, in particular Barbados.[24]

This pattern of vulnerability exhibited by the most heavily deforested and plantation-centric colonies continued throughout the nineteenth century. In 1898, Barbados, St Vincent and St Lucia were hit by a notably strong hurricane whose rains triggered severe landslides on St Vincent, in particular, in an area which had been heavily deforested.[25] St Lucia also suffered landslides, especially around its cocoa estates, causing £217 10s worth of damage and claiming the lives of seven children.[26] In 1901, Barbadians living in the Scotland district of the island were again subjected to dangerous landslides following a period of intense rain.[27]

The plantation had a clear role in increasing the dangers of hurricane impacts, in particular but, in its monopolisation of arable land, also significantly prolonged the time it took to recover and exposed survivors to further risk in the process. In addition to sapping the fertility of soil, plantations marginalised both the land and the time available for the enslaved and smaller free populations of the British Caribbean to grow crops for subsistence. As a result, since the eighteenth century, British planters had been heavily dependent on imported food stuffs, particularly from the US, to feed the enslaved population. Due to the uncaring nature of planters and the fragility of trade links in the era of sail, importing goods in this manner was never guaranteed and so there were frequently periods where the enslaved and sometimes the free population experienced food shortages, colloquially known as 'hungry or hard time[s]'.[28]

To offset these risks, plantation owners had, in the interest of lowering the overall amount of food they had to import (and thus the cost to themselves), long allowed enslaved people small plots of land around the plantation. The idea was that enslaved people would be enabled to provide for themselves and lessen the financial burden on planters. It was, however, hamstrung from the outset. Planters were obviously not willing to give up prime land and so allotments were often allowed only on the most marginal areas of what was already sapped soil. Furthermore, planters were also not keen for enslaved people to direct the majority of their energies anywhere but the plantation and so the time afforded to work these pieces of land was limited and usually only occurred after long workdays. With their time and energy so tightly constrained, most enslaved people preferred to plant crops such as plantains that were not as labour intensive, despite it being well known that they were more vulnerable to hurricanes.[29]

In the nineteenth century, after abolition cut them off from a seemingly limitless supply of labour, some planters, in an effort to stem a population drop, did moderate their approach to allow enslaved people more time to tend their allotments. However, seeking a means to some limited economic agency, enslaved people tended to grow crops they could sell rather than grow for their own subsistence.[30] This was a trend which only increased over time; Joseph Sturge, a British traveller, noted that in Dominica 'all the money which the negroes acquire, is earned by taking the surplus products of their grounds to Roseau, and other markets ... Of their privilege of attending market they are so jealous'.[31] Typically, during the period of slavery, the crops planted by enslaved people were selected for their market value and not their hardiness; plantains, corn and other above-ground crops were more common than deep rooted tubers such as yams, which were far more wind resistant.[32] As a result, these allotments only provided a fraction of the necessary calories for enslaved people, and hence the importation of staples such as guinea corn persisted throughout the eighteenth and nineteenth centuries.

Disasters were capable of simultaneously destroying both normal import arrangements and the allotments of the enslaved, and in the process, often immeasurably and sometimes fatally amplified 'hard times'. Not only did disasters expose the precariousness of the Caribbean colonies' import dependence, but so too did wars and other disruptions to shipping. In some cases, disaster and disruption arrived at the same time. When the hurricanes of 1780 hit, it was in the middle of the American War of Independence, which had halted much trade with the Caribbean, and these two combined had devastating effects for the African-Caribbean population. In Jamaica, at least five hundred perished after the hurricane. Mulcahy suggests that in Barbados more than a thousand people died after the hurricane. In both cases, communications between the islands and Britain suggest that food shortages and consequently starvation played a significant role in the death tolls.[33]

No loss on this scale would occur in the long nineteenth century but the plantation remained at the centre of life in the Anglophone Caribbean, and thus the vulnerability it created runs like a through line in this period. On 12 October 1812, Jamaica was hit by a storm that 'did great damage to houses, and destroyed immense quantities of growing provisions, a calamity more serious on account of the war with the US preventing importations from that quarter'.[34] Again, the import dependence fostered by the plantation economy was exacerbated both by disaster and existing disruptions to shipping. In that same year, plantation owners on St Vincent reported that the 'dread of famine' stalked the island in the wake of the eruption of its volcano La Soufrière.[35] Only the arrival of provisions from Barbados in the weeks after the eruption appear to have averted major starvation. Disasters were events that heightened societal tensions, and hunger only ratcheted that potential further. As shown in chapter 3, the lack of provisions and the resulting hunger on Barbados following the 1831 hurricane was a key driver of conflict between white authorities and the enslaved population.

The dominance of the plantation created a perverse situation in which despite these colonies being devoted almost solely to agriculture, they were quite often unable to avoid prolonged periods of hunger even in the absence of disaster. After the ending of coerced labour in 1838, planters desirous of maintaining a coerced labour force tried to enclose and prevent the sale of land to drive the African-Caribbean population to wage labour. There is some evidence to suggest that in the same period the free population, perhaps in an effort to work outside of the confines of the plantation, did change their approach somewhat to farming, incorporating more subsistence crops. For example, on Tobago, after a hurricane in 1847, mention of starvation and famine otherwise replete in post-disaster colonial communications throughout the long nineteenth century are conspicuous in their absence. Instead, the colonial report detailing the losses from the storm indicates that the provision grounds of the African-Caribbean population were planted with cassava and yams, which both survived the hurricane.[36]

In many ways, however, Tobago proved to be the exception. Where land was less fertile and less accessible for the African-Caribbean population, the trend toward import dependence continued throughout the long nineteenth century. After hurricanes in 1898, St Vincent and St Lucia needed to rapidly import food. In 1902, following the next eruption of La Soufrière, St Vincent would again need imports, with the US characteristically supplying them.[37]

In 1903, after a hurricane, Jamaica became temporarily reliant on the import of provisions from America to prevent starvation.[38]

Only enhancing the problems some colonial authorities faced, import dependence was a vulnerability that could be readily exploited by those wanting to make a quick profit. In 1866, after a hurricane, the Bahamas found itself in need of rapid food imports and, with them not being quickly supplied by a neighbouring British colony or the US, the authorities became reliant on local merchants who, whilst importing the food, raised their prices significantly.[39]

Even when there were mass casualties after a disaster, such as in 1902 when the eruption of La Soufrière killed an estimated 1,600, there are no specific numbers for those who died after disasters due to starvation; in 1902 the governor wrote that the 'true number will never be known'.[40] Though there was rarely an accurate count kept of those dying of starvation after disasters there can be little doubt of the hardships that disasters caused. If not resulting in death, then malnutrition certainly helped the spread of disease, as in the case of the cholera outbreak that occurred after the Barbadian hurricane of 1898.[41]

Food was not the only material that plantations prevented a ready supply of. The deforestation occasioned by their building, expansion and fuelling also left many of the British Caribbean colonies dependent on timber imports. For all of the long nineteenth century, timber was an essential component in rebuilding after disaster, but import dependence again slowed down recovery. In 1831, heavily deforested Barbados needed timber to rebuild houses, plantations and sugar manufacturing equipment but found itself more starved of timber than ever when even the timber reserves of Tobago, the island from which it had imported timber since the seventeenth century, had been drastically reduced. Similarly, Antigua too, after an earthquake in 1843, had to reach out to Puerto Rico for timber.[42] In both cases, timber scarcity dragged on the recovery.

By the middle of the century, Tobago's forestry stocks appear to have recovered enough that it did not have to import timber after the hurricane of 1847, but any building material that was available was deemed important enough that the island's authorities passed a new law that permitted the open flogging of free people for the theft of timber.[43] Over half a century on from the hurricane of 1831, both Barbados and St Vincent were still so reliant on imported timber that its importation was considered to be the only way to rebuild the infrastructure of the two islands, and so limited was the amount of timber coming into the island that it had to be extensively rationed.[44]

Through these examples we can see clearly the consequences of the all-consuming plantation complex at the heart of the British Caribbean; it required the simplification of its surrounding environment, directed all labour to it and hobbled these islands' natural abundance, hamstringing any chance of self-sufficient recovery from disaster. In this, we see one of the ways in which the relationship the British had with the Caribbean environment shaped the British response to disaster: it changed the very scope of the disasters the British had to respond to. Disasters were accompanied by a whole range of epiphenomenal issues such as landslides and food shortages that, as shown below, also required their own response, stretching both the resources and energy available for the relief of suffering and prolonging recovery.

The question that readily emerges is why, with these vulnerabilities, particularly the frequent food shortages that occurred even outside times of disaster, was little ever done to attempt to ameliorate them? This is not an anachronistic question to ask, as the stockpiling of food in disaster-prone areas is a centuries-old technique for preparing for disaster.[45]

The answer to this question is a broad one. In brief, the whites ruling the British Caribbean shared what is perhaps best termed a 'plantation mindset': they saw the Caribbean as a place to extract wealth from and they saw the plantation and slavery as the means to do that, and fought vociferously to ensure the survival of both, regardless of the consequences. Though whites certainly experienced the harsh reality of Caribbean disaster, those most heavily invested in plantation society did not. They were absentees, and disasters threatened their profits rather than their lives. Finally, this white population had an obvious racialised contempt for the lives of African-Caribbean people, which persisted far beyond the acts of abolition and emancipation. To have remedied the vulnerabilities induced by the plantation would have meant a fundamental restructuring of British Caribbean society in order to control the externalities of the plantation and would have placed a new, higher value on African-Caribbean life; such a reconfiguration was simply not possible within the bounds of the plantation mindset.

The persistence of the plantation

The externalities of the plantation complex were not invisible and were subject to criticism both implicit and explicit. Joseph Sturge, on his visit to Dominica in 1837, describes the peculiarities of the plantation system to his British audience and provides us with a basic example of the plantation mindset:

> The island imports great quantities of timber, and numbers of cattle and horses, though valuable trees grow on every estate ... if it be asked, why man does not put forth his hand and gather the good things which nature provides with

such spontaneous bounty, the reply is, that there is no surplus labor to devote to such minor matters; the sugar and coffee cultivation absorb all the resources of the island.[46]

Speaking more pointedly to the plantation owners or 'plantocracy', botanist Alexander Anderson, in his 1799 book, *Geography and History of St Vincent*, expressed frustration at their 'fruitless' deforestation and exasperation at the fact that timber had to be imported from Demerara and Puerto Rico at 'vast expense and on a precarious footing'.[47] Anderson clearly understood the benefits of forest; he notes in the same text that it played an essential role in making the climate tolerable, promoting rains and screening the land (one assumes from storms).[48] He appears to be a lone voice, however; by contrast, the plantocracy were unable and seemingly unwilling to fully grasp the impact that the plantations were having on the Caribbean environment.

It is fair to say that in some cases there were exceptions. On St Vincent, no doubt because of Anderson's writings, laws were passed in the early nineteenth century to prevent deforestation at the sources of the island's rivers. This was probably in recognition of the fact that, like Madden had observed in Barbados and Jamaica, the felling of trees around river heads meant their waters filled with soil and silted the ports and irrigation channels cut to feed plantations.[49]

Colonial governors received no direction from the Colonial Office to deal with these issues, but with their office came great latitude in the projects they could choose to pursue. Some did try to strike new directions for their colonies but quickly came up against resistance from other planters. Sir William Young became Governor of Tobago in 1807 and stayed in office until his death in 1815. In his time as governor, Young tried to decrease the island's dependence on American food imports but found planters and estate managers reluctant to fully embrace his proposal. Even as a planter himself, Young was unable to persuade them and at the time of his death the island remained a keen consumer of American provisions.[50] It must be said, some planters did recognise the precariousness of the import regime. At the beginning of hurricane season, Jamaican planter Simon Taylor went to some effort to store food to 'prevent want even in case of storms'. However, as Nicholas Crawford points out, Taylor was particularly wealthy planter and more careful than many others.[51]

The plantation was the source of wealth and power for the coterie of planters who quickly came to control the British Caribbean colonies. The overall impact of their profits on Britain and its industrial revolution remains a contested topic, but there can be little doubt that plantations and slavery made many individuals fabulously wealthy. In this context, there was obviously little incentive to attend to the environmental externalities the plantation created. Madden, as quoted in the introduction, noted that where he saw Barbados as a land with 'no claim to picturesque attractions', Barbadians, by which he no doubt meant white plantation owners, felt very differently from him. Madden put this difference down to the denuded environment providing 'them with advantages to which they were most want of'.[52] Most planters were unwilling and unable to see the damage the plantations caused and how they exacerbated disaster outcomes.

Over the eighteenth century, as absenteeism became endemic through the region, plantation owners were further removed than ever from the externalities caused by their enterprise. For the planters and whites who remained in the Caribbean, the plantation remained at the centre of society because, by physically concentrating the labour in one place it also served as the main means through which the power of the white minority could be most effectively exerted on the African-Caribbean majority.

Even as the influence of the plantocracy waned in the face of the equalisation of sugar duties and the general turn to India, the plantation still persisted at the heart of Caribbean society. This was in part the result of a lack of imagination on the behalf of the British. Even when, in the 1890s, the region began to face serious competition from European sugar beet, which triggered a serious economic downturn, the British response effectively amounted to a doubling down on agriculture.

Joseph Chamberlain, Secretary of State for the Colonies between 1895 and 1903, signalled in his 1897 speech titled *True Conceptions of Empire* that he was prepared to take a new direction in colonial management, suggesting that he wanted to move beyond the thinking that saw the colonies only 'as possessions valuable in proportion to the pecuniary advantage which they brought to the mother country'.[53] Chamberlain envisioned a more direct role for Britain in developing its 'underdeveloped estates' but in practice, his Caribbean policy displayed itself to be as wedded to plantations as that of the planters who had gone before him.

In the same year he gave his speech, Chamberlain called a Royal Commission specifically to investigate the causes of the economic downturn in the Caribbean. It identified the declining price of cane sugar as the key source of the downturn, but it proposed few remedies beyond the introduction of new methods to enhance agricultural efficiency. In the case of Barbados, for example, it was suggested that the island should move to centralised sugar factories, a move that would have only intensified the rate of extraction from the soil, thus worsening the environmental externalities of the plantation.

Wisner et al. argue that disasters often 'deeply reflect failed or skewed development', and the British Caribbean could not be a more perfect example of how skewed development increased vulnerability.[54] The British were never able to imagine the Caribbean as more than a land for profit, and this lack of vision kept it 'underdeveloped'. The near-constant focus on the plantation and agricultural extraction that had guided British Caribbean politics since the seventeenth century meant that, as Michael Craton puts it, the region was 'denuded of political and cultural leadership'. In this way, the plantation mindset had a profound impact on both vulnerability to disasters and the response to them.[55] It shaped the Caribbean's built environment in a manner that rendered even those outside of the physical plantation more vulnerable to disaster and, as shown in chapter 5, played a fundamental role in the apportioning and targeting of post-disaster financial relief from Britain.

A land for profit

Part of the reason why the British lacked the willingness to develop the Caribbean was not just that the plantation provided wealth, but also because the planters who controlled Caribbean society never saw the region as a home – it was only ever a land for profit. With land quickly concentrated in a few hands and those looking for opportunity already turning elsewhere, by the early eighteenth century, the sense that the Caribbean had the same potential as the American colonies as a place for settlement had diminished significantly. Even for those who had obtained positions of wealth and power in the region, their personal affection for it appears weak at times. Indeed, Andrew Jackson O'Shaughnessy argues that the planter class never really saw the Caribbean truly as their home. He sees them more as mere 'sojourners', firmly attached to their British identity.

Above all, they sought to distance themselves from those they enslaved, resisting anything that suggested a creolisation of their lifestyles. As a result, as Michael Connor puts it:

> The English colonists did what they could to continue their familiar modes of fashion and style in the tropics, whether in dress, diet, or architecture. The English plantocracy tried to retain the mother-country's architectural styles in the eighty-degree heat.[56]

This was seemingly a distinctly British view that put them at odds with the other European powers in the region well into the nineteenth century. For example, in the journal of his travels through the Caribbean, Frederick Bayley, a visitor from Britain remarked that:

> The French must be amused, and their colonists are not like our English people, always going backward and forward, to and from the mother country. France only *was*, but Martinique *is* the home of its inhabitants, and they are attached to it as such.[57]

Bayley's observation is borne out in the few letters left by French planters. The Martinican Pierre Dessalles was born and educated in France and yet, when making trips back there, frequently expressed a homesickness for Martinique.[58] Toward the end of his life when an acquaintance asked him to stay in France to protect his health Dessalles confided in his diary that the acquaintance would not succeed in their pleas and that he was 'very anxious to go home'.[59] The experiences of some British planters offer a stark contrast.

Jamaican born planter Simon Taylor, who became one of the most successful British planters in the eighteenth century, not only owned property on the island but was also an active participant in its politics. Taylor was a member of the island's assembly, its legislature, the chief magistrate of his parish and, for a time, the lieutenant general of its militia.[60] Yet, despite both it being his birthplace and the myriad business and political connections he maintained there, he never saw the island as home; Britain was fixed as that in his mind and in direct contrast to Dessalles, it was the place he envisioned journeying to when his health declined in later life.

Part of this wider attempt to maintain a connection with Britain as their true home was that, as far as they could, and often in the face of rejection from the upper echelons of British society, planters resisted any creolisation in their identities and habits. This trend probably had an effect on disaster resistance, as effective adaptations to environmental hazards were rejected. For example, Mulcahy notes that during the eighteenth century there was a trend toward building hurricane shelters, not just in the Caribbean but also through South Carolina. These shelters were designed as small, stout bunkers sunk into the ground and were reportedly effective enough at protecting those who used them that they drove up the value of a property.[61] In South Carolina they continued to be built throughout the nineteenth century, while in the Caribbean they dropped off in popularity despite the efficacy at saving lives. One can imagine that for the planter class determined to maintain a British character in their houses, the hurricane shelter may have represented a dangerous creolisation.

Planters did make some sensible climactic adjustments to their houses such as limiting their height and the extent of their decorative features, but this seems to have been in constant tension with their desire to retain their British character and display their wealth. Writing in 1841 of her travels in Jamaica, Nancy Prince remarks that the 'best houses' were usually built with reduced height to make them more resilient to earthquakes and hurricanes.[62] Implicit in Prince's words is the suggestion that some houses were not built like this and indeed the observations of other visitors in the nineteenth century bears this out. Bayley relates that a friend of his, also a visitor to the Caribbean, commented that 'the great houses of the estates, as we cruised along the coast appeared to me more like the country seats of our English gentlemen than any other others I had seen in the West Indies.[63]

These plantation houses often became death traps in the face of hurricanes and earthquakes, in particular, their heavy walls and floors crushing those unlucky enough not to make it out in time. Typically, the African-Caribbean population fared little better. Though the huts to which they were largely restricted were rarely built of materials that threatened to crush their inhabitants, the region's hazards often made short work of them, leaving most with not even the remnants to begin repairing after a disaster.

As chapter 5 shows, African-Caribbean people were also almost never given any financial aid to help them in the rebuilding of their properties even if they were to survive a disaster in a substantial way. This situation got no better over the course of the nineteenth century. Despite the arrival of legal freedom in 1838, many Barbadians were trapped in precarious land rental agreements and as such lived in chattel houses, designed to be physically moved if these agreements changed. They were portable but at the cost of deep foundations and were consequently very vulnerable to hurricane winds. In 1898, after a hurricane hit Barbados, 9,937 homes of African-Caribbean people were destroyed, leaving 50,000 homeless.[64]

The built environment

The centrality of the plantation, the power of the planters and the racially bifurcated nature of British Caribbean society meant that while some planters adapted their own residences to the climate, these adaptations were spread very unevenly around the rest of society. In fact, urban centres in the Anglophone Caribbean suffered neglect that marked them out against other colonies in the Caribbean. Recounting a visit to the Barbadian capital of Bridgetown, British traveller Daniel McKinnen described the town in particularly disparaging terms, remarking on its refuse-filled streets lined by warped, crumbling and dilapidated buildings.[65]

In the next twenty years, little changed. In the 1820s Bayley described Bridgetown as: 'for the most part, irregularly built, without any regard to order, or the slightest attention to the rules of architecture'.[66] By contrast, an acquaintance of Bayley's whom he quotes, found St Pierre in French-controlled Martinique to be a 'beautiful place – perfectly European' and, more importantly, incomparable to any place in the British Caribbean.[67] This perspective did not go away over the course of the nineteenth century. Returning again to Froude's *The English in the West Indies*, he was similarly disparaging of Kingston, capital of Jamaica and made an explicit comparison to what else had been achieved by the Spanish in Cuba: 'Kingston is the best of our West Indian towns, and Kingston has not one fine building in it. Havana is a city of palaces, a city of streets and plazas, of colonnades, and towers and churches and monasteries.'[68]

Upon arriving in these places, white visitors found them hollowed out and devoid of culture. Bayley remarks that the arts were entirely neglected in the British Caribbean and that on his travels he encountered few places of public entertainment, Bayley's friend in Martinique made the explicit comparison that the French colonial theatres were far superior to anything available in the British colonies.[69] Bayley also goes on to make further comparisons between the shops of the French colonies and the decidedly more basic stores of the British colonies. What they were experiencing was a society completely skewed in the direction of the plantation and whose leaders had little interest in developing or building anything of substance. Planters recognised and occasionally railed against this too. Jamaican planter Edward Long blamed absentee plantation owners for ensuring that Caribbean society would never become more than a 'simulacrum' of British society.[70] This critique of the hollowness of the colonies' society and its linkage to the plantation had in fact been made almost from the very beginning of English settlement. In his *History of Barbados* published in 1657, Richard Ligon remarked on the artistic tastes of Barbadians and wrote, 'though I found at Barbadoes some, who had musicall mindes; yet, I found others, whose souls were so fixed upon, and so riveted to the earth, and the profits that arise out of it, as their souls were lifted no higher'.[71]

The sense that many British seemed to share, that the Caribbean was not a place for them to permanently settle, had an impact beyond the aesthetic or the frivolous entertainment expected by white visitors. The plantation mindset and control over the direction of Caribbean society had a tangible impact on how disaster relief funds were apportioned, as shown in chapter 5, but these underdeveloped towns also increased their inhabitant's exposure to disasters and prevented the sort of reengineering efforts that other colonies, considered as true settlements, were employing throughout the eighteenth and nineteenth centuries.

It is true that, in many ways, there was no perfect set of adaptations that the British could have made. They were frequently caught between a multitude of hazards, not least, hurricanes and earthquakes. For many urban centres in the Caribbean, small, squalid, and often unplanned as they were, buildings with bricks and stone emerged as straightforward defence against hurricanes. While hurricane winds did often blow bodies and decaying matter into narrow unplanned streets, sometimes causing outbreaks of disease, it was rare that winds would completely level brick buildings and as such, building with brick emerged as a relatively successful strategy.[72] However, earthquakes then posed a huge threat. Wooden buildings, with their natural flex, could withstand earthquakes but were often blown away in hurricanes and also increased the chance of major fires breaking out not just in normal times but also during disasters.

Natalie Zaceck tells us that in the first two centuries of British settlement in the Leeward Islands, fires were such a regular occurrence that townspeople became accustomed to them.[73] In Bayley's observations on Barbados, he relates that fires were extremely common in Bridgetown and details one that he witnessed, noting that, in a reflection of the chronic under-preparedness of British Caribbean societies, it was particularly destructive because it burned for a long time, fire engines being few and far between.[74] Antigua's capital, St John's, suffered a major earthquake in 1843, and appears to have only avoided a substantial fire afterwards because the town was still so decimated from a fire 1841 and the importation of materials had been so slow as to prevent a complete rebuilding. The large gaps between the buildings that had been created in 1841 acted as unintentional firebreaks and stopped a blaze from spreading.

Adaptations to the region's hazards were ad hoc at best and, where they were deployed, focused on buildings that benefitted the colonial regime. In his book *Empire Divided*, O'Shaughnessy also observed this trend, saying that where the planters and colonial officials did spend money developing infrastructure in the Caribbean it was on 'fortresses, naval dockyards, and military barracks', all structures designed to ensure the maintenance of British power and the protection of its commerce.[75]

The efforts of the Royal Engineers who were sent to Barbados after the hurricane of 1831 reflect this trend clearly. They arrived to assist with the rebuilding and their efforts appear to have primarily focused on rebuilding the island's barracks. Since 1824 there had been some attempts by Colonel Sir Charles Felix Smith, commanding the Royal Engineers in the region, to standardise the construction of barracks in the Caribbean colonies. His primary focus, informed by miasmatical understanding of disease, was making them as ventilated as possible, but he was also interested in increasing their hurricane resilience.[76] By the time of the 1831 hurricane, one building, the Ordnance Hospital, had been built in accordance with Smith's recommendations and it was one of the few buildings said to have survived the storm in good condition.[77] Indeed, remarking on its survival, a key eyewitness, the anonymous author of the *Account*, was keen for its construction to form a blueprint for more buildings in the colony:

> The plan of the whole is admirable, and there is no apparent reason why it should not be adopted in the construction of private houses. It is much cheaper than the common mode of building, very desirable for cleanliness and durability, and is not only proof against fire, but evidently the most secure in case of the island being again visited by storms.

Lieutenant Colonel William Reid oversaw the replacement of elements of the original barracks with stone features to better withstand future storms. The Royal Engineers were also involved with making other, unmentioned buildings more hurricane-resilient through the use of metal embedded into the foundations.[78] In his time on Barbados, Reid not only expressed a broad apprehension at the lack of resilience building efforts through the region but tied this directly to a persistent desire to appear British:

> There cannot be a doubt but that some difference of construction should be made in buildings, between countries subject to the most violent hurricanes, and countries which are not. Yet it is too often the practice, simply to place a roof on its walls, as is the custom in Europe, and to copy the details of construction from the modes adopted in England.[79]

Evidently the adaptations being deployed in the Barbadian barracks did not inform the housing of the wider community. Indeed, funding adaptations, even with collective benefit to the planter class, appears to have been difficult in Caribbean society. In 1835, the establishment of a hurricane resistant lighthouse was proposed on Barbados, with Parliament even volunteering to cover half of the cost of its erection. Despite this relatively generous offer, the island's planter-dominated legislature could not agree on providing the other half of the necessary funds.[80] As Cynthia Kierner tells us, throughout the preceding centuries lighthouses had become a key pillar of efforts to build disaster resilience in both Europe and America; the planters of Barbados again demonstrated a narrow conception of public interest that showed them to be out of step with their contemporaries outside of the Caribbean.[81]

Due to the frequency with which it experienced hurricanes, inexpensive adaptations such as wooden shutters were common in Barbados, in contrast to the extensive use of glass windows in Antigua, Tobago and the Grenada islands, long regarded as being out of the regular path of hurricanes.[82] However, through the example of the 1835 lighthouse scheme, we can see just how quickly the limits of what Barbadian planters were willing to spend on their own protection were exceeded.

The ad hoc nature of adaptations to the region's hazards stands out particularly when compared to other contemporary societies and even other colonies within the British Empire. As discussed in chapter 1, after the earthquake of 1755, Lisbon had been wholly rebuilt and redesigned, as far as possible, in an earthquake-resistant 'Pombal style' (named for the Marquess of Pombal who oversaw the rebuilding effort). One could argue that this effort reflected Lisbon's status as the capital of Portugal and the seat of an empire, and this was certainly an important factor, but even in more marginal places, as a providential understanding of disasters gave way to a more scientific one, some societies worked to collectively render themselves more resilient. When the town of Providence, Rhode Island was levelled by a storm on 23 September 1815, its residents responded by completely redesigning the worst affected areas. They raised the riverbanks, repositioned buildings and redesigned a crucial bridge and buildings in new, more durable forms.[83] This flurry of post-disaster resilience building is made all the more striking in comparison with the British Caribbean by the fact that the 1815 storm was the first to hit Providence in 180 years.

This rebuilding of Providence was no doubt uneven in its own way and it is not a stretch to imagine that the new durable building practices did not benefit everyone in Providence – in 1815, America was, after all still a slave society. However, the rebuilding represented something that was seemingly impossible in the Caribbean: a collective, cross-societal effort. The impetus driving the improvement of Providence was not uniquely American; in Britain the eighteenth century marked the emergence of the era of local government, improvement projects proliferated, and the nineteenth century only saw this drive to improve accelerate. David Eastwood informs us that between the years 1800 and 1845 almost four hundred Local Improvement Acts were passed.[84]

Such contrasts mark out the impact of the planter class who controlled Caribbean society but saw it as a land of 'exile', never a place to 'live, prosper, and die'.[85] The role of the planters in perpetuating the region's disaster vulnerability is further isolated when we consider that others outside of the planter sphere were calling for change. Not only praising the changes made to military buildings, the author of the account of the 1831 hurricane made a wider plea:

> would it not be advisable so that the colonists, to the utmost of their ability, should be at all times prepared to encounter the impending danger – not alone by a life of virtue and religion ... but also by a commendable precaution in constructing buildings more calculated to withstand the force of the elements than those usually erected?[86]

As to why the anonymous author of this account might have made a plea so at odds with the perspective of the planter class, Stuart Schwartz has suggested that the author was probably Samuel Hyde, the editor of *The West Indian*.[87] Hyde was a creole, born in Barbados and, like many creole people, may have seen the island as his home and thus, unlike the planters, made a plea for development on the island. By contrast, other than building themselves mansions that emphasised their Britishness and doing all they could to sustain the short-term profitability of their plantation holdings, the planters were clearly loath to invest in and develop the Caribbean. It was not a land they wanted to live in, nor, through the typical crude climatic racialisations of the day, was it one in which they considered themselves racially suited to.

The racism of the planters no doubt had a role in precluding resilience building efforts because unlike the white citizens of Providence who were primarily building to protect themselves, similar efforts in the Caribbean would have meant planters, often situated comfortably in Britain, expending capital to primarily protect the African-Caribbean people who, not least because they were the majority of the population, were the most affected by disasters.

As shown in chapter 5, in the nineteenth century, the planters could mostly count on Parliament to deliver some form of aid, circumscribed and conditional though it may have been, to repair their investments. Neither planters nor MPs were interested in making safer Caribbean society for non-white people, however, as they did not value their lives or their property as much as their own. After the hurricane of 1898, MP Henry Labouchère exclaimed in Parliament that:

> the houses in Barbados are simply bamboo huts ... no doubt a great deal of injury has been done, but it is only of a temporary character, because these huts which have been destroyed can be built again for £1 or £2.[88]

The racially bifurcated nature of Caribbean society also precluded the emergence of mutual aid and ensured that disasters almost always became the site of racial conflict. By contrast, pre-colonial societies in the Caribbean and Latin America deployed a number of wide-ranging adaptations to their climate and its hazards. Some were at the level of individual buildings, which used windbreaks and were otherwise small and easily rebuilt. More broadly, there was a focus on reciprocity on a scale unseen in the colonial Caribbean. In his exploration of Incan responses to earthquakes in Peru, Anthony Oliver Smith shows that the systems of reciprocity embedded in their social structure, as well as the creation of *Qollqas* points for food storage, were part of their constant long-term preparation for disasters.

Some planters did take precautions, as in the above-mentioned example from Simon Taylor. Some went further and created granaries to store limited provisions, but these were often defeated by the climate, pests and the fact that, as Nicholas Crawford puts it, the logic of these adaptations was driven by the planter desire to save money and preserve the health of their slaves in order to more efficiently and frequently extract labour from them.[89]

As demonstrated throughout this book, there was reciprocity between British colonies during disasters but, reflecting planter short-termism, it was always organised on an ad hoc basis. For much of the time the British occupied the Caribbean, the Colonial Office was seemingly not interested in promoting resilience building efforts. The formal guidance given to colonial governors heading for their first appointments in the Caribbean rarely, if ever, mentioned the regions' common natural hazards and offered no instructions for the event that disaster did strike.[90]

In this context, we can see the power not just of the planter class but also of the very nature of colonialism to deter resilience building efforts. When discussing Incan strategies for resilience, Smith argues that Spanish colonialism not only physically destroyed them but stopped them being possible; it created in their place an 'infrastructure for disunity' that would ultimately render it an agricultural nation dependent on imported food.[91] The applicability of those statements to the British Caribbean is clearly demonstrated by this chapter. In the nineteenth century, there was a particularly unique lack of resilience building efforts in the Caribbean. Research into hurricanes in particular did take place in the region, but the developments it spurred were deployed elsewhere.

Scientific developments

The experience of reconstructing Barbados after the hurricane of 1831 clearly had a major impact on Royal Engineer William Reid. It seems to have spurred a lifelong interest in hurricanes that developed into a book titled *The Law of Storms*, which was published in 1838. It was the first major nineteenth-century study of hurricanes and represents the first comprehensive study of the atmospheric origins of hurricanes and strategies for limiting their damage. The strategies focused particularly on trying to limit their damage to shipping in the Atlantic. For example, the book set out techniques for sailors, giving the direction in which they should tack when encountering hurricanes to avoid their ships being devastated.

The book was a huge success and became a required part of the inventory of every British ship of war.[92] It also led to both Reid's election to the Royal Society and his becoming a Knight Companion of the Order of the Bath. This success was also most probably behind his being made Governor of Bermuda in 1839. The colony was of significant strategic importance for the British in the Atlantic, who feared that it could be a potential invasion point for the US. What is most interesting about Reid's tenure as governor is that despite him being one of the premier hurricane researchers of his day, he did not deploy his knowledge on the island even though it had a long history of suffering from hurricanes and was hit by one shortly after his arrival in 1839. Instead, he focused his attention, unlike any previous governor, on resolving the island's dependence on American imports, developing the island's productive capacity, and making the island ready for an invasion attempt. Reid's main fears were not hurricanes but that, were the island invaded, because of its import dependence, its people would starve.[93] This was not something borne out of compassion. Reid appears to have been a particularly pragmatic man. After the 1839 hurricane, he argued against setting up a board to distribute charity, stating that to do so would: 'bring a very serious evil upon the community ... and might cause more harm than the storm itself'.[94] As shown in chapter 3, Reid's response to relief was characteristic of many governors throughout the British colonies in the region.

Emphasising the uniqueness of Britain's relationship with the Caribbean, while Reid's knowledge was not employed to build resilience in the region, it was used to great success in the Indian Ocean. Retired British sailor Henry Piddington who had settled in Calcutta was inspired by Reid's work and set about recording and studying cyclones in the Indian Ocean.[95] He would go on to publish *The Horn-Book for the Law of Storms for the Indian and China Seas* in 1844 which, like Reid's book, would focus on providing practical instruction for sailors. Piddington also made recommendations for the development of colonial infrastructure on the basis of his knowledge. For example, he recommended that Port Canning not be constructed on the east of Calcutta, which was vulnerable to cyclones – his advice was ignored and it was later destroyed by storms in 1867.[96]

Piddington died in 1858 but his work continued to be an important resource, as the prediction of storms continued in colonial India at a pace never witnessed in the Caribbean. The British Government responded to a decade of devastating storms from 1864 by setting up and funding the Indian Meteorological Office in 1875. While certainly not perfect, it subsequently developed into the 'largest and most complete' system of cyclone prediction across all of the tropical empires.[97] It should also be said that we should not celebrate these developments uncritically. Tirthanker Ghosh argues that the colonial desire to expand the state's metrological knowledge was borne of a preoccupation with ensuring its maritime grip over India after the 1857 mutiny.[98]

Elsewhere in the British Empire, as the nineteenth century progressed, developments in disaster resilience did emerge but in a sporadic manner. Charles Bruce, noted thinker on the responsibilities of colonial governance, took up the governorship of Mauritius in 1897, not long after it was struck by a devastating hurricane in 1892. Bruce subsequently directed the overhaul of the island's political structures to render them more flexible in the face of disasters and recalibrated the beginning and end of the financial year to minimise the impact of storm losses for sugar planters on the island's plantations.[99] Under Bruce there was also greater communication between the island's civil service and community leaders from the indentured Indian population to best ensure that needs were being met during times of disaster.[100]

His successful reforms were not wholly positively received in Britain, however. The report of a Royal Commission sent to the island in 1909 implies that Bruce did face criticism from some in the Colonial Office who suggested he had unnecessarily increased the colonies' expenditure.[101]

It is worth restating that responses like Piddington's and Bruce's were not without their shortcomings and were certainly not driven by a wholly humanitarian desire, but they do reflect a pragmatic response to natural hazards that was simply not present in the British Caribbean. This absence tells us much about the position of the Caribbean within British elites' understanding of Empire. With the loss of slavery and the failure to replace it with the dynamic wage economy envisioned by liberal abolitionists, many considered the Caribbean to be a region in decline. This framing is crucial to understanding both the persistent vulnerability of the region and the shape of British disaster responses over the course of the long nineteenth century.

The lack of attention to the Caribbean meant that at the end of the nineteenth century, as the imperial map of the region was beginning to be reshaped by the expansionist drive of America, Britain found itself dependent on the emergent hegemon to protect its underdeveloped colonies from hurricanes. Like the British in India, America had been spurred to develop a pragmatic response to hurricanes because they threatened its imperial grip. When fighting the Spanish in Cuba, America was heavily reliant on its navy to project its military might, and hurricanes were considered such a threat to that projection that President William McKinley is reported to have said: 'I am more afraid of a West Indian Hurricane than the entire Spanish Navy.'[102] The American fear of hurricanes drove them to establish the first hurricane warning system in the Caribbean in 1898. Despite Britain having developed its own unparalleled early warning system in the Indian Ocean, American developments in the Caribbean filled a gap the British had never bothered to amend and quickly exposed the shortcomings of their failure.

In 1898 a hurricane swept through the Windward Islands, causing widespread destruction but primarily affecting Barbados, St Vincent and St Lucia. In the colonial communications that accompanied this disaster, the British Caribbean authorities struck a terse tone with the US's consul in Barbados, accusing them of a failure to notify the island in advance of the hurricane's landfall. The reality was not that the British were victims of US maliciousness, but rather that they had fallen foul of protocol designed by Americans for Americans. To reduce the potential for errors, American observers were not permitted to make warnings without first subjecting their observations to a review by a second station. In line with that policy, the American station in Barbados had to send it its observations back to

US Agricultural Department regional headquarters in Kingston, Jamaica where a collective decision could be made with a fuller picture of regional data. After the diplomatic fracas of 1898, however, in an attempt to maintain their permission to run these stations on British territory, the US amended its policy, allowing the observer on Barbados greater latitude to make early warnings on their own, including to the benefit of the British authorities on the island.[103]

It is striking that despite having been subjected to hurricanes since the early seventeenth century, by the end of the nineteenth the British were reliant on what was effectively a rival power to provide hurricane warnings. The Windwards did not receive an early hurricane warning in 1898, and this was as much a product of the shortcomings of US protocol as it was the plantation mindset and the underdevelopment and neglect that flowed from it. This underdevelopment and its roots in the economics of the plantation are rendered all the more visible when we see that it took a new economic opportunity, potentially superseding the plantation, to generate a meaningful change from this course.

The new economic opportunity arrived in the form of the American commitment to finish the Panama Canal project started but later abandoned by the French. Jamaican elites, in particular, considering the island's proximity to the canal, envisioned it instigating a renaissance for the island with it becoming the major entrepôt for trade in the region. There was also growing interest in the island from Lancastrian textile producers interested in developing its agricultural focus to include cotton. This dream was part of a wider moment in which the Caribbean briefly remerged in the British colonial imagination with a perceived glimmer of a new profitable dynamism, or, as Eric Williams put it more pithily, '[the Caribbean colonies were] forgotten until the Panama Canal reminded the world of their existence'.[104]

In 1907, as this dream began to crystallise, the envisioned entrepôt, Kingston, capital of Jamaica, was utterly levelled by the worst earthquake in the British colonies since 1692. What the tremors did not reduce to rubble was reduced to ashes by the fire that swept through docks district for days afterwards. The dream of a reinvigorated Jamaica was quite literally at risk of going up in smoke. Henry McNeil, a member of the Council of the British Cotton Growing Association, the group keen to invest in Jamaica, observed that 'unless something striking is done to counteract the misconception, investments within the earthquake zone will for years be taboo'.[105] It was the first time that a request like this had not fallen on deaf ears and, to allay investor fears amongst other things, plans were quickly drawn up by the West India Committee (WIC) to rebuild Kingston 'on such scientific lines as would render it, as far as possible, immune from the effects of earthquakes, hurricanes, and fire'.[106] The WIC also encouraged members of the Colonial Office to attend a lecture given by John Milne on the 'Construction of Buildings in Earthquake Countries' in February 1907. Having spent twenty years of his life studying earthquakes and seismology in Japan, Milne was a leading expert on the topic.

Building codes distinctly different from those that went before them were passed in June 1907, though there is no record of exactly how the WIC's pressure and the Milne lecture influenced them. In the case of individual properties, there were efforts to enforce minimum standards in construction materials to make buildings less susceptible to collapse. For example, roofs were mandated to be constructed of durable and incombustible material as well.[107] The legislation also specified a minimum distance between buildings to try and minimise the potential for fires to spread and there were new rules enforcing a minimum width to the city's streets to try and reduce the threat of fires. Kingston's council was given greater oversight to review buildings and extensions and fine anyone not adhering to newly specified clauses related to building materials and foundation requirements. The rebuilding of Kingston did not go entirely smoothly, however. Controversy about whether existing building insurance policies covered fires started by earthquakes carried on through Kingston's courts until late 1908 when the Law Lords of the Privy Council in London dismissed an appeal from the Scottish Union and National Insurance Company finding them liable to cover the costs of several burned-out businesses in the city.[108]

Similar legislation had been passed in Kingston in 1883 following a fire in 1882, but it was clear that it had not gone far enough or been properly enforced. The building codes of 1907 represented a broader step forward for the British Caribbean and show the incentive needed for state-driven resilience building in the region: opportunity for profit outside of the plantation. In 1907, it was more important than ever that those envisioning a new future for Kingston had to physically rebuilt the city and its trade infrastructure to ensure its survival but also – as British business interests were courting investment and the entire disaster was exposed to an unprecedented level of media scrutiny – to demonstrate to parties interested in investing that they were more than just passing visitors.

Ultimately, though it represented a break with the British lack of resilience building in the Caribbean, the response to the 1907 earthquake still followed the central trend of British responses to disaster in that it was driven primarily by economic considerations. Throughout this chapter we have seen that the short-term, profit-driven focus of the planters and their unwillingness to develop the Caribbean beyond a land for their profit worsened disaster outcomes across the long nineteenth century. Planters clearly assumed that the risk posed by disaster was worth enduring above and beyond the cost of building a more resilient society. As I have made clear, this willingness to forego serious and methodical adaptations even as they were being deployed elsewhere reflects that those in control cared little for the lives and property of those whom disasters primarily affected: the African-Caribbean population. The plantation mindset, as I have termed it, had profound consequences for how disasters were responded to and the 'relief' that was provided for the African-Caribbean population. It brought into sharp focus the racial divisions of Caribbean society and their persistence long beyond the end of slavery.

Notes

1 James Anthony Froude, *The English in the West Indies, or, the Bow of Ulysses* (London: Longmans, Green and Co., 1888), p. 256.
2 James Froude's white supremacist views are readily apparent through much of his writing, but the point about his views being out of step with his contemporary intellectuals is made clear by his own hand when he remarks in his 1896 book, *English Seaman*, that 'The transport [slave trade] over the Atlantic became a regular branch of business … The full consequences could not be foreseen; and I cannot see that as an experiment it merits the censures which in its later developments it eventually came to deserve.' James Anthony Froude, *English Seamen: In The Sixteenth Century: Lectures Delivered At Oxford Easter Terms 1893–4* (London: Longmans, Green and Co., 1896), p. 40.
3 Elizabeth DeLoughrey, 'Yam, Roots, and Rot: Allegories of the Provision Grounds', *Small Axe*, 15:1 (2011), p. 74.
4 B.W. Higman, *Slave Populations of the British Caribbean, 1807–1834* (Kingston: The University of the West Indies Press, 1995), p. 52.
5 Griffith Hughes, *The Natural History of Barbados in Ten Books* (London: Printed for the author, 1750), pp. 20–22.
6 Richard Robert Madden, *A Twelvemonth's Residence in the West Indies; During the Transition from Slavery to Apprenticeship; With Incidental Notices of the State of Society*, Vol. I (London: James Cochrane and Co., 1835), p. 35.
7 Ibid.
8 Ibid., pp. 35–36.
9 Griffith Hughes, *The Natural History of Barbados in Ten Books*, pp. 20–22.
10 Sir Robert Hermann Schomburgk, *The History of Barbados: Comprising a Geographical and Statistical Description of the Island, a Sketch of the Historical Events Since the Settlement, and an Account of Its Geology and Natural Productions* (London: Frank Cass, 1848), pp. 67–68.
11 Nancy Prince, *The West Indies: Being a description of the islands, progress of Christianity, education and liberty among the colored population generally* (Boston: Dow & Jackson, 1841), p. 4.
12 Robert Baird, *Impressions and experiences of the West Indies and North America in 1849* (Philadelphia, PA: Lea & Blanchard, 1850), p. 140.

13 *Baptist Magazine*, 'The Late Hurricane in Jamaica: With Reflections', 31 October 1815, p. 106.
14 Ibid., p. 106.
15 Editor of *The West Indian, Account of the Fatal Hurricane by Which Barbados Suffered in August 1831*, p. 47.
16 Ibid., p. 23.
17 TNA, CO 31/51 (Barbados) Sessional Papers. Assembly, 20 December 1831.
18 TNA, T1/4397, Long Papers, bundle 852, part 3: West Indies relief, Extract of a letter sent by Rev George; TNA, CO 71/78 (Dominica) Correspondence, Original – Secretary of State: Despatches; Offices and Individuals, J. Colquhoun to Spring Rice, 12 November 1834. Clarke to (recipient not given), Dominica, 20 September 1834.
19 TNA, T1/4397, extract of the *Dominica Colonist*, 27 September 1834.
20 B.W. Higman, *Slave Populations of the Caribbean*, p. 55
21 Joseph John Gurney, *A winter in the West Indies, described in familiar letters to Henry Clay of Kentucky* (London: J. Murray, 1840), p. 72.
22 On a tour of Jamaica in 1837, James Thome and Joseph Kimball noted that, following a hurricane in 1812, coffee production increased while sugar production decreased because the former did not suffer from the 'effects of a storm'. James Armstrong Thome and Joseph Horace Kimball, *Emancipation in the West Indies: A six months' tour in Antigua, Barbadoes, and Jamaica in the year 1837* (Philadelphia, PA: The American Anti-Slavery Society, 1838), pp. 119–120.
23 TNA, T1/4397, Colquhoun letter addressed to St James's Place, 7 April 1835.
24 Joseph Sturge, *The West Indies in 1837: Being the journal of a visit to Antigua, Montserrat, Dominica, St Lucia, Barbados, and Jamaica; undertaken for the purpose of ascertaining the actual condition of the negro population of those islands* (London: Hamilton, Adams & Co, 1838), p. 96; Joseph John Gurney, *A winter in the West Indies*, p. 72.
25 Bonham C. Richardson, *Economy and Environment in the Caribbean: Barbados and the Windwards in the Late 1800s* (Kingston: The University of the West Indies Press, 1997), p. 180; PP (1898), HoC [C 9205], West Indies. Correspondence relating to the hurricane on 10th–12th, 1898, and the relief of the distress caused thereby, Governor Moloney to Secretary of State, 15 September 1898, p. 2.
26 HoC [C 9205], Governor Moloney to Secretary of State, 12 October 1898; HoC [C 9205], King-Harman to Moloney, 15 September 1898.
27 *Barbados Advocate*, 4 October 1901.
28 B.W. Higman, *Slave Populations of the British Caribbean*, p. 214.
29 Justin Roberts, 'The "Better Sort" and the "Poorer Sort": Wealth Inequalities, Family Formation and the Economy of Energy on British Caribbean Sugar Plantations, 1750–1800', *Slavery and Abolition*, 35:3 (2014), p. 464.
30 Ibid., p. 207.
31 Joseph Sturge, *The West Indies in 1837: Being the journal of a visit to Antigua, Montserrat, Dominica, St Lucia, Barbados, and Jamaica; undertaken for the*

purpose of ascertaining the actual condition of the negro population of those islands (London: Hamilton, Adams & Co, 1838), p. 101.

32 Kenneth F. Kiple, *The Caribbean Slave: A Biological History* (Cambridge: Cambridge University Press, 2002), pp. 67–68.
33 Matthew Mulcahy, *Hurricanes and Society*, p. 108.
34 William James Gardner, *A History of Jamaica from Its Discovery by Christopher Columbus to the Present Time* (London: Elliot Stock, 1873), p. 249.
35 TNA, CO 260/29 (St Vincent) Correspondence, Original – Secretary of State, Robert Paul to Earl of Liverpool, 16 May 1812.
36 'Summary of the Damage done to the Sugar Estates of this Island by the Storm of the 11 October, 1847'. Historical Documents of Trinidad and Tobago No. 3.
37 PP, HoC [C 9205], West Indies. Correspondence, p. 16, Moloney to Chamberlain, 29 September 1898; PP (1902), HoC [Cd 1201], St Vincent. Correspondence relating to the volcanic eruptions in St Vincent and Martinique in May 1902, p. 70, Enclosure no. 1 in Admiralty to Colonial Office, 13 June 1902.
38 *Lebanon Daily News*, 'Thousands are Destitute', 14 August 1903.
39 TNA, CO 23/185 (Bahamas) Correspondence, Original – Secretary of State: Despatches, Governor Rawson to Earl of Canarvon, 17 October 1866.
40 HoC [Cd 1201], Governor Sir R.B. Llewellyn to Mr Chamberlain, 13 May 1902.
41 Bonham C. Richardson, *Economy and Environment in the Caribbean*, p. 91.
42 TNA, CO 7/74, G.H. Fitzroy to Lord Stanley, 10 February 1843.
43 W. Reid to Earl Grey, 20 November 1847. Historical Documents of Trinidad and Tobago No. 3.
44 HoC [C 9205], Moloney to Chamberlain, 25 September 1898, p. 7.
45 An example of this in the same hemisphere as the Caribbean is the *Qollqa* used by the Inca to preserve grain in case of crop failure or other disasters.
46 Joseph Sturge, *The West Indies in 1837*, p. 98.
47 Richard Grove, 'The British Empire and the Origins of Forest Conservation in the Eastern Caribbean 1700–1800', in Islands, Forests and Gardens in the Caribbean: Conservation and Conflict in Environmental History, ed. by Robert S. Anderson, Richard Grove and Karis Hiebert (Oxford: Macmillan Education, 2006), p. 164.
48 Ibid., p. 163.
49 TNA, CO 263/4 (St Vincent) Legislative Council; Privy Council, 'An Act to Prevent the clearing away of wood at the fountainheads of rivers running to any town or shipping place in this island or that supply estates with water', 3 December 1811.
50 Nicholas Crawford, 'Calamity's Empire: Slavery, Scarcity, and the Political Economy of Provisioning in the British Caribbean, c. 1775–1834' (unpublished PhD thesis, Harvard University, 2016), p. 27.
51 Ibid., p. 65.
52 Richard Robert Madden, *A Twelvemonth's Residence in the West Indies*, p. 15.

53 Charles W. Boyd (ed.), *Mr Chamberlain's Speeches*, Vol. 2 (London: Constable and Company, 1914), pp. 1–6.
54 Ben Wisner, J.C. Gaillard and Ilan Kelman, 'Introduction to Part I', in *The Routledge Handbook of Hazards and Disaster Risk Reduction*, ed. by Ben Wisner, J.C. Gaillard and Ilan Kelman (Abingdon: Routledge, 2011), p. 11.
55 Michael Craton, 'Reluctant Creoles: The Planters' World in the British West Indies', in *Strangers Within the Realm: Cultural Margins of the First British Empire*, ed. by Bernard Bailyn and Philip D. Morgan ('Chapel Hill, NC: University of North Carolina Press, 1991), p. 315.
56 Michael Connors, *Caribbean Houses: History, Style, and Architecture* (New York: Rizzoli, 2009), p. 126.
57 F.W.N. Bayley, *Four years' residence in the West Indies* (London: W. Kidd, 1830), p. 268. Emphasis author's own.
58 Pierre Dessalles, *Sugar and Slavery, Family and Race: The Letters and Diary of Pierre Dessalles, Planter in Martinique, 1808–1856*, ed. by Elborg Forster and Robert Forster (Baltimore, MD: Johns Hopkins University Press, 1996), pp. 196–197.
59 Ibid., p. 123.
60 Christer Petley, '"Home" and "This Country": Britishness and Creole Identity in the Letters of a Transatlantic Slaveholder', *Atlantic Studies*, 6:1 (2009), p. 46.
61 Matthew Mulcahy, *Hurricanes and Society in the British Greater Caribbean*, p. 128.
62 Nancy Prince, *The West Indies*, p. 4.
63 F.W.N. Bayley, *Four years' residence in the West Indies*, p. 265.
64 HoC [C 9205], Hay to Chamberlain, 27 September 1898, p. 8.
65 Daniel McKinnen, *A Tour Through the British West Indies, in the Years 1802 and 1803: Giving a Particular Account of the Bahama Islands* (London: J. White, 1804), p. 15.
66 F.W.N. Bayley, *Four years' residence in the West Indies*, p. 31.
67 Ibid., p. 266.
68 James Anthony Froude, *The English in the West Indies, or, the Bow of Ulysses*, p. 292.
69 F.W.N. Bayley, *Four years' residence in the West Indies*, p. 268.
70 Andrew Jackson O'Shaughnessy, *An Empire Divided*, p. 3.
71 Richard Ligon, *A True and Exact History of the Island of Barbados*, ed. by David Smith (e-text, 2014, 5th edition), p. 163.
72 Bonham C. Richardson, *Economy and Environment in the Caribbean*, p. 91.
73 Natalie A. Zacek, *Settler Society in the English Leeward Islands, 1670–1776*, p. 23.
74 F.W.N. Bayley, *Four years' residence in the West Indies*, p. 74.
75 Andrew Jackson O'Shaughnessy, *An Empire Divided*, p. 3.
76 Henry Rowland Brandreth, 'Memorandum relative to a System of Barracks for the West Indies, recommended by Colonel Sir C.F. Smith, C.B., R.E., and approved by the Master-General and Board of Ordnance', *Papers on Subjects*

Connected with the Duties of the Corps of the Royal Engineers, Vol. II (1838), p. 239.
77 Editor of *The West Indian, Account of the Fatal Hurricane by Which Barbados Suffered in August 1831*, p. 92.
78 William Reid, 'On Hurricanes', *Papers on Subjects Connected with the Duties of the Corps of the Royal Engineers*, Vol. II (1838), p. 149.
79 Ibid.
80 HoC [715], Lighthouse (Barbadoes), 1847, pp. 1–28.
81 Cynthia Kiener, *Inventing Disaster*, pp. 63–64.
82 In *the Seaman's Practical Guide for Barbados and the Leeward Islands* the author commenting on Grenada remarks that 'It is said the hurricanes never reach this Island, as proof of which, the windows are without outer shutters, and are fitted with glass, which cannot resist the force of these terrible winds'. A captain in the Royal Navy, *The Seaman's Practical Guide, for Barbadoes and the Leeward Islands; with observations on the islands from Blanco to the Rocas on the Coast of La Guayra* (London: Smith, Elder & Co. Cornhill, 1832), p. 24.
83 Rob Emlen, 'The Great Gale of 1815: Artifactual Evidence of Rhode Island's First Hurricane', *Rhode Island History*, 48:2 (1990), pp. 51–61.
84 David Eastwood, *Government and Community in the English Provinces, 1700–1870* (New York: St. Martin's Press, 1997), p. 66.
85 Andrew Jackson O'Shaughnessy, *An Empire Divided*, p. 3.
86 Editor of *The West Indian, Account of the Fatal Hurricane*, p. 25.
87 Stuart B. Schwartz, *Sea of Storms: A History of Hurricanes in the Greater Caribbean from Columbus to Katrina* (Princeton, NJ: Princeton University Press, 2015), p. 134.
88 HoC Deb 10 March 1899, vol. 68, cols 496–497.
89 Nicholas Crawford, 'Calamity's Empire', pp. 65–66.
90 One example I found was an eighty-eight-point instruction guide for the incoming Governor of St Vincent which covered many aspects of colonial administration but failed to mention hurricanes or volcanic eruptions and what steps to take if the colony was struck by a disaster. TNA, CO 260/3 (St Vincent) Correspondence, Original – Secretary of State, untitled file, 1783.
91 Anthony Oliver-Smith, 'Peru's Five-Hundred-Year Earthquake', in *Disasters, Development and Environment*, ed. by Ann Varley (Chichester: John Wiley & Sons, 1994), p. 83.
92 Olwyn Mary Blouet, 'Sir William Reid, F.R.S., 1791–1858: Governor of Bermuda, Barbados and Malta', *Notes and Records of the Royal Society of London article*, 40:2 (1986), p. 175.
93 TNA, CO 37/100, Despatches from Sir Stephen Remnant Chapman (items 1–17) and Sir William Reid (35 onwards), successive governors of Bermuda, Governor Reid, A report upon the military defence of Bermuda, 28 October 1839.
94 TNA, CO 37/100, Printed note recording W.M. Reid's appraisal of New Poor Law Act of 1834, 1 July 1839; TNA, CO 37/100, Reid to the Marquis of Normandy, 15 October 1839.

95 Henry Piddington, 'Researches on the Gale and Hurricane in the Bengal on the 3rd, 4th and 5th of June, 1839; being a first memoir with reference to the theory of the Law of Storms in India', *Asiatic Society of Bengal*, Vol. III, 1838, p. 559.
96 C. Blyth, 'Piddington, Henry (1797–1858), meteorologist', *Oxford Dictionary of National Biography*.
97 Tirthanker Roy, '"The Law of Storms": European and Indigenous Response to Natural Disasters in Colonial India, c. 1800–1850', *Australian Economic History Review*, 50:1 (2010), p. 7.
98 Tirthanker Ghosh, 'Historicizing Earthquake and Cyclones: Evolution of Geology and Cyclonology in Colonial India', *Indian Historical Review*, 46:1 (2019), pp. 22–40.
99 *The Times*, 'Death of Sir Charles Bruce', 14 December 1920.
100 Sir Charles Bruce, *Milestones on my long journey: memories of a colonial governor* (Glasgow: Robert Maclehose, 1917), pp. 108–109.
101 Report of the Mauritius Royal Commission, 1909: Presented to Both Houses of Parliaments by Command of His Majesty, June 1910, Vol. II (London: H.M. Stationery Office, 1920), p. 16.
102 David Longshore, *Encyclopedia of Hurricanes, Typhoons, and Cyclones* (New York: Infobase Publishing, 2010), p. 303.
103 TNA, CO 28/251, Letters received from various government offices (departments), other organisations and individuals relating to Barbados, Enclosure in Henry White to the Marquis of Salisbury, 21 January 1899.
104 Eric Williams, *Capitalism and Slavery* (Chapel Hill, NC: University of North Carolina Press, 1994), p. 153.
105 TNA, CO 137/662 (Jamaica) Letters from individuals on matters relating Jamaica, Henry McNeil to Earl of Elgin, 4 February 1907.
106 HoC [Cd 3560], Jamaica. Correspondence Relating to the Earthquake at Kingston, Jamaica, on 14 January 1907, The West India Committee to the Colonial Office, 25 February 1907, p. 75.
107 TNA, CO 137/661, Letters from the Foreign Office (March to December 1907) and 'miscellaneous offices' (Government departments and other organisations) relating to Jamaica, Jamaica Law 13 of 1907, 10 June 1907.
108 *Daily Gleaner*, 'Insurance Judgement', 30 October 1908.

3

'Aid' in the absence of freedom

Despite their wealth, when hurricanes hit, the planters of the nineteenth-century Caribbean could do little but cower in their houses. As we have seen already, many of them had gradually abandoned the once-popular hurricane shelters and instead chose, as far as possible, to emulate the palatial residences of their aristocratic counterparts in Britain. In times of disaster, the aspirational grandeur of these plantation houses caused grievous injury and, on occasion, death.

This was the fate of much of the Edgehill family as, on the night of 9 August 1831, they sheltered in their Barbadian mansion, Fustick Hall. Thomas Edgehill, the patriarch, had spent much of the evening trying to nail down all the shutters in the property in the face of escalating winds. In some respects, one can imagine that the storm had already turned their world upside down by flattening some of the emotional distinctions that whites liked to imagine set them apart from the enslaved population. Edgehill and family were sheltering with their enslaved house servants and no doubt their shared distress was conspicuous. By the early morning the hurricane had mostly taken apart the house around them, that great edifice of planter wealth and power shattered. Edgehill, sensing a lull in the wind, tried to lead his family and those he had enslaved to an outhouse on the property, but he was not quick enough and the remaining walls of Fustick collapsed as they set off, killing his mother and seven enslaved people.[1]

For the planters who sat at the top off Caribbean society, the destruction of the most obvious symbols of their power and wealth was no doubt galling. Disasters presented a clear challenge to a class of people who, threatened by abolition as they were, wanted to portray themselves to African-Caribbean people as the ultimate arbiters of freedom and enslavement, life and death. Disasters could puncture this image and leave planters feeling open to a challenge of their authority. In 1834, having spent the night hiding in his bed as a hurricane took apart his house around him, the owner of the Rosalie estate on Dominica emerged in the morning to find nothing but one corner of his house left standing. To make matters worse, on trying to extricate himself from the wreckage, a rusty nail drove its way through his foot leaving him crippled for a week. Much to his chagrin, the apprenticed labourers on his estate saw him in his hobbled state.[2] Those same apprentices would go on to directly challenge his orders later in the day, arguing to his face that their time would be better spent attending to their surviving cassava than rebuilding his plantation.

In the British Caribbean, disasters precipitated heart-wrenching losses across the spectrum of society. However, though these losses of life and property were felt keenly by both white elites and African-Caribbeans, rarely did any meaningful sense of shared suffering emerge. At the beginning of the nineteenth century the planters of the Caribbean appeared to be fighting and losing a number of rear-guard actions against a diverse range of enemies, seemingly determined at the very least to fundamentally change the order of the Caribbean, or in some cases to overthrow it at any cost. The success of the Haitian Revolution was for many planters their very worst nightmares made manifest, and it was followed by abolitionist successes in 1807 and 1811, when engagement with the slave trade was actually made illegal.

Disasters, in creating moments of flux in which normal structures of authority and control were suspended, became a stage on which planter concerns about rebellion and abolitionism were played out. Contrary to some rosy pictures of disaster, these events did not bring Caribbean society together, rather they exacerbated existing societal divisions. They created mutual, albeit unequally shared, losses, but planters and colonial officials primarily responded to disaster by prioritising the restoration of normality and order. Though this became the central organising principle of British disaster response, not just during slavery but also after emancipation, it did not create uniform responses to disaster.[3] White elites reflexively used violence, coercion and often disingenuous benevolence, depending on their assessment of how best to restore order in the circumstances facing them.

The preoccupation with the restoration of order was not just born of the difficult circumstances facing Caribbean planters in the first half of the nineteenth century, but also of an understanding of the ways in which disasters could fundamentally disrupt the key methods of white minority control. First and foremost, there was destruction of the plantations; hurricanes, earthquakes and eruptions all had the potential to destroy not just the homes of planters but also the boiling houses, the watermills and the sugar crop itself. The destruction of crops, in particular, posed an obvious threat to the planter as, overly mortgaged and notoriously indebted as they were, they now faced long-term financial difficulty. In the immediate term, however, the disruption and sometimes destruction of plantations also prevented them from functioning in their role as not just sites of African-Caribbean enslavement and labour, but also sites of spatial and temporal discipline.

Amongst many things, the rhythms of plantation labour dictated when people woke, who they spoke with during the day and when they could rest at the end of the day. The open vistas created by deforestation and the building of watchtowers allowed overseers and other whites to constantly surveil the enslaved population, in what was effectively an 'open-air panopticon'.[4] The whites running the plantations had relative impunity to act and punish as they saw fit. Central to the entire model was the racist and infantilising perception commonly shared amongst whites involved in the Caribbean colonies that people of African heritage were fit only to labour. Furthermore, because of the crude climatic similarities drawn by whites, it was also held that they were uniquely suited to labour in tropical climates. Many whites therefore argued that freedom was a danger to enslaved people and suggested that without labour to drain their energies enslaved people would turn against their supposedly beneficent masters. Crucially, amongst whites, these views coalesced to form a general conclusion that white control was contingent on the continuation of African-Caribbean labour and thus, by extension, the continued existence of the plantation to facilitate it.

It must also be noted that the plantation's role in controlling and disciplining the African-Caribbean population extended beyond its walls and fields. Typically, enslaved people were not allowed to leave the plantations without the express written permission of an overseer or other senior white person. These so-called 'pass systems' that sprang up throughout the Caribbean and America were broadly conceived as a way to prevent strikes and other large gatherings that could have easily overwhelmed white minority control. When we talk of white minority populations on Caribbean islands and think about how this played into white racial anxiety, I think it is important that we remember just how severe the population imbalances were. For example, a census from St Vincent in 1812, the year its volcano erupted, shows that, even after the abolition of the slave trade, enslaved people on the island numbered 22,020 whereas the white population numbered just 827.[5] In this context, the plantation is in part what allowed planters to achieve what Hilary Beckles has called an 'impressive record of minority socio-political control'.[6] Given the plantation's role as the nexus through which white minority control was exercised and racial anxieties soothed, it is perhaps no coincidence that it was on Barbados, the island most dominated by plantations, that their destruction by a hurricane occasioned one of the most violent responses to disaster in the era of slavery.

Violence and coercion

In 1831, Barbados was hit by a hurricane of destructive power unparalleled in the region for more than a century. Eyewitness reports of the storm that hit the island on 10 August do not lack for superlatives to describe its violence and its effects on the island and its people. Trying to capture its sheer enormity, one eyewitness wrote:

> The sheltered observer of the storm, amazed and in a state of stupor, was fixed for a time to the spot where he stood, the sight and the hearing were overpowered, and the excess of astonishment refused admission to fear. What must have been the mental agonies of those wretched fugitives who destitute of a place of refuge were the sport of the dreadful tempest.[7]

This dramatic description was warranted; we know that in one night the hurricane destroyed nearly all the sugar plantations on the island, killed somewhere in the region of 1,787 people and injured many more. By the estimations of those who had the misfortune to experience both the hurricanes of 1780 and 1831, the latter was regarded as 'far greater in its force and devastating in its consequences'. When morning broke on 11 August, those who had survived faced dire circumstances. In their communications with London, colonial officials wrote that the island's inhabitants were 'destitute of the common necessaries of life'.[8]

Though the proximate cause of these dire circumstances was the hurricane, even in these reports written less than a day after the hurricane we can see the manifestations of the vulnerability created by the plantations. It was said that 'the whole face of the country ... [was] laid waste [with] no sign of vegetation' and communication with neighbouring colonies disrupted. Predictions of famine were already being made.[9]

The first recorded response of the British authorities to the devastation was to publicly issue a proclamation on 15 August that had been authored by the island's Governor Sir James Lyon. The proclamation commended all to 'exert themselves, to the utmost of their power, in preserving on this melancholy occasion peace and tranquillity of the island, and to prevent ... the depredation and plunder by such evil disposed persons'. Though the proclamation was ostensibly written to all Barbadians, by virtue of access to education, its audience would have primarily been the island's white population, though some may have taken it upon themselves to read it out to the illiterate. Going on, Lyon called upon the island's militia, membership of which was restricted to whites, to assemble 'for the purposes of preventing disturbances and preserving the general peace'.[10] This line in particular tells us that, from the outset, those in control of the island feared the hurricane's trail of destruction might precipitate a challenge to the established order.

As the British response to the hurricane unfolded over the following week, one gets the sense that rich, white Barbadians saw the situation on the island as akin to a rapidly expanding pressure cooker whose lid needed to be forcibly put back on. Initially, what seems to have sparked their ire was the fact that from the day following the hurricane some of the African-Caribbean population had begun to leave their ruined dwellings on the plantations and head toward Bridgetown, the island's capital. In response, the governor published a second proclamation, this time published in the island's colonial newspaper the *Barbados Advocate*. He called for the recapture of the now 'vagrant' enslaved people who had left their plantations and ordered whites to seize any African-Caribbean person guilty of vagrancy and put them to work at a number of newly created public work schemes, where they would be left until picked up by an overseer or their owner.[11] The public work schemes had been created by the island's Legislative Council, who, simultaneous to the publishing of the governor's proclamations, had created a commission for clearing the capital's streets and had called on all those who owned slaves to provide their labour and to enforce the attendance of any enslaved person they encountered.

In his communications with London, Lyon explained the necessity of these coercive measures in a racialised observation very typical of his white contemporaries throughout the region; he wrote of the enslaved population's 'apathy and unwillingness to work' and of their strong 'inclination to pilfer and steal'. What is more, in the same communication, no doubt in an effort to highlight his prudence as governor, he also informed London that in anticipation of this and more violent behaviour, he had pre-emptively strengthened guard outposts throughout the island.[12]

Given that our insights into the behaviour of the enslaved population after the hurricane almost entirely come from white planters and colonial officials who, immured in their racialised view of the world, tended to think the worst of enslaved people, there is strikingly little recorded that suggests there were any plots and/or organised resistance emerging after the hurricane. And yet, in the context of the disaster, the fear of such a challenge seemed to mean that whites saw potential conspiracy in the smallest transgressions.

On 13 August, before the publication of Lyon's first proclamation, a militia headed by plantation owner and council member Sir Reynold Alleyne was deployed around the island. Despite the 'menace' of famine being reported to London, the initial focus of this militia seemed to be doing all it could to stop enslaved people feeding themselves with the sparse crops that had survived the storm. Arriving at one plantation, Alleyne's militia put a stop to the salvage of surviving crops and threatened punishment for any who persisted and refused to submit again to the authority of estate managers.[13] The militia seems to have repeated this approach as it visited the estates across the island, tactically encircling them to prevent any escapes.

The actions of Alleyne's militia in concert with the rhetoric of the governor's two proclamations clearly shows us the extent to which the restoration of racial 'order' and thus normality factored heavily in white elites' responses to the hurricane. Dispatching the armed militia was a clear and purposeful show of force by the island's white population, but Alleyne, the seeming de facto leader of the militia, seems to have considered that the use of violence alone would have inflamed the delicate situation. He initially attempted to balance his explicit threats of violence with rhetoric that sought to play up the shared suffering of the enslaved and their masters. On arriving at the Spring Hall plantations, Alleyne told the gathered enslaved people that he came to them as a 'friend' and informed them that it was only due to their behaviour that he was induced to summon the militia, the implicit suggestion being that it would be withdrawn if they acted in accordance with his wishes. He also, in attempt to further soothe discontent, spoke to them of the 'common distress' that 'involved both master and slave'.[14] He also continued this line of rhetoric by stressing that the 'uproar of the elements could never sever the ties that existed between them and their owners, but that it ought if possible, to have united them more strongly'.[15]

As one might predict, Alleyne's overtures of friendship would prove to be disingenuous. His conciliatory tone was quickly dropped when it did not achieve its intended aim. A second-hand account detailing the aftermath of the hurricane tells us that this address was met with 'insolent language' and agitation from certain 'ringleaders'.[16] Alleyne had the most disobedient offenders brought forward from the crowd and punished with fifty lashes. Later, on another plantation, he had an enslaved person shot dead for striking one of his militiamen. That Alleyne simultaneously deployed paternalistic rhetoric alongside violence might appear incongruous, but his approach to restoring order was broadly reflective of how many wealthy plantation owners managed the enslaved population, particularly in an era in which they and the institution of slavery were under attack.

In 1824, Alleyne had been interviewed as part of a report by the Council of Barbados that sought to defend slavery.[17] In his interview, just as he did after the hurricane of 1831, Alleyne portrayed himself as a paternalistic master who, while not afraid to physically punish enslaved people on his estates, only did so in the most egregious of circumstances, noting, with seeming pride that he had forbidden the use of the thong whip and replaced it with a more 'humane' five-strand small cat.[18]

The second-hand account that details the actions of this militia tells us that the majority of those being punished were 'guilty' of little more than taking corn and butchering animals in what were clear efforts to survive the scarcity proximately induced by the hurricane. In the documents that survive, there is little to suggest that there was any serious threat to white authority. How can we then account for the relatively violent response of the militia, particularly in the context of it being led by Alleyne, a planter who liked to at least give the impression that he was fair and even handed?

For Alleyne, and by proxy much of the island's white population, the mere presence of enslaved people existing outside of the confines of the plantation was in itself a threat to their control. In this context, Alleyne's rhetoric functioned to remind the enslaved population of their place within the colonial hierarchy, and the violence later meted out by his militia physically reasserted the asymmetrical power relationship that whites saw as essential to the continuation of their control.

As this violent response to the disruption induced by the hurricane unfolded, Governor Lyon, in his communications with the Colonial Office, painted a conspicuously more harmonious picture of what had happened on the island in the days after the 10 August. In a dispatch of the 30 August, he wrote that while initially following the hurricane the African-Caribbean population were 'idle', they were once again 'perfectly obedient to their masters' and working alongside whites with 'firmness and resignation'.[19] Lyon's dispatch belied the fact that many on the island thought that they were but a hair's breadth from full-scale rebellion. In the anonymous account that chronicles much of the aftermath of the 1831 hurricane, the author records their belief that had Alleyne not stepped in, 'the flame [of insurrection] would soon have been kindled, and would have spread with rapidity into every part of this devoted island'.[20] In the context of that author's remark, I think it is also important that we understand the response to disaster on Barbados as not just born of fear that the disruption to the plantations might lead to unrest, but also of the island's recent history.

In 1816, only fifteen years earlier, the island's enslaved population had engaged in a large-scale revolt against the island's authorities, later called 'Bussa's Rebellion'. During the rebellion, one white civilian and at least fifty enslaved people were killed during small skirmishes. Though it would eventually be put down by the island's militia, resulting in the further deaths of around a thousand enslaved people, the suppression, as Michael Craton puts it, 'seems to have downed neither the slave's unrest nor the master's brutally awakened fears'.[21] The lasting effect of the rebellion of 1816 was that, although the white population had long seen the potential for rebellion on the island, the rebellion convinced them they only held the island by military force.[22]

In reality, in the wake of the hurricane of 1831, not only do we not see any evidence of a rebellion emerging, but what descriptions we do have of the island's population suggest that there was very little appetite for violence following the hurricane. One eyewitness observing the general population of Barbados as they mingled in Bridgetown wrote:

> The heart of each was surcharged with distress, the voice was paralyzed and denied the power of utterance; neither could congratulate the other on the

safety of his life, or recite his disconsolate tale; but the silent, convulsive grasp of the hand emphatically expressed 'my affliction is greater than I can bear!'[23]

From this observation, and what we know of the actions of those scavenging food on the plantations, the energy of most people seems to have largely been focused on simply surviving the aftermath of the hurricane. Indeed, another white eyewitness, a missionary and member of the British Bible Society also remarked that the enslaved population 'conducted themselves like Christians giving assistance and keeping clear from the accursed thing plunder'.[24]

While explicit shows of force, coercion and violence emerged as the early hallmarks of the British response to disaster in early August 1831, as the month progressed, reports suggest that their use had begun to recede. While the restoration of order and racial hierarchy remained the central preoccupation of the island's authorities, these goals were increasingly realised through an expansion of the public work schemes that initially emerged in the days following the hurricane. The first true disaster relief arrived in the form of wages that were offered to those participating in the public work schemes.

On 23 August, the *Barbados Globe and Advocate* reported that those who participated in the clearing of Bridgetown and the island's roads would be paid for their efforts. Here, it is worth noting that it would not have been easy work, given what eyewitness accounts report; the capital's streets and the island's roads were said to be awash with the putrefying corpses of humans and animals and clogged with rotting vegetable matter. What is interesting is that the paper reported that those who participated would not be paid a flat rate. Rather, despite ostensibly doing the same work, labourers were paid at different rates to reflect their pre-disaster position in society. Day labourers were paid 2s 6d, common carpenters and masons 3s 9d, and master workmen 6s 3d.[25]

The rates offered to day labourers appear to reflect the recommendations of the Jamaican consolidated Slave Act of 1792 (an act later adopted by other British colonies). This act suggested that when circumstances arose that prevented enslaved people from feeding themselves, planters should provide them with relief equal to 2s 6d. The act was intended to cover a range of circumstances such as periods of crop failure, but, reflecting the seeming unwillingness of most planters to prepare for disasters, the act made no mention of hurricanes or other hazards.[26] All of this is to say that, while a form of relief did arrive just under two weeks after the hurricane, the amounts offered seem to have made no allowances for the exceptional circumstances and, if we broaden out from the Caribbean, were comparatively low by British standards; the daily rate for day labourers in Britain during this period was, on average, 11s a day.[27]

Under normal circumstances, a single pound of pork or fish would have cost around 7½s, or a third of the wages of someone labouring for 6s 2d.[28] As the price of provisions rose in the widely reported scarcity after the hurricane, these wages could have done little to stave off hunger. Yet for the planters and British officials the efficacy of these schemes at relieving hunger was of low importance. They rebuilt the social hierarchy amongst enslaved and free people and restarted the market mechanisms that allowed the authorities to limit their responsibilities towards the populace and thus engendered a situation where, as the *Barbados Globe and Colonial Advocate* put it, 'on the good behaviour of the slaves, principally depends their own comfort'.[29] It is also important to note at this point that there is no record of what happened to those who could not participate in the public work schemes due to injury or age.

So seemingly important was it for the planters and colonial officials to restart these disciplining forces that they even turned down outside relief when they could not wholly control its distribution. On 2 September, a large donation of foodstuffs arrived at Bridgetown by boat, gifted to Barbados by the government of the Berbice region of British Guiana. Even though just three weeks earlier the island's planters had been penning dire warnings of famine, and articles in the island's newspapers detailed frantic searches for food, John Drake, the Barbadian charged by the Legislative Council with overseeing 'relief' ensured that this relief never left the ship. When the boat docked, he had it promptly turned around and sent back to Berbice, despite knowing that the provisions would rot on the return journey. Drake was under no pressure to publicly justify his actions, but in a private letter sent to the Legislative Council he explained that he had returned the provisions because they were 'wholly unnecessary and unsolicited' and 'were not required on Barbados either by the troops or by the inhabitants, nor at any other station'.[30] He further explained that, because 'they could not be housed anywhere', his returning of the provisions was in the 'public interest'. As shown in chapter 5, it took Barbados at least two years to fully recover from the destitution caused by the hurricane, so Drake's actions should not be seen as evidence of a miraculous turnaround in the island's fortunes in the month following the hurricane.

How can we explain Drake's seemingly counterintuitive actions? Firstly, they suggest that the planters of Barbados had some other way of feeding themselves. Records do not tell us how they avoided hunger, but on nearby St Vincent, which had also been affected by the hurricane, stores of food did survive, and the wealthy were able to purchase them, though prices increased significantly. It is not unreasonable to conclude that something similar happened on Barbados; if rich whites did not have access to provisions, it seems reasonable to assume that they would have taken the donated supplies from Berbice for themselves. There was, however, still great hunger among the enslaved population and so the question remains: why did Drake turn the provisions away? I think we can begin to understand why the supplies were returned when we remember that the restoration of white control over the African-Caribbean population remained the ultimate priority of the island's authorities. One of Drake's justifications for the return of the provisions was that there was nowhere to house them, which suggests that simply distributing them freely from the boat directly to those in need was not acceptable; he and by extension the colonial government had to retain control over who could access them. Free distribution of relief would have de-incentivised the indigent from participating in the public work schemes, which, from the perspective of the island's white elites, would have undermined their goal of restoring order to Barbados.

We can see the white fixation with getting African-Caribbean people to resubmit to their authority and, by extension, to the disciplining force of labour, running throughout the different phases of the British response to the Barbadian hurricane of 1831. Violence and coercion were deployed initially, and then a more pragmatic and punitive approach to the distribution of relief emerged as whites became confident that no rebellion was imminent. In such a rigidly, racially divided society built so fundamentally on abhorrent physical and mental violence, we might expect British responses to disaster in the era of slavery to frequently play out as they did on Barbados in 1831. But, while the preoccupation with the restoration of order characterised many British responses to disaster, the violence on Barbados in many ways actually appears an outlier perhaps best explained by the island's relatively recent rebellion. In fact, as this book shows, there were many different shades to disaster response in the Caribbean. The 1812 eruption of La Soufrière on the island of St Vincent provides an interesting example of how changing attitudes, informed by the abolition of the slave trade and the shifting fortunes of the planter class, coalesced to produce a different, altogether less violent response to disaster.

Disaster opportunism

On 27 April 1812, the people of the island of St Vincent felt a 'severe concussion of the earth' and, looking to the north of the island, they saw a plume of smoke so thick that it blocked out the sun.[31] Everything pointed to the imminent eruption of the island's volcano, La Soufrière. Tremors continued throughout the island until, on 30 April, the noise from the volcano became incessant. At some point after 7 pm on that same day, the volcano began the march towards its terrible, inevitable conclusion; lava poured from the volcano's crater and fiery pumice and ash rained down on the northern portion of the island until at least 6 am the following day.[32]

The eruption caused both the indigenous people who lived at the base of the volcano and the enslaved people who worked on plantations in the vicinity to flee to the island's capital, Kingstown. Eyewitness accounts of the eruption and the days leading up to it provided by planters characteristically focus primarily on detailing the behaviour of the enslaved population and display all the characteristic prejudices of the period and their authors. They detail how the enslaved population 'became confused, forsook their work' and 'trembled with the dread of what they could neither understand or describe'.[33]

The one eyewitness account that details events in Kingstown as the eruption took place comes from planter Hugh Perry Keane. It is sparse in detail, but it does tell us that the capital was 'in great confusion'.[34] Descriptions from the early nineteenth century described Kingstown as small, consisting of three streets intersected by six others and containing only three hundred houses.[35] It was once larger but was said to have been levelled in the 'Great Hurricane' of 1780 and seems to have never fully recovered its size or original, albeit limited, grandeur. We can only imagine how it would have looked accommodating panicked whites, fleeing enslaved people and the island's indigenous population, who rarely left their lands on the north of the island. St Vincent was notable as one of the only British colonies in the region to have any indigenous Caribbean people living on it in the nineteenth century. In the present day this population refer to themselves as the Garifuna. In the nineteenth century, they were known generally as Caribs, with the population of St Vincent being divided into 'black' Caribs and 'yellow' Caribs, black here referred to the offspring of 'yellow' (indigenous peoples) and escaped enslaved people. The Garifuna numbered only 120 in total, making them a small part of the 7,000 people who were said to have fled to Kingstown, but their presence seems to have caused enough of an issue that members of the island's government felt something needed to be done about them.

Though his motives for doing so are unrecorded, on 5 May, the president of the island's Legislative Council, Robert Paul, put before the council a request for aid for the Garifuna. His request was refused by the planters who comprised the council because they argued that the losses from the eruption were too great to justify the expenditure. Circumstances after the eruption were dire. Reflecting the vulnerabilities characteristic of a plantation colony, many of the early reports from St Vincent detail the lack of foodstuffs to be found throughout the island and, as a result, the fear of famine gripping the planter class.

Seemingly unwilling to give up on the Garifuna, Paul wrote an appeal to George Beckwith, then Governor of Barbados. Despite the Barbadian legislature having just assented to donate between £1,000 and £2,000 (records conflict on the amount) to St Vincent, Beckwith replied to Paul stating that it was not within his power to authorise expenditure for the Garifuna.[36] Determined to resolve the situation, Paul, on 16 May, wrote to the Earl of Liverpool, Robert Jenkinson, asking for permission to incur expenditure on St Vincent's public account for the Garifuna. When writing to Jenkinson, Paul felt it necessary to reassure him that, were he to authorise any expenditure, he would do his utmost to not 'incur any expense that it [was] possible to avoid', which is indicative of the limited 'relief' that Paul envisaged providing. Jenkinson's response is not recorded; however, it seems likely that it was favourable because by July 1812, St Vincent's Council had agreed to a plan for the Garifuna which Paul had laid before them.

Agreed in a letter on 8 July and then put into action on 3 August, Paul's plan for the Garifuna involved them being transported from St Vincent to the district of Toco on the nearby island of Trinidad. Toco is located on the most north-easterly point of Trinidad, and at the time was not yet entirely given over to sugar cultivation; there were in fact, according to the minutes of the St Vincent Council, unoccupied lands for the Garifuna to be settled on. Crucially, the Garifuna themselves were said to have 'numerous relatives' in the district.[37] In keeping with the assurances of frugality that Paul had made to Jenkinson, St Vincent's Council made it clear to Major General Hector William Munro, the Trinidadian official receiving the Garifuna, that they would not support them and that they must 'depend entirely on their own industry'.[38] There is no record of how, or indeed if, the details of this scheme were presented to the Garifuna taking refuge in Bridgetown. What we do know is that eighty-eight of their number agreed to the transportation, including their leader, rendered in colonial records as Captain Baptiste, leaving approximately thirty-two of their number behind, who are recorded as having refused the 'opportunity'.[39] It cannot have been an easy decision for either party; one left behind their ancestral homelands, the other, friends, family and leadership.

Sometime not long after the 3 August, the eighty-eight Garifuna who agreed to travel to Trinidad were transported on two sloops, the *Victualler* and the *Mentor*. Their passage was accompanied by extensive provisions of dried salt fish, rice, dried plantains and a proportion of rum and sugar.[40] This was a generous accompaniment provided by the Council of St Vincent who, less than three months earlier had refused to help the Garifuna and were reporting the likelihood of famine on the island. The obvious questions that remain are: why were the Garifuna afforded this, in some respects, generous opportunity, and what does it tell us about British responses to disaster?

The Garifuna were offered relocation because it fitted in not only with the characteristic colonial desire to restore productivity to the island, but also long-standing patterns in the island's history. This was not the first time that Garifuna had been transported from the island by colonial hands. They fought the British throughout the eighteenth century and, perhaps most galling to the British, in 1773 and 1795 they fought with and were armed by the French.[41] The conflict of 1795 alone was said to have cost British proprietors a third of the value of their estates and left them with deep animosity toward the Garifuna. In 1797, the British went on the offensive and subdued the Garifuna, after which a treaty was signed between the two groups that meant a portion of the Garifuna were deported to Ruattan in Honduras and a portion were given land in the north of St Vincent around the base of the volcano.[42] This, however, was far from the end of the antagonism between the two groups. In the following years, the British consistently pushed for more concessions.

Following the arrival of Governor Henry Bentick in 1802, the British began increasingly encroaching on the Garifuna reservations.[43] Their reservations were coveted because the soil around the volcano was known to be some of the most fertile and productive on the island.[44] What is more, the Garifuna offered little utility to St Vincent's planters. Unlike the enslaved population, they did not work the plantations, they occupied fertile land and, now rendered homeless by the eruption, they represented a future drain on the island's public funds. From the outset of the eruption, the island's government had prioritised providing provisions to the enslaved population as the central labour force. Precisely at the moment when the island's council were refusing Paul's initial request to provide relief to the Garifuna, they were already sending a member of their Legislative Council to Barbados with a mission to procure food specifically for the enslaved population. The Barbadian legislature would go on to donate a sum of £2,000, with the island's governor, George Beckwith, the same governor who refused President Paul's request for aid for the Garifuna population, personally donating £400 of that sum. In the context of both the history of conflict with the Garifuna and what planters felt was necessary to restore productive enterprise, a motive starts to emerge.

Moving even a proportion of the Garifuna population represented an opportunity to both open up new land for plantations on the island – precisely at a moment when an economic recovery was needed most – and lessen the Government of St Vincent's relief obligations. Further underscoring this motive is the fact that in 1812, members of the island's Government feared more conflict with the Garifuna population. In a meeting in September of that year, a member of the Legislative Council 'lamented that the scheme of taking the Yellow Caribs to Trinidad could not be expanded to the entire population of Caribs on St Vincent. As they must ever view us with a degree of resentment'.[45] Other members of the council saw the continued existence of the Garifuna population on the island as corrosive to the master and slave hierarchy they so prioritised; a collective statement from the Privy Council read: 'We beg leave to add that they [the Garifuna] may be the means at some future period of carrying on a dangerous intercourse with the Enemy [the French] and any disaffected slaves in the colony'.[46]

This seeming 'limited benevolence' with which the Garifuna were treated in 1812 and the opportunism that actually lay just beneath its surface shows how British responses to disaster, while fixated on the plantation, could pragmatically and opportunistically respond to situations with more than just violence. From the British perspective, there was little incentive to aid those who contributed nothing to the plantation economy while occupying some of the most fertile land on the island. They were, however, incentivised to aid those, the enslaved, who in the immediate aftermath of the disaster could be forced into rebuilding the plantations and on whose entire labour the long-term operation of the plantations relied.

Viewed in the context of both the recent passage of the Act for the Abolition of the Slave Trade in 1807 and the ending of the inter-island trade in enslaved people in 1811, the enslaved population, cruelly rendered as commodities, now had more value than ever. Planters across the Caribbean faced a new reality where they were unable to easily replace those they condemned to death on their plantations and so maintaining a positive natural increase in the enslaved population became another preoccupation for them.[47] White, slaveholding solidarity in the face of this new reality might also explain the generous donations from Barbados and its governor and also the fact that both Berbice and Demerara dispatched, unbidden, provisions expressly for St Vincent's enslaved population.[48]

The archival records that detail the British response to the eruption of 1812 tell us little of how aid was distributed to those who survived but, in his diary, Keane records that the island's militia was deployed just two days after the eruption.[49] Unlike on Barbados in 1831, there is no record of violence being visited on the African-Caribbean population. While it is certainly possible that it could have occurred, as demonstrated in the case of Barbados in 1831, planters and officials often detailed any perceived infractions African-Caribbean people committed against the established order.

As chapter 5 shows in greater detail, Parliament was often reticent to hand out large sums of relief money and so those in the Caribbean petitioning for it usually marshalled evidence of a collapse in the social order to legitimate and justify their requests for financial aid. Instead, the planters of St Vincent petitioned for relief, not on the basis of some potential rebellion, but rather by painting themselves not just as the victims of an eruption but also of injurious government policy. Just as they used the eruption as an opportunity to remove some of the Garifuna from the island, so too did they use it as an opportunity to try and shore up their enterprise as the contours of British rule in the region seemed to be changing so drastically at the beginning of the nineteenth century.

Prior to 1812, tensions had been building between America and Britain, and the Caribbean in many ways was caught in the middle. America had long provided British planters, particularly in times of scarcity, with the necessary provisions to feed the enslaved population. Often in exchange for these provisions, Caribbean planters also maintained a small but nonetheless financially important export trade in sugar, rum and molasses. As tension built between the two nations, Britain consistently tried to restrict America's ability to trade in the Caribbean, something which particularly aggrieved British planters, coming as it did after the passing of abolition in 1807.

In January 1812, a petition from Barbadian planters shows how these issues were being used to try and leverage Parliament for financial assistance. The planters complained that 'partial export of sugar from the West Indies was formerly allowed in American bottoms [barrels], the prohibition of which has proved extremely injurious to the planters'. They also stated:

> the present population of their negroes can only be kept up by an unremitting care and liberal attention to their comforts; and … that the depreciated value of their produce, and the heavy and disproportioned imposts laid on it … will operate as a severe check to the slave population.[50]

Further into the petition, the planters were keen to stress that they were not out of step with public opinion and that they accepted the humanity of ending the slave trade, but argued that with American trade closed, unreasonable duties imposed on their produce, and now the extra 'burden' of maintaining the enslaved population, they were deserving of aid.

These same lines of argument emerged in the petitions written by the planters of St Vincent in 1812. They sought permission to reopen trade with America on the basis of losses caused by the eruption and while they did not name abolition explicitly, they did stress that the island had been subject to a 'rapid succession of calamities'.[51] However, in a later petition, it is clear that the politics of abolition were not far from their minds, as they deployed characteristically paternalist rhetoric that painted them as having the best interests of the enslaved at heart: 'If we do not get relief, I fear we must abandon our estates, and our poor Negroes must be divided into lots and sold for the benefit of our creditors, and the families torn from each other'.⁵² Just as they had done with the Garifuna, the planters of St Vincent were successful in turning the eruption to their advantage, and trade with America was restored in November 1812.

This battle between planters and abolitionists continued to flare up during disasters as the nineteenth century progressed. Amongst the planters of the Caribbean, the abolition of the slave trade created a permanent sense of injustice, and their sense of having been punished only worsened in the 1820s as Parliament sought to intervene more directly to regulate the conditions of slavery. In 1823, a revitalised anti-slavery movement, led by Thomas Buxton and James Cropper, began pushing for a new set of regulations to ameliorate the conditions of enslaved people in the Caribbean. The government, seeking to avoid being wrong-footed by Buxton, quickly followed with a statement delivered by the Foreign Secretary, George Canning, setting out its intent to implement a programme of 'amelioration'. A large-scale and violently suppressed revolt of enslaved people on Demerara in August 1823 cemented the perceived need for amelioration amongst British liberals.

Measured by tangible improvements to the conditions of enslaved people, amelioration was certainly not a resounding success. However, it did result in enslaved people having, for the first time, notional representatives in the form of the offices of the Protector of Slaves and the Registrar of Slaves. These offices were supposed to provide enslaved people with a legal guardian and a check on planter abuses, and were the object of much derision by the planter class. After the hurricane of August 1831, Barbadian planters opportunistically sought to use the disaster as cause for eroding the legal advancements that had been made to protect enslaved people.

On 30 November, a group of planters wrote to Viscount Goderich, Secretary of State for the Colonies. In the petition it is obvious they saw themselves as on the virtuous side in the ongoing battle between white Britons over the best interests of enslaved people. They stated that: 'the class of persons upon whose support the wellbeing of the community rests is composed of those planters whose estates have in the greatest degree suffered from the late dreadful calamity ... since upon depended the subsistence and comfort of the rural community'.⁵³ Perhaps because it was being sent to a member of the British Government, the petition struck a more subtle tone than the article which, earlier that year, had appeared in the *Barbados Globe and Colonial Advocate*. This article, published in late August not long after the hurricane, read: 'We will soon observe the real friends of the negro slaves; whether the oppressed and nearly bankrupt planter, who struggles to feed, clothe, and educate him, or the enthusiast who, in his amiable zeal for liberty, considers nothing but his unconditional and immediate emancipation'.⁵⁴

In petitioning Parliament for financial assistance, the planters knew they were no doubt setting themselves up for a lengthy and uncertain wait, so they wasted little time in trying to use the ongoing crisis to their advantage in the meantime. In August 1831, at a meeting of the island's assembly group of planters, it was suggested that reducing the island's expenditure on colonial officials would not only be necessary to protect the island's finances but also to increase the amount of money available for relief and rebuilding. Tellingly, the two offices for which they suggested significantly reducing the salary were the Protector of Slaves and the Registrar of Slaves.[55] These requests obviously represented a naked attempt to use the disaster to weaken legal protections for enslaved people and to reassert the social order off the British Caribbean's perceived late eighteenth-century heyday, when planter power was all but unchecked.

Records do not show whether the planters were successful with these requests but, ultimately, we can view them as some of the final salvos in a conflict they had all but lost. At the end of 1831 and continuing into January 1832, Jamaica experienced the largest revolt of enslaved people in its history. The so-called 'Baptist War' and its brutal oppression by the island's planters and colonial officials demonstrated that amelioration measures had done little to quell enslaved people's desire for freedom. Where emancipation had been something that abolitionists had perpetually kicked into the long grass, there can be little doubt that the Baptist War played a key role in forcing their hand. In 1833, Parliament voted for the complete emancipation of enslaved people throughout the Caribbean, with the act to come into force on 1 August 1834.

Tentative benevolence in the era of apprenticeship

For many enslaved people, 1 August 1834 was for the most part a disappointment; only Antigua, Bermuda and the Cayman Islands opted to proceed directly to freedom. Instead, the majority of the British Caribbean colonies proceeded to bind the formerly enslaved to a new framework of coercive labour known as the apprenticeship system. Under this system, the newly apprenticed population was obligated to give forty hours unpaid labour on the estates of those that had previously enslaved them. Whites envisaged them spending the rest of their time growing crops above subsistence and for sale at markets.

Both planters and abolitionists had long viewed African-Caribbean people as unfit for immediate freedom and planters particularly feared that complete emancipation would precipitate the total abandonment of the plantations.

Consequently, apprenticeship emerged as a compromise; African-Caribbean people would remain tied to the plantations and planter authority, but over the period of apprenticeship would gradually be made ready for freedom in 1840. Apprenticeship eventually ended prematurely in 1838, but as shown in chapter 4, concerns about how to coerce, control and retain labour on the plantation would remain a point of constant consternation for whites in the Caribbean beyond 1838. Apprenticeship was no doubt an important milestone, but for African-Caribbean people, the reality of life changed little from slavery and some first-hand accounts suggest that whites, feeling the sting of lost power, inflicted cruelty that in some respects exceeded their abuses under slavery.[56]

Apprenticeship remedied none of the racial disparities of Caribbean society, nor did it lessen whites' assuredness that their control was contingent on African-Caribbean labour. Consequently – though as detailed in chapter 2 British disaster response was never formally codified – responses continued to be shaped by the same preoccupations as when the post-slavery era began, albeit treated with more caution as whites navigated the new social terrain of apprenticeship.

On the night of 20 September 1834, Dominica was visited by a ferocious hurricane and became the first Caribbean island to suffer a major disaster in the era of apprenticeship. The details of what took place on that night come from an article in the *Dominica Colonist* in which the author, clearly keen to impress upon readers the scale of the disaster, drew heavily on the aesthetic of the 'plantation pastoral' to provide a shocking contrast with what followed. On the day of 20 September, the sun set on Dominica's 'fair and verdant fields', its acres of 'mountain cabbage and stately cocoa trees' and on the 'humble but comfortable cottages of the happy labourers'. On the following day, it was said that the 'same sun rose on blighted and withered wastes' and on 'the houses of masters and on the huts of servants involved alike in one mass of ruins'. Striking a particularly despairing tone, the author finished the article by writing that 'the awful Equinox of September 1834 can never be obliterated from the memory of the inhabitants of Dominica'.[57]

Florid descriptions of the destruction aside, in comparison with the casualties following the disasters of 1831 and 1812, the number of deaths directly resulting from the hurricane was relatively low, estimated at around twenty-nine. Yet, again reminding us of how the plantation rendered Caribbean colonies more vulnerable, the survivors of the hurricane faced the same immediate crisis that Barbados and St Vincent did before it: a severe shortage of food. The hurricane was reported to have destroyed provision grounds of every description as well as all of the coffee crop and half the sugar crop.

The majority of the population was largely reduced to scavenging food from the ground where it had been uprooted but was still edible. It was said that the scavenged foodstuffs were themselves very meagre and would only last a fortnight or at most three weeks before the famine began.[58] In his initial communications with the Colonial Office, Governor Evan Macgregor detailed the effects these losses were having on the mood of the populace, writing that the 'extreme change from great abundance of food to perhaps the reverse, has thrown gloom over all'.[59]

Characteristic of their class, the planters of Dominica responded to the disaster by prioritising putting the African-Caribbean population back to work. Writing to the governor just three days after the hurricane, the Speaker of the House of Assembly, James Corlet, wrote of the pressing need to have the African-Caribbean population clear the island's roads of soil and other debris so that they could then return to work rebuilding the plantations. Elsewhere, eyewitness accounts tell us that the African-Caribbean population were directed to work on rebuilding their housing on the plantations. However, the new apprentices appear to have chafed at these directions, preferring instead to focus on what they clearly saw as a more pressing need: feeding themselves. Apprentices on one plantation implored the estate owner to allow them to attend their cassava, which was beginning to rot and was their 'best stand by, as it may be preserved for any length of time'.[60] According to the planters, transgressions against their authority abounded in the aftermath of the hurricane and their frustration is palpable in the letters they sent to each other. For example, writing to a fellow planter, Dugald Laidlaw expressed his indignation that:

> The rich, respectable founders the planters [have] with every disposition sought to assist them [the labourers] [but that] ever since the hurricane, the negroes have been behaving ill, and have done little towards rebuilding their houses – on which they have been exclusively employed. Finding that my brother was nearly dead from being buried in the ruins of the great house, they robbed and plundered everything they could lay their hands upon.[61]

And yet, despite the anger planters clearly felt, unlike their counterparts in Barbados in 1831, they did not turn to violence and coercion. Laidlaw, for example, angry at what he saw as the 'looting' of his house, still purchased imported food for the apprentices noting that it was an 'unavoidable expense'.[62] In a batch of letters that were sent to London to illustrate the situation on the island and to underscore its need for relief, Laidlaw was also keen to highlight the number of apprentice children whom he and other planters were doing what they could to feed.[63] Even the island's governor publicly called on the island's legislature to provide immediate shelter to all those without it.

While we should not take at face value the writings of those who benefited from the daily abuse of those they now purported to help, the tone struck here is notably different from communications after the hurricane of 1831 and eruption of 1812. It would be easy to put this tentative benevolence down to the fact that the apprenticeship system was in its infancy and some planters feared that harsh treatment would drive apprentices to work on other estates. However, I think we must also bear in mind both the island's very recent history and slightly more distant, but nonetheless relevant, events. On 15 August 1834, there had been female-led resistance to the implementation of the apprenticeship system.[64] In colonial records this resistance is recorded as having been suppressed through 'firm but temperate measures', a vague phrase that may elide the reality of those measures, but nonetheless no widespread violence was reported. Perhaps, in the aftermath of the disaster that left them weakened, the planters did not wish to inflame existing tensions. It is also worth noting that, between the years 1813 and 1815, Dominica's planters had been engaged in a series of violent struggles with Maroon communities on the island. The planters had eventually subdued the Maroons, but as Polly Pattullo suggests, dissent on the island and the conflict permanently weakened the planters' ability to violently enforce their will.[65]

Across the Caribbean, as planters and the formerly enslaved adjusted to the realities of apprenticeship, unsurprisingly white anxieties around control and labour continued to be key factors in shaping British responses to disaster. However, what is surprising is that the use of violence and coercion continued to recede. On 12 August 1835, the island of Antigua was visited by a particularly devastating hurricane, which destroyed much of the island's sugar industry and many of the administrative buildings. The immediate response of the island's white elites continued the post-slavery trend of tentative benevolence like that exercised on Dominica in 1834.

On 17 August, members of the island's legislature met to discuss how those without shelter might be provided with it and noted that daily meals were already being supplied to the poor of the island.[66] We do not know the racial composition of the 'poor' referred to here, but the fact that only two weeks later planters were said to be actively involved in aiding the reconstruction of labourers' cottages suggests that there was some genuine relief being given to the African-Caribbean population.[67]

This seemingly more benevolent approach to disaster response – compared to that of Lyon in 1831 – continued in a proclamation issued by the governor, Evan Macgregor, and written by his private secretary in late August.[68] While it lacked the harsh tone used by James Lyon, for example, in his 1831 proclamations it retained a characteristic focus on African-Caribbean labour and firmly recommended against the African-Caribbean population using the hurricane as an opportunity to withdraw their labour. In a particularly key section, the governor's private secretary, Henry Loving, wrote:

> nothing can be gained, upon [the labourers'] part, from combination and attempted intimidation, nor anything, on the other hand, exacted from them but what the law prescribes ... to the labouring population, in particular, his excellency [the governor] would point out the necessity, as well as moral obligation, of striving to better their condition in life, not by idleness and uniting to withhold the required labour for the culture of the land.[69]

There can be little doubt that Macgregor, via Loving, was using the proclamation to warn against a repeat of events on the island in the previous week. On 3 August, at least 1,800 labourers had abandoned their work and participated in a strike which was serious enough that the authorities deployed the island's police force. To break the strike, the superintendent of the police force, Richard Wickham, had made it his mission to 'strike terror into the minds of the disaffected'. When he and his troops were deployed to the Popeshead district of the island, he ordered them to stand on an elevated position overlooking the estates with the express purpose of making their strength visible to the labourers on the plantations below. He also ordered the sounding of a bugle to call the labourers to work and then sent his troops into the apprentices' quarters to drag out any of those still striking from work.[70]

The context of such widespread strike action occurring just prior to the hurricane helps us explain the seemingly benevolent response to the disaster. Indeed, there can be little doubt that there was a similar relationship between the strike action that took place on Dominica in August 1834 and the apparently benevolent response of the planters to the hurricane of September that year. It is perhaps surprising that, for such a racially divided society in which the minority population exercised and abused extreme power, disasters did not foment widespread violence more often. In fact, the violence of the British response to the hurricane of 1831 appears not quite an outlier, but at the very least an extreme example during the era of slavery.

All of these examples, however, are bound together by one clear thread: the fixation on quickly reasserting the colonially imposed racial order. This fixation was not unique to the British Caribbean; in the same period the British in India similarly directed their energies when responding to periodic famines. However, in contrast to British responses to famine in Ireland and India, which became increasingly formalised over the course of the nineteenth century with the institution of work camps and relief eligibility tests, responses to disaster in the Caribbean remained relatively ad-hoc.[71]

What characterised British responses in the Caribbean during this period was an ability to respond, to some degree, pragmatically to the situation to achieve their goals. Crucially, with their dominance in assemblies and legislative and privy councils throughout the region, it seems that in the era of slavery and then later apprenticeship, it was primarily planters defining these goals and responding to disaster. Interestingly this seems to also be the case in other rival colonies where plantations were the primary means of economic growth.

In 1830 and then in 1832, the French colony of La Réunion was hit by two powerful cyclones. To ameliorate the scarcity that emerged in the wake of the hurricane, the governor took a market interventionist approach and lowered the duties on imported foodstuffs. Alessandro Stanziani shows us that planters on the island quickly took advantage of these adjustments and 'attempted to pass the cost of bad weather and poor markets onto their workers by increasing their working hours and retaining their wages'.[72] French planters seem to have shared with their British counterparts a view that their governments did not always have their best interests at heart and seem to have similarly sought to use disaster to their advantage.

As the nineteenth century progressed, the importance of the island colonies of the Caribbean within Britain's imperial design waned, and with it, so too did the power of the planters. As the next chapter shows, this meant that governors and colonial officials increasingly took control of disaster response. Governors, while broadly sharing the objectives of the planter class, brought with them a more codified approach to disaster response informed by British approaches to domestic poor relief, but they were also afforded great latitude in their actions and so, particularly as the geopolitics of the region changed, their actions could have dire consequences as disasters increasingly became the focus of international attention.

Notes

1 Editor of *The West Indian, Account of the Fatal Hurricane by Which Barbados Suffered in August 1831*, p. 108.
2 TNA, T1/4397, Extract of a letter from Rosalie Estate, 28 September 1834.
3 The focus of this chapter is on *British* responses to disaster, because as the ones in control of Caribbean society, how they responded affected all others in a colony. Those separate to the British colonial apparatus had their own responses on both an individual and communal level, but the focus here is on the British as it was they who most shaped the realities of post-disaster situations.
4 James A. Delle, *The Colonial Caribbean: Landscapes of Power in Jamaica's Plantation System* (Cambridge: Cambridge University Press, 2014), p. 106.
5 TNA, MS. Nos. 206–253, CO 262/11 (St Vincent) Return of the population of the island of St Vincent, 10 March 1812.

6 Hilary Beckles, 'Social and Political Control in the Slave Society', in *General History of the Caribbean: The Slave Societies of the Caribbean*, ed. by Franklin W. Knight (London: UNESCO, 1997), p. 215.
7 Editor of *The West Indian*, *Account of the Fatal Hurricane by Which Barbados Suffered in August 1831*, p. 37.
8 CO 31/51 (Barbados) Sessional Papers. Assembly. 'The humble Petition of the Legislature of Barbados'.
9 Ibid., p. 47.
10 Jerome S. Handler, 'Freedmen and Slaves in the Barbados Militia', *Journal of Caribbean History*, 19 (1984), p. 10.
11 *Barbados Globe and Colonial Advocate*, 23 August 1831.
12 TNA, CO 28/107, Governor of Barbados to Colonial Office, 16 August 1831.
13 Editor of *The West Indian*, *Account of the Fatal Hurricane by Which Barbados Suffered in August 1831*, p. 119.
14 Ibid.
15 Ibid.
16 Editor of *The West Indian*, *Account of the Fatal Hurricane by Which Barbados Suffered in August 1831* (Barbados: Printed for Samuel Hyde, 1831), p. 120.
17 A Report of a Committee of the Council of Barbadoes, appointed to inquire into the actual condition of the slaves in this island (London: W. Sior, 1824).
18 Ibid., p. 102.
19 Editor of *The West Indian*, *Account of the Fatal Hurricane by Which Barbados Suffered in August 1831*, pp. 77, 117.
20 Ibid., p. 117.
21 Michael Craton, 'Proto-Peasant Revolts? The Late Slave Rebellions in the British West Indies 1816–1832', *Past & Present*, 85 (1979), p. 105.
22 Michael Craton, *Testing the Chains: Resistance to Slavery in the British West Indies* (New York: Cornell University Press, 2009), pp. 265–266.
23 Editor of *The West Indian*, *Account of the Fatal Hurricane by Which Barbados Suffered in August 1831*, p. 39.
24 Letter written by M. Jackson of the Barbados Bible Society to the British Bible Society, 15 August 1831. Accessed online 15 July 2021, Adam Matthew Digital, Church Missionary Society Archive.
25 *Barbados Globe and Colonial Advocate*, 23 August 1831.
26 Bryan Edwards, *The history, civil and commercial, of the British colonies in the West Indies*, Vol. II (London: John Stockdale, 1801), p. 190.
27 Arthur Bowley, *Wages in the United Kingdom in the Nineteenth Century* (Cambridge: Cambridge University Press, 1900), p. 34.
28 F.W.N. Bayley, *Four Year's Residence in the West Indies*, p. 149.
29 *Barbados Globe and Colonial Advocate*, 18 August 1831.
30 TNA, T1/4395 Long Papers, bundle 852, part 1: West Indies Relief, Drake to Stewart, 17 February 1832.
31 Description of the eruption of the *Souffrier Mountain*, on Thursday night the 30th of April 1812, on the island of Saint Vincent, printed by J.T. Calliard in HoC [182], St Vincent. Report from committee on petition of persons interested in estates in the island of St Vincent, pp. 5–7.

32 Ibid., p. 7.
33 Ibid., p. 6.
34 Virginia Historical Society, Keane Family Papers, Mss 1 K197 a23, Hugh Perry Keane, Diary, 2–4 May 1812.
35 Charles Shephard, *An Historical Account of the Island of Saint Vincent* (London: W. Nicol, 1831), p. 5.
36 National Library of Scotland, Ms 6, 396, Stuart Rothsey Papers, Stuart Rothsey, 'Account of the Eruption at St Vincent in May 1812 [&] its effects on Barbadoes', pp. 141–143; TNA CO 28/81, George Beckwith to the Lord of Liverpool, 13 May 1812.
37 Christopher Taylor, *The Black Carib Wars: Freedom, Survival and the Making of the Garifuna* (Jackson, MS: University of Mississippi Press, 2012), p. 152.
38 TNA CO 263/4, St Vincent, Privy Council, 3 August 1812.
39 Ibid.
40 Ibid.
41 Patrick Colquhoun, *A Treatise on the Wealth, Power, and Resources of the British Empire* (London: J. Mawman, 1814), p. 558; A.C. Carmichael, *Tales of a Grandmother* (London: Richard Bentley, 1841), p. 141.
42 Robert Montgomery Martin, *History of the West Indies: Comprising Jamaica, Honduras, Trinidad, Tobago Grenada, The Bahamas, and the Virgin Isles* (London: Whittaker & Co., 1836), p. 227.
43 Joseph Spinelli, 'Land Use and Population in St Vincent, 1763–1960: A Contribution to the Study of the Patterns of Economic and Demographic Change in a Small West Indian Island' (unpublished PhD thesis, University of Florida, 1973), p. 64.
44 So notable was the fertility of the soil in the north of the island, that in February 1812 a man claiming to have commanded the British fleet when it recaptured St Vincent in 1797 wrote to the governor of the island from London requesting that he be personally considered in any future redistribution of the valuable land.
45 TNA, CO 263/4 (St Vincent) Privy Council Meeting, 16 September 1812.
46 Ibid.
47 To underscore just how significant an effect the Abolition had on the slave populations it is worth bearing in mind that between 1816 and 1834 only Barbados and the Bahamas maintained an increasing enslaved population.
48 TNA, CO 263/4, J. Barker, John Tapier, J.H. Schlarhow, John Douglas, W.M. Jordan, Angus Fraser, Robert Douglas to Governor and Legislature of St Vincent, 8 June 1812; TNA, CO 263/4, Acting Governor of Demerary Lyle Carmichael to Robert Paul 31 May 1812.
49 Hugh Perry Keane, Diary, 2 May 1812.
50 Hansard, HoC Deb 22 January 1812, vol. 21.
51 TNA, CO 263/4 (St Vincent) Privy Council Meeting, 1 September 1812.
52 HoC [182], St Vincent. Report from committee on petition of persons interested in estates in the island of St Vincent, 7 May 1813, p. 4.
53 TNA, T1/4396, Petition signed by J. Woodhouse, Holquhoun, Haran, J.P. Mayers, H.M. Paul, H. Bouverie, P. Cruickshanks, J. Mayal to Viscount Goderich, 20 November 1831.

54 *Barbados Globe and Colonial Advocate*, 25 August 1831.
55 TNA CO 31/51, Barbados, Assembly, 25 August 1831.
56 Jamaican Apprentice James Williams' account of life as an apprentice provides us with perhaps the clearest example of this phenomena. James Williams, *A Narrative of Events since the First of August, 1834*, ed. by Diana Paton (Durham: Durham University Press, 2001).
57 *Dominica Colonist*, 27 September 1834.
58 TNA, T1/4397, Extract of a letter sent by Rev. George Clarke to (recipient not given), 20 September 1834.
59 TNA, CO 71/78 (Dominica) Correspondence, Original-Secretary of State: Despatches; Offices and Individuals, E.M. McGregor to C.M. Schomberg (Governor in Chief Antigua).
60 TNA, T1/4397, Extract of a letter from the Rosalie Estate contained within Laidlaw to Gregg, 2 October 1834.
61 TNA, T1/4397, Colquhoun to Spring Rice, 2 October 1834.
62 Ibid.
63 Ibid.
64 TNA, CO 71/78, Lt Governor Sir C.M. Schomburg to Spring Rice, 15 August 1834.
65 Polly Pattullo, *Your Time is Done Now: Slavery, Resistance, and Defeat: The Maroon Trials of Dominica (1813–1814)* (London: Papillote Press, 2015).
66 TNA, CO 71/79 (Dominica) Correspondence, Original – Secretary of State: Despatches; Offices and Individuals, Sam Horner, Nicholas Nugent to Evan Macgregor, 22 August 1835.
67 TNA, CO 71/79, Richard Wickham to Evan Macgregor, 3 September 1835.
68 Macgregor governed Dominica and Antigua simultaneously along with some of the smaller colonies grouped together as the Leeward Islands.
69 TNA, CO 7/42, Correspondence, Original – Secretary of State: Despatches, Macgregor (1835, August–December) 'A Proclamation', 20 August 1835.
70 TNA, CO 71/79 (Antigua) Privy Council notes, report from the Superintendent of the Police, 5 August 1835.
71 Joanna Simonow, 'Understanding Humanitarian Action in South Asia: Responses to Famine and Displacement in Nineteenth and Twentieth Century India', working paper, *Humanitarian Policy Group*, 2015, p. 3.
72 Alessandro Stanziani, 'The Impact of Cyclones on Nineteenth-Century Réunion', in *Bondage and the Environment in the Indian Ocean World*, ed. by Gwyn Campbell (Cham: Palgrave Macmillan, 2018). pp. 151–152.

4

'Freedom', decline and fear

Though it was not immediate, the shine of the compromise 'apprenticeship' system wore off for abolitionists. Over time, it gained a rightly deserved reputation as 'slavery by any other name'. This reputation emerged in no small part through the actions of the apprenticed who, from the outset of the system, resisted its imposition and offered their testimony where they could despite the violent reprisals it might provoke in whites. James Williams' testimony, provided to Quaker abolitionist James Sturge, is perhaps the most famous of these. It offers a richly detailed account of his life as an apprentice in Jamaica; perhaps one of the most striking insights it provides is Williams' belief that he received better treatment overall as a slave.[1] In elaborating on this, Williams describes a white class who, shorn by the abolitionists of total legal authority over African-Caribbean people, found themselves insecure about their power and felt a compulsion, through increased physical and mental punishment, to disabuse non-whites of the notion that 1833 had initiated any weakening of whites' power.

In 1838, with the exception of Antigua, which had chosen to proceed to legal freedom in 1833, the apprenticeship system was brought to a premature end by Parliament two years before its intended end date. The insecurity whites felt about their grasp over the Caribbean's land and people only persisted, festering into anxieties that would permeate their daily interactions with non-whites and their governance more broadly.

Throughout the period of apprenticeship, but especially as its end loomed, the planter class intoned to all who would hear it that the advent of free labour in the region would bring about a complete collapse of Caribbean society. For them, freedom beckoned to an apocalyptic future in which their estates lay untended, and they were harried and murdered by the formerly enslaved population out for revenge. Liberal abolitionists countered by imagining a future in which, while some paternalist, white guidance would still be needed, the invisible hand of the market would inevitably drive the African-Caribbean people to 'sturdy independence'. In the end, for both of the groups directly affected, legal freedom proved to be a disappointment.

At the most basic level, by virtue of continuing to control the plantations, planters still retained a great deal of control over the everyday lives of the formerly enslaved, and they fought fiercely to sustain this power. They sought to curtail any attempts by the African-Caribbean at the sort of self-sufficiency that would have allowed them to have lives independent of their plantations. In rural areas, planters took steps to stop the formerly enslaved owning land, and in urban centres, subjected them to new regimes of surveillance and punishment.

For the British observing at a distance, those who had been anti-slavery found themselves disappointed that the end of coerced labour did not bring about the quick emergence of a self-improving, wage earning African-Caribbean labour force. The formerly enslaved had a multitude of ideas about how they wanted to exercise their freedom, which often did not correlate with what the white, liberal classes of Britain had envisioned for them. For those invested in the economic success of the Caribbean, the post-emancipation era marked a steep decline in their fortunes. Not only were abolitionist claims of higher output post-slavery not realised, but with the economic motor of slavery gone, the Caribbean's enviable place within the British Empire slipped.

Less than ten years after the ending of the apprenticeship system, 1846 saw the equalisation of import duties on sugar across the British Empire. For planters, this signalled the loss of the preferential tariffs that had sustained their business for decades previous and forced them to compete not just with East Indian sugar from within the British Empire, but also Cuban and Brazilian sugar still produced with enslaved labour. The position of the Caribbean planters and the value of their cane crop was also undergoing a slow erosion at the hands of beet sugar. Experiments in extracting sugar from beet had been ongoing in Europe since 1747, but in the nineteenth century they came into their own with the first high yields of sugar being extracted in France from 1812 onwards.[2]

These trends converged in the minds of the British elites to create a general sense that the Caribbean had entered a period of terminal decline. At the midpoint of the nineteenth century, the sense of antipathy felt for the Caribbean colonies is perhaps best summed up by Benjamin Disraeli. In 1852, whilst Chancellor of the Exchequer, he wrote to Lord Malmsbury, Foreign Secretary, describing Britain's colonies as 'millstones' around the country's neck.[3] Even for those more enamoured with Britain's territorial acquisitions, by this time, the Caribbean colonies did not give the appearance of possessions dynamically involved in enriching Britain. India and, to an extent, Africa, became the new polestars of the British Empire.

Acting upon on the shifting sands of British power in the Caribbean, disasters only exacerbated emerging anxieties over the British grasp of the region and its people. Interventions in the last three decades of the study of the post-emancipation Caribbean have suggested it would be unwise to paint a binary between slavery and freedom. British disaster response provides us with a new view onto the stark inequalities that persisted despite the transition away from slavery. Disasters continued to bring to the surface tension between African-Caribbean and British people. Colonial disaster response continued to be an exercise in, at best, neglect, and at worst, antagonism and violence. In addition to this and in line with many doom-laden pronouncements of Caribbean planters who saw their collapsing enterprises as presaging the collapse of the British Caribbean, disaster response in the post-emancipation era was also coloured by a new insecurity over British authority that manifested at multiple levels.

On the ground, there is much continuity in white elites' preoccupation with ensuring that disaster did not allow non-whites to slip free of the disciplining forces of labour. If anything, this was easier during the period of slavery; there was a binary between slave and master, in which master had total legal control. In the post-emancipation era, things were less clear. Planters had lost the ability to punish the apprenticed and later the free population, which was instead now the purview of the 'special magistrate'. The magistrates were employed by the British state and while they could be from the island which would become their jurisdiction, they could not be planters.

In response, whites increasingly levelled at African-Caribbean people a developing lexicon of racial stereotypes, particularly concerning their perceived inherent laziness. Insecure about their control, whites increasingly drew on these stereotypes and changing approaches to poor relief in Britain to create a new 'objective' reality that justified their punitive response to disaster. This insecurity was particularly visible in the strength with which they still presumed the disasters would provoke a challenge to their authority.

Complicating this picture, however, is the fact that this period also witnessed expansion of governmental apparatus and displacement of planters as the sole source of authority. In the latter half of the nineteenth century and in to the twentieth century came a new era in which Caribbean people could expect for the first time some, though extremely limited, indiscriminate relief. The immediate aftermath of disasters was no longer entirely managed by planters and thus a complete *laissez faire* free-for-all. The colonial state did begin to make efforts to provide genuine relief to further limit loss of life. That said, the driving principle of coercing the African-Caribbean population back to labour remained at the centre of British disaster response; after the era of slavery a new vocabulary, imported from domestic developments in British poor relief came to shape relief, categorise its claimants and, where possible, exclude them.

'Freedom'

On 8 February 1843, the Leeward Islands were struck by a severe earthquake, with buildings on all of them suffering damage in one form or another. Guadeloupe and Antigua, in particular, however, were harshly affected. Almost all of the buildings in the French colony Guadeloupe's capital were destroyed, with an estimated cost of fifteen hundred lives.[4] Comparatively, Antigua suffered much less. There the earthquake did significant damage to the buildings of St John's, the capital and to plantations throughout the island but there were only between eight and forty deaths caused by the quake.[5]

Despite this relatively limited damage, Governor Charles Fitzroy's communications with the Colonial Office suggest he feared immediate unrest. He notes that 'pillage' was much dreaded and that as a result he had taken measures to protect private property such as swearing in a number of new special constables and, on the day following the earthquake, sending out a detachment of the 47th Regiment to assist the police in cases of 'necessity'.[6]

Fitzroy made a presumption that the African-Caribbean population would turn the disaster into an opportunity to loot and otherwise transgress against white-owned property. There can be little doubt that his fears were stoked by the fact that the earthquake had greatly damaged the key physical manifestations of colonial power. The court, the jail, the house of correction, the lunatic asylum and the main barracks were all reduced to rubble.[7] Speaking to the island's council, Fitzroy described these buildings as the 'primary points' which required the quickest attention, expressing particular concern that there was nowhere suitable to hold existing or potentially new prisoners.[8]

In the days the followed the quake, however, these concerns about civil disobedience were quickly confounded. Fitzroy reported to the Colonial Office that 'with only one trifling exception no attempt at plunder has been made'.[9] Colonial prejudices were further wrong-footed, as Fitzroy reported that the African-Caribbean population came forward and volunteered to help with the clean up on St John's and made it clear that they would not take advantage of the distress and raise the price of their labour.[10] Later, on the basis of observations gained riding through the streets of St John's to personally assess the damage, Governor Fitzroy was keen to stress to the Colonial Office that 'the conduct of the labouring population [had] been most praiseworthy'.[11]

What is interesting is that, in this instance, the 'labouring population' did not work alone. Fitzroy noted that 'all classes' worked together to pull down ruined buildings and clear the capital's streets.[12] Though Fitzroy was speaking the language of 'class', Antigua, unlike Barbados, had no substantial white labouring population, and in this sense, though his observations only concern the capital, he describes a scene of relative racial harmony. While the records describing the aftermath of the earthquake do not allow us a detailed picture of events beyond the capital, given the fear the colonial authorities had over unrest, I think it is fair to say that had unrest been taking place it would have made its way into the record. These events stand in stark contrast to those in Barbados in 1831 and even to the frustration and annoyance expressed by planters after the Dominican hurricane of 1834. Thus the question of what was different in Antigua arises.

I would argue that we are not seeing a picture of harmony born from emancipation but rather one rare instance in which the priorities of white elites aligned with those of the African-Caribbean population. Unlike in the disasters discussed up to this point, the availability of food on Antigua was not significantly disrupted. The earthquake destroyed buildings across the island but unlike a hurricane, did not uproot crops, meaning that unlike in previous disasters, where whites were anxious to restart labour while the African-Caribbean population understandably prioritised food and shelter, there was a broad unity of purpose. In effect, with an availability of provisions and willing labour, the circumstances after the earthquake were not sufficiently dire to pose a threat to the colonial hierarchy.

Circumstances on Antigua could have been much worse. In the capital of Guadeloupe, Pointe-à-Pitre, material shortages after the earthquake and a subsequent fire dragged out the colony's recovery. On Antigua, it appears a similar conflagration was only narrowly avoided because the capital had already suffered a devastating fire in 1841 that consumed much of the capital. As of 1843, much of what had been destroyed by the fire remained neglected and unbuilt. Thus there were significant gaps between buildings, which probably prevented a fire spreading. The fact that the aftermath of the disaster was not followed by fire and material shortages likely prevented a ratcheting of tensions between the white elites and African-Caribbean people: the hallmarks of slavery-era disaster response had a tendency to quickly re-emerge when disaster shortages did occur.

When Tobago was visited by a hurricane in 1847 it was, for many, a surprise. The colony had long been considered out of the path of hurricanes. The houses and plantations of the wealthy and the cottages of the labouring class were utterly destroyed across the island. The response of the authorities was in some respect more moderate than that of the Antiguan authorities in 1843 and troops were not deployed, but insecurity about African-Caribbean conduct was nonetheless clear. On 15 October, three days after the hurricane, Laurence Graeme, the Lieutenant Governor, issued a public petition stressing that he had issued directions for the punishment of anyone found taking advantage of the destruction to misappropriate property. That this warning was intended for the African-Caribbean population is clear because Graeme made it the duty of all magistrates, ministers and members of the colonial authorities to publicly read it out.

Five days after this proclamation was issued, the Lieutenant Governor followed it up with a particularly harsh, new law, which is very informative of the insecurity whites felt. To start, the targets of the new law were very broad: it was directed to any 'idle and disorderly persons' who were found 'roving about the country and refusing to work, and whose object [was] evidently to avail themselves of the present opportunity of plunder'.[13] The scope of the items that could render someone liable for persecution was similarly broad:

> money or valuable security, or any goods or chattels, wares, or merchandise, or any lumber, shingles, staves, bricks, tiles, copper, zinc, lead, tin, iron or other building materials in or from any store, shop, house shed, or other building, or exposed in any street, highway, or other place, or attached or detached from any freehold wholly or partly destroyed or damaged in the later hurricane.[14]

Such a scope reflects a colonial authority desirous of enacting new legal barriers, to prevent any slippage in a social order built on the sanctity of white property.

The law effectively rendered just about any form of salvage a crime and, in the fine print, purposely lowered the bar for conviction as ordinary tribunals were not 'summary enough'. The law also gave Justices of the Peace enlarged powers. They were now allowed to convict and punish on the spot with just the testimony of one witness. The punishments listed in the law were, for men, public flogging via thirty lashes of a cat o' nine tails and, for women, imprisonment and hard labour for up to three months.

Like most public punishments, the flogging of men in this instance was obviously prescribed with the intent of sending a clear message to any other would-be looters. That women were not to be flogged but imprisoned reflected the gendering of punishment since the era of amelioration by colonial authorities. There was a worry that the flogging of women risked their potential indecent exposure and would thus undermine their sense of 'gender difference'.[15] In effect, it was considered that public punishment degraded women and undid the 'civilised', feminine qualities that whites were supposedly working hard to raise in the African-Caribbean population. The final two clauses of the law made it clear that only not did the Justices of the Peace have indemnity whilst convicting under this law, but there were to be no appeals as every decision was final.

This law is also striking because it reflects a clear reversion to the punishments of the era of slavery. Flogging had largely been abandoned in the

Caribbean, and had even been abolished in Jamaica in 1840 (though there was an exception granted for young adolescent males).[16] Confinement and fines instead became the primary means to discipline the African-Caribbean population; in an era of wage labour these punishments took on a new weight that they did not have for those already without freedom in the era of slavery. Therefore, this act tells us much about the level of anxiety that the colonial authorities felt in the post-disaster moment and how quickly the advances made since 1838 could dissolve.

The language of this act, specifically the use of the terms 'idle and disorderly', reflect the desire to maintain social order in the face of the collapse of the defined barrier provided by slavery, and to reproduce the hierarchy deemed essential to British rule in the region. At least rhetorically, the line between those who would submit to waged labour (read white authority) and those who would not, emerged to replace the old dichotomy between slave and master. The descriptors idle and disorderly did not emerge in a vacuum in the Caribbean, however, but were very much part of the lexicon that accompanied the 'rationalisation' of poor relief in Britain in 1834. The new Poor Law Amendment Act of that year, emerging out of a climate of rising poverty rates and population growth, sought to decrease state spending by discouraging what was seen as rampant dependency on relief, and arrived with a new vocabulary to categorise and distinguish between the deserving and undeserving poor. Idle, lazy and disorderly were just some of the most common pejoratives used by the state and wider society to describe those they saw as unwilling to work despite being 'able-bodied'.[17]

These terms made their way to the Caribbean but, unlike paupers in Britain, who had a chance of transcending their 'idle and disorderly' categorisation, for the African-Caribbean population, idleness came to be seen as a racial characteristic and thus one that they could not be rehabilitated from. This supposed 'inherent' racial difference not only acted as a means to maintain a doctrine of racial difference but also the justification for the programmes of punitive relief that were replete throughout British responses to disaster in this era.

After 1838, one gets the sense that white elites were looking for new, solid ground on which to reconstruct their authority after the ending of slavery, and a moralising rhetoric around wage labour emerged to provide that. As in the era of slavery, whites still saw disasters and their associated hardships as a potential catalyst for a contestation for their authority. However, where they had looked for slave conspiracies, the authorities now sought to coerce and shame those who would not work after disasters. The focus on work remained but the tenor shifted.

The new Poor Law Amendment Act had also been part of a wider reconfiguration of the new industrialising state's relationship with its citizens.

It sought to limit state intervention and to make claiming relief from the state an absolute last resort. The intent was to drive paupers away from charitable relief (which, it was believed, encouraged idleness) and, because the tests for aid were so stringent and conditions in the new workhouses so poor, towards whatever work they could find. In all, state relief was to be made an absolute last resort. That said, in his history of humanitarianism, Michael Barnett notes that although the 1834 Act discouraged relief, it did not do away with relief entirely. There was still a recognition that the state did have some responsibility to help the deserving poor, albeit, in a manner that expedited their return to the labour market and 'sturdy independence'.[18]

It is hard to pinpoint how these attitudes crossed over the Atlantic to the Caribbean, but it is clear that they did. The workhouse had been a feature of Caribbean life since the first had been constructed in Jamaica in 1780. Inside the workhouse, enslaved people were subject to a regime of work that sought to replicate the discipline of plantation labour but in a manner that 'tended to exacerbate the most negative and demeaning aspects of [it]'.[19] After the end of slavery, the workhouse remained and actually took on an even more important role in that it was a site dedicated to the reproduction of racial hierarchy.[20] The language of idleness appears to have developed in the Caribbean as a means to continue to buttress the existence of workhouses and colonial control more broadly. As demonstrated in the case of the 1866 Bahamian hurricane, it was not until later in the century that these attitudes would really crystallise and begin to thoroughly shape British disaster response.

The hurricane began early in the morning of 1 October 1866, with squalls, deluges of rain and choppy waters in the harbour of Nassau, the capital of the Bahamas. At seven in the evening, there was a brief moment of calm, but sailors and those with prior experience of hurricanes knew what was coming and spent time readying their dwellings. The governor, Rawson W. Rawson, records that others less experienced with hurricanes 'flattered themselves' into thinking the storm was over.[21] At nine, the hurricane hit again, with a renewed and constant fury. This continued until two in the morning when the wind finally began to decline.

Surveying the damage to Nassau the next morning, Rawson wrote that 'a bombardment could hardly have inflicted greater mischief'.[22] He also wrote of obstructed roads throughout the city and buildings that, in their damaged state, posed a threat to its citizens. Nassau, however, was seemingly where difficulties were felt least. On the following day, Rawson reported that with clear weather, the citizens of the town displayed an inclination toward 'self-help, neighbourly kindness, and cheerfulness'.[23]

Rawson painted a rosy picture in his description of the inhabitants of Nassau, and from his perspective, things were indeed as good as they could be. There was full employment available to those who could work, and for others who had lost property or wealth, opportunities were presenting themselves. The storm had wrecked a great many vessels, but the citizens of Nassau, long experienced salvagers, were quickly finding compensation for their losses in these wrecks. Rawson was thus able to cheerfully note that applications for charitable relief had been very few.

While the picture may have appeared, at least to his eyes, positive, in Nassau, the distress of many was only just beginning and he had far from a complete picture of the colony. As Governor of the Bahamas, he was in charge of not just New Providence, the island home to Nassau, but also seventeen 'out-islands' whose only connection to New Providence was via ship. In the days that followed the hurricane, even without information on circumstances in the out-islands, Rawson expressed not only apprehension at the situation that might be unfolding there but also a characteristically colonial preoccupation with returning African-Caribbean people to labour:

> The pressure will be felt most in the out-islands, where the greater part of the population live upon the produce of their fields, with no opportunity of earning wages as labourers, and where there are few gentry, or persons of capital, or enterprise, capable of aiding them in distress, or stimulating them to industry.[24]

Alongside his clearly paternalistic framing of the situation, as he began to send out police officers and magistrates to assess the damage, not just in New Providence but also in the out-islands, Rawson was very determined to set clear expectations of the state. Writing back to the Colonial Office, he stated that his actions had been guided by a desire to inspire feelings of 'independence and self-help' and disabuse Bahamians of the 'erroneous' notion that the colonial government was going to aid in the reconstruction of the general populace's housing.[25]

As it happened, the situation was predictably dire across many of the out-islands. For example, on Long Island, the magistrate reported that the people were suffering 'all but starvation' living on what crabs and fish they could find. The majority of the island's population were sheltering in the local prison and police station, having experienced the total destruction of their dwellings. They had not only lost their homes but also had no chance of rebuilding them as traditionally they were roofed with palmetto leaves, and the hurricane had either destroyed or stripped the island's palmetto trees. As a result the magistrate concluded that 'the population will, therefore, remain exposed to serious inconvenience and discomfort for a period of nearly six months'.[26] While Long Island certainly seemed to experience the worst destruction, the governor was of the opinion that, given the destruction of crops throughout the out-islands, until new crops could be planted and harvested (in itself a gamble), severe want and hardship would persist for two to three months.[27]

Despite this clear and immediate need, Rawson, preoccupied with returning the African-Caribbean population to labour, had different priorities; as he later put it in a speech to the Legislative Council in 1867: 'giving direction to industrial efforts, and by far removing existing impediments to successful enterprise far outweigh[ed] the removal of an immediate, but temporary, pressure'.[28] Notwithstanding those strong words, Rawson did send out some initial relief to try avert starvation but, even then, he attached conditions to that relief that still advantaged his ultimate goal of curtailing indiscriminate relief.

Rawson sent to Cuba for a supply of both seed corn and cotton seed, which was then distributed amongst the out-islands by a schooner. However, he attached nakedly exploitative conditions to the distribution of the seed corn. Cotton seed was given freely, probably because this was part of restarting the colony's economy, the 'productive powers of the community' that Rawson was so concerned about restoring.[29] By contrast, the seed corn, which people were to plant and feed themselves with, was to be distributed on credit and later paid for through money or labour. Given both the destruction of property by the hurricane and the paucity of property owned by the Bahamian labouring population, one can assume they had little choice but to accept the corn and pay with their labour. As transparently exploitative as we might see these conditions, it was exactly this sort of governance that the Colonial Office favoured. An undated and anonymous note on the reverse of a letter from Rawson to Earl of Carnarvon (then Secretary of State for the Colonies) on 17 October 1866 reads: 'The Gov. seems to have met the emergency with much alacrity and judgement. I think his proceedings should be commended.'[30]

This exploitative response to the hurricane and the typical food shortages that followed did not go unresisted, however. Reporting on conditions on the out-island Eleuthera, Rawson, in a manner illustrative of hardening British attitudes to state welfare, wrote that 'the people seem to expect that the Government will continue to support them, and that the losses by the hurricane will furnish an excuse for protracted destitution, without any effort on their part to supply their own wants and to restore their dwellings'.[31] On Exuma, reception of the governor's approach escalated beyond inaction. The local Justice of the Peace who was in charge of distributing the relief was surrounded by locals who threatened to lynch him and tear down his office if he did not distribute the aid fairly and equally and dispense of the requirement of labour to access the seed corn.[32] No doubt because he was located on an out-island with little chance of support, the Justice of the Peace acquiesced.

Despite this obvious rejection of his approach to relief, Rawson was not willing to concede or negotiate. In fact, he doubled down, arguing that the hurricane presented a necessary opportunity for the labouring classes to work harder than ever. Addressing the Legislative Council in 1867, Rawson called on the people of the island to 'imitate nature, which hastens with redoubled forces to repair the mischief she has committed, imparting twofold fertility to the soil ... and thus teaches us to apply ourselves at such seasons with redoubled energy'.[33] He also noted his conviction that industry was not only the means to recover present losses but to build economic resilience for the future.

Whilst extolling the virtues of work and industry at every level, Rawson was also using the hurricane as an opportunity to try and shape the colony's future. In his report to the Colonial Office, he notes that he had encouraged people to quit the exhausted and disaster-vulnerable soils of the out-islands and move to seek more consistent employment in more 'favoured localities'. Even without a formal plantation economy, Rawson was clearly desirous of using the hurricane as means to exert more control over the people who had previously had limited engagement with the colonial state and its market.

Decline

This discouragement of relief-seeking and the addition of punitive conditions when it was given only intensified as the economic situation in the British Caribbean worsened. Idle and lazy more than ever became the adjectives the governing classes reached for to describe those more often than not stunned and traumatised by disasters.

The last years of the nineteenth century and the first of the twentieth saw an economically crippled Caribbean battered by three disasters that only compounded its economic woes. While other colonies, such as Cuba, had continued to use slave labour, since 1838, output had consistently fallen on British plantations. This was combined with the equalisation of sugar duties in 1846 and then competition with European sugar beet. With many of their dreams for self-sufficiency after emancipation never realised, life was particularly hard for African-Caribbean people in this period. Wages were low and work hard to come by. Racial tensions simmered and protests occurred sporadically throughout the British Caribbean. Barbadians in particular struggled; unlike Jamaica, which had an abundance of land, Barbados had a scarcity of land and was considered, in colonial eyes, overpopulated.[34]

As mentioned in chapter 2, under the direction of Joseph Chamberlain, in the 1890s the British Government began, for the first time in a long time, to take an interest in the Caribbean colonies. It was mostly moved to do so by the economic depression, to which it responded by convening a Royal Commission which was sent to the region to investigate and recommend solutions. The Commission arrived in 1897 but, a hurricane would visit the Lesser Antilles in 1898 and send conditions plummeting much further still before the Commission was able to recommend and action solutions.

The hurricane of 1898 swept through the Lesser Antilles in early September, making landfall in Barbados on the tenth and St Vincent and St Lucia on the twelfth, where it did the most damage. Unlike with previous disasters, in which many of the communications are written or at least received far after the event, the deployment of telegraphic cables to the region in the 1870s gives us a far more in-depth, day-by-day look at the British response. That said, initial reports out of the Lesser Antilles were slow because the storm had damaged much of the infrastructure. Governor of Barbados, Sir J.S. Hay, had to divert his messages via Trinidad to get them across the Atlantic.

His initial report on Barbados stated that the hurricane had lasted ten hours, cost sixty-one lives and destroyed almost all property on the island. He reported that 2,000 of the labouring population's huts were destroyed and that there were already 1,500 homeless people sheltering in the island's churches; this number would later be increased to 50,000 homeless.[35] Governor of the Windward Islands, Cornelius Moloney, reported similarly that thousands were destitute and in need of basic necessities.

Further telegrams from both St Vincent and St Lucia added detail to the suffering being experienced, particularly by the labouring population. On St Vincent, 41,000 were said to be without shelter and on both St Lucia and Barbados, characteristically, acute food shortages quickly began to threaten the lives of those who had survived the initial storm.[36] Across these islands, estimates of deaths added up to around three hundred, with many more injuries. However, given the confusion, the colonial authorities themselves acknowledged that these were most likely severe underestimates.

At least on St Vincent, the initial response of the government indicated a marked shift in the approach of the British authorities. Moloney noted that the destitute were flocking to the capital, Kingstown, and that he was already borrowing money from the colony's funds to provide them with what necessities he could. Moloney specifically borrowed this money on the presumption that charitable or imperial aid would be forthcoming. That he did this, indicates how attitudes toward disaster had changed favourably, at least on an international level.

The growth of the telegraph network in tandem with print media had made disasters far more visible spectacles, and this accessibility often expanded the charitable relief that was forthcoming in their wake. Telegraphic messaging allowed Queen Victoria to extend her sympathies to the colonies in less than a week following the hurricane.[37] The second half of the nineteenth century had also witnessed the further growth of what Michael Barnett calls 'Imperial Humanitarianism'.[38] Through technology and the work of missionaries, in particular, the fringes of empire were brought ever closer to those living in the metropole. Though it was almost entirely through a paternalistic lens, this fostered a connection not just with distant colonists but also native people. While it largely resulted in the destruction of their cultures as the British sought to 'uplift' others by imposing their own culture, it did, in aid of enhancing Britain's reputation, also occasion a broadening of who was considered deserving of sympathy and charity.

Another important factor driving Moloney's presumption of aid was the reforming energy present in the Chamberlain's Colonial Office. Indeed, this would also shape Governor Hay's response to the crisis. Much of his early communication with London, for example, presumed that relief would be forthcoming on the basis that the Royal Commission had given London an independent and accurate account of how bad a financial position the estates were in even before the hurricane. The Commission painted a picture of many planters surviving on such meagre credit that they would not have been able to afford to rebuild the plantations.

On the face of it, these changing sentiments may have led to a more proactive approach than the British had employed in the Caribbean previously but old tensions around race and labour simmered just under the surface. They would quickly emerge, proving to be, as ever, the key factors in the colonial authorities' response.

The money that Moloney drew from government funds was spent on ordering food from Trinidad to deal with the typical post-hurricane shortages: 500 barrels of crackers and flour, 100 barrels of fish and 100 bags of rice were purchased to meet immediate demands. Similarly, on Barbados, Governor Hay reported that he had provided some initial indiscriminate relief to the labouring population as they flocked to Bridgetown. He authorised £1,500 for the repair of public buildings and £3,000 for the immediate feeding, clothing and sheltering of the poor. Corresponding with London, he also painted a rather harmonious picture of planters who 'unbegrudgingly ... fed, housed and helped to clothe many thousands of their poorer neighbours'.[39] We sadly do not have a second perspective from which to judge the reality of Hay's claims. I would argue that if this picture was playing out, it was because, like Moloney, these planters were working on the belief that charitable and/or imperial relief would later be forthcoming and allow them to recoup their outlay.

Even with authorities in Barbados and St Vincent working on the assumption that some form of financial aid would be forthcoming, there was a characteristic uneasiness about government expenditure. Those lower down the colonial hierarchy felt they had to pre-empt criticism for attempting to provide effective relief to the poorer survivors of the hurricane. Harry Thompson, an administrator in St Vincent involved with the distribution of aid, wrote to Governor Moloney stating:

> Your excellency will understand that in what I am doing I am taking a very grave responsibility – a responsibility which in view of the emergency, I felt bound to assume, but which I feel, may be open to criticism. I will not at this moment attempt to justify the course I am taking beyond saying I have a starving population with no one to look to but the government. So far the expenditure has not been so large that if my action were disapproved I could not bear the whole cost.[40]

Even with his apparent attempts to provide genuine aid, it is striking how circumscribed these efforts were. Writing just two days after the hurricane, Thompson stated that where possible, he was refusing 'able-bodied' men indiscriminate relief out of fear that with no work they would quickly become a source of 'social disorder'. Going forward, Thompson was anxious to ensure that plantation owners made long-term decisions about repairing their estates so that he could provide a more long-term source of work. With no shelter and thus almost certainly no sleep, added to a rapidly diminishing food supply, one can only imagine the physical difficulties men of the labouring class had to face to earn relief, and that is before we even account for the mental pain they might be suffering from losing loved ones and worldly possessions. They were being paid an unrecorded wage but as was typical after disaster there was nowhere for this wage to be spent. The roads around the island were blocked by landslips and food quickly running out.

Implicit in Thompson's actions is the recognition that for order to be restored, African-Caribbean people – men in particular – needed to be put back to work. When that did not happen smoothly, others were quick to make what was implicit in Thompson's report more explicit. J. Leslie Burr, a Naval Captain, remarked after the hurricane that a ship of war needed to remain at St Vincent because: 'riots may at any moment show themselves if there is no adequate protection, as there are hundreds of negro loafers about the towns who have no employment, and would not work if they had employment offered to them, but are ready to get all they can by thieving and incite [sic] others to disturb the peace'.[41] While Burr tacitly acknowledged that there was no work to even offer these men, he was convinced that the blame still lay with them.

While Thompson did not fear a full-blown challenge to his authority, he made it clear that he was pursuing this course of action not just to stymie resistance but also to control the movement of the labouring population. Putting them to work was a means of getting them out of the island's capital of Kingstown. Thompson's concern about the size of the crowds massing in the capital reflected a long-held concern that whites had had since emancipation. Crowds of African-Caribbean people in urban spaces were a physical manifestation of their fears about being a demographic minority. For Thompson in 1898, this need to dissipate the crowds took on a new importance because the food shortage was affecting not just the African-Caribbean but also the white population.

It clear that Moloney wanted to avoid a situation in which the white population looked as conspicuous in their distress as the African-Caribbean. Having them waiting for aid in the same overcrowded capital would no doubt have undermined attempts to restore the racial 'order' that so preoccupied the colonial authorities. Moloney allotted £400 of relief for private distribution through the island's parishes. This was explicitly intended for what he called a 'better class' of people, rather than the 'motley crowd' which had resorted to crowding into Kingstown for aid.[42] Unlike the African-Caribbean population, there was no indication that able-bodied white men would have to work for this relief.

In the days and weeks that followed the hurricane, with materials for reconstruction almost non-existent, the homeless labourers on both St Vincent and Barbados were forced to find shelter in churches and other vacant buildings. Given the scale of the hurricane damage, safe buildings were few and far between. In the words of Moloney, these temporary shelters were crowed with people herded together like 'animals'.[43] Disease spread quickly and meagre medical facilities were quickly overwhelmed. Districts in St Vincent, in particular, were desperate for more doctors as the scale of injuries became clear.

Genuine suffering abounded, but, as ever, sympathy from the authorities was in short supply. Instead, they focused their energies on expanding the programme of 'outdoor works'. In a paternalistic turn of phrase, Moloney maintained that such works were necessary to avoid the 'wholesale demoralisation' of the labouring classes.[44] They were instructed to clear roads of refuse, bodies and soil and repair the banks of agricultural irrigation systems. Colonial records do not detail how this work was adjudicated, but, based on other instances that will be covered later, it would certainly have been overseen by a white authority which made judgements about what constituted enough work to earn wages. No doubt many needed these wages and would have had little choice but to engage with these schemes, but this soft coercion reinforced a power dynamic that, post-emancipation, African-Caribbeans fought to avoid.

Similar schemes of outdoor relief had been deployed in Ireland during the famine and in India during a number of famines that occurred throughout the nineteenth century. The schemes were ineffective for a number of reasons, not least because the calories labourers expended to earn provisions often outweighed the calorific content of the provisions themselves. In 1898, though food shortages were acute, the situation does not appear as dire as it had been in Ireland and India. What is more, in contrast to those schemes, and to poor relief in Britain, the labouring population in the Caribbean received wages instead of provisions directly.

Besides the perceived benefits to restoring order, this form of relief had further benefits for the colonial authorities. First, it individualised relief because it became the responsibility of the individual to seek out relief then work for it. The state then had to proactively make sure that all were cared for. Secondly, paying wages as opposed to directly providing food resuscitated the market forces that white elites had long seen as an essential part of 'disciplining' African-Caribbean people and making them 'fit' for freedom.

As stated already, in 1898, individuals earning wages in this manner would have found themselves hard pressed to spend them. The damage caused by the hurricane had destroyed or suspended most business on the island. Furthermore, the colonial authorities themselves were facing difficulties importing food. The Spanish–American war, which was occurring concurrently to the crises in the Leewards and Windwards, had raised the price of imported food by around 20 per cent. Again, we are reminded of the vulnerability and risk these colonies exposed themselves to with their plantation-centric, export-focused economies.

In the months after the hurricane, in light of these difficulties and their own ideological concerns about indiscriminate relief, governments on both islands began to look toward ending all relief. In October, London and Barbados were discussing ways to decrease the relief bill. By the third week of September Chamberlain proposed to Hay that an emigration route be opened for five hundred labourers from Barbados to go to British Guiana under an indenturing scheme. Trinidad would later also express a willingness to accept Barbadian labourers. By November, colonial administrators on Barbados were being instructed to only provide relief where 'employment was impossible'.[45]

Hay, having been governor already for seven years, knew the island and its people, and was sceptical of the Guiana plan. As he put it: 'the labouring classes have such a rooted hatred for leaving their island that even in poverty, except it means starvation, will as a general rule fail to induce them to go

[sic]'.⁴⁶ An indenture, while not slavery, was a constriction of freedom and on top of every anguish the hurricane brought, it is not hard to see why this scheme would have been resisted. Despite his own reticence, Hay did not seem to entirely abandon the plan. Writing to the Colonial Office later in November he stated: 'every inducement is being given that can be given, but I fear that no facilities, however great they be, will be of much avail'.⁴⁷

Hay does not provide us with any more detail as to what that those inducements were, but worsening circumstances on the island, combined with shrinking state help, might have been inducement enough for some. By the end of November, just as all indiscriminate relief was curtailed, dysentery and typhoid were running rampant through the island's villages. Despite the compounding crises, Hay took leave of the colony and was temporarily replaced by Ralph Williams. Williams later reported that ninety-seven had taken up the indenture but believed at least a further one hundred and three would take it up. Given the informed scepticism of Hay's initial response, we can only imagine how dire the circumstances had got for some in Barbados.

Moloney was far more communicative with London than Hay's replacement and as the months progressed, he provided a great deal of detail on the actions he took to further curtail relief. On St Vincent, he placed further conditions on relief. Even with the labour test in place for able-bodied men, in November he made the decision to limit the amount of work people could undertake for relief to three days per week. This was a move designed to wean survivors of the hurricane off even these hard-earned rations and induce them to replant their own provision grounds and rebuild their houses. In early December, Moloney then wrote to London that he was going to end nearly all food relief on the island. He directed inspectors to be sent out on foot around the island to discern the eligibility of ongoing claims, particularly where someone had argued that it was absolutely impossible for a person to earn wages. Moloney made it clear to the Colonial Office that he was desperate to avoid continued government expenditure and in doing so, implicitly reveals the value, or rather lack thereof, that he placed on African-Caribbean life. He acknowledged that he was ending relief whilst 'many genuine cases of absolute destitution still exist[ed]', but that this was preferable to a 'wholesale condition of state aided-pauperism' which was 'to be avoided at all costs'. We do not have exact detail on the conditions of the majority of the populace as relief was curtailed in December, but it is fair to say that they had not recovered from the hurricane or its disruptions. In November, as on Barbados, dysentery and fever were still raging through the capital.⁴⁸

It is worth noting at this point that Moloney, Hay and later Williams were making the decision to limit relief independent of each other. That many of their actions mirrored each others' demonstrates the strength of feeling around indiscriminate state relief and the extent to which this was suffused through the elite circles from which most governors were drawn. Like Rawson before him, Moloney also felt the need to impress the government's direction on the people in person. Travelling on *H.M.S. Pearl*, Moloney visited the Leeward coast of St Vincent to impress upon the labouring population the need for them to independently work to recover, and to remind them that government aid could not continue indefinitely. After this tour, Moloney shared some of the government administrators' frustration with what they saw as the slow speed of rebuilding. While he publicly admonished the labouring population, in private he effectively admitted that their current destitution was not their fault. The island was deforested and reliant on imported timber. In 1898, these imports were arriving very slowly and the government had to impose a limit of eighty feet of timber per person, something he himself described as 'far from ideal'.

This callous indifference toward the African-Caribbean population only intensified as the need for support persisted and as the population also subverted colonial expectations about how the relief was to be used. J. Hughes, a police magistrate, wrote to Moloney in exasperation to report that throughout his district 'men [were] living on the rations issued to their wives and women and hoarding up their wages'.[49] So where free food was still being distributed to women, they were able to use it to feed their whole family, whilst men claimed wages from the public works, a clearly strategic decision no doubt based on the precariousness of life throughout the island. However, from the colonial perspective, not only did this look like families claiming twice from the government, but the 'hoarding' of wages represented a failure to engage with the market economy.

Demand continued to be great into the following year, despite the strict thresholds for claiming relief, with 1,300 people still being provided relief by the government as of January 1899. Despite the rhetoric of Moloney's communications, it is clear that he was unprepared to let the larger part of the island's population starve; it was, as ever, an informally negotiated process. Resistant as the authorities were to relief, they needed a workforce, but continued to express their aggravation at the continuing claims being made by the labouring population. One colonial administrator noted that within the 1,300, 'large numbers of persons ... entirely undeserving' were trying to draw on government largesse.[50] Even if one were to side with the colonial perspective that some of those attempting to claim relief were attempting to take advantage of government provision, that would still leave many who, nearly five months after the hurricane, were still in distress.

Perhaps in reaction to this administrator's comments, Moloney felt it necessary to employ a special officer for six months starting in January

1899 who was intended to supplement the work of magistrates and work specifically to investigate relief claimants, to make sure only 'bona fide' claims were honoured. This action reminds us of the ideological importance placed on discouraging the view that the state was there to provide relief on a long-term basis. Moloney was concerned about government expenditure but was nonetheless willing to fund a new position purely to investigate claimants.

The instructions drawn up for this new position of 'Relieving Officer' have this attention to stringency woven through them too. They include the characteristic requirement that no one who was able to work was offered relief but there were also directions for those disabled by the recent hurricane. In cases of temporary disablement, the officer was directed to end relief as soon the period for which it had been granted ended, not necessarily when the injury healed. Furthermore, the document implicitly encouraged the officer to act from a default position of distrust. It suggested that no written certificates of disability were to be accepted as proof of relief alone and that the officer should make wider inquiries to prove the genuineness of such an injury. Finally, these instructions also made it clear that no man was to receive relief if he had relations able to support him. Men were nearly always the central providers for families by virtue of them earning higher wages. Women did typically augment family income but also provided much unpaid labour. For a man to have relief refused because there was some other meagre household income would have placed strain on families still recovering from the hurricane.

In the long run, the disaster also presented an opportunity to Moloney. First, he used it as a pretext to reduce the amount the colony spent on everyday relief. Prior to the disaster a small 4s dole had been due to the aged and 'destitute paupers', but after the hurricane, Moloney reduced this to 3s, a sum he openly acknowledged was 'barely sufficient to support existence', but had, from his perspective, the benefit of 'compelling those who can work to seek employment'.[51] Second, he also began implementing more long-term plans about the colony's future organisation.

One of the more forward-thinking aspects of the 1897 Royal Commission's report was its recommendation to begin the resettlement of labourers on empty lands within the colony to start a limited form of peasant proprietorship. While this did have potential benefits for the labourers themselves, for Moloney this was primarily about stemming the flow of labour to non-British territories and having a reason to withdraw state assistance. Evidently, Moloney had been previously reticent about beginning the resettlement process because to him the chaos occasioned by the hurricane represented the 'perfect opportunity' to begin resettling labourers whilst the devastation limited their will to resist.

In 1898, on both Barbados and St Vincent it is clear that discouraging the claiming of relief where possible and withdrawing the state's offer as quickly as possible defined the response of both governments to the disaster. Faced with food and material shortages out of their control, the African-Caribbean population were subjected to punitive and conditional relief. They were, however, on St Vincent at least, able to strategically make the best of the government's offering and clearly represented enough of a potential threat to the authorities that the governments were unwilling to entirely withdraw state relief. As much as the goals of the respective governments had changed little from earlier in the century, their actions also represented a significant bureaucratisation of disaster response. Clearly bearing the hallmarks of Britain's domestic approaches to pauper relief, this subjected survivors of the disaster, though all affected by the universal chaos and destruction, to different regimes depending on gender and their 'deserving' or 'undeserving' status. Though the planters still held sway in Caribbean society, here we see the colonial state beginning to take the reins of disaster response, replacing the planters' random violence with a new systematic approach that still caused damage to claimants, just in different ways. Not uncoincidentally, this increasing bureaucratisation of disaster response also marked the first time that colonial governments began to receive challenge on their actions, not just from the African-Caribbean population but also from other whites. Bureaucratisation provided the means for making complaints.

For the majority of the population of St Vincent, struggling to recover from the hurricane of 1898, the advent of the twentieth century very quickly brought new challenges. In the first week of May 1902, a minor earthquake shook the island. Despite there not having been an eruption since 1812, correctly identifying the quake as an indication that there was one imminent, hundreds of inhabitants from the volcano's immediate vicinity fled south to the coastal town of Chateaubelair. The colonial government found itself in the strange position of having to respond to the disaster before it had even begun and having to feed at least three hundred of those who had fled. On 7 May, the uneasy wait was over, and with a sound that was described as like 'artillery fire' the La Soufrière erupted at around three in the afternoon.[52]

As the eruption took place, the governor of the island, now Sir R.B. Llewelyn was visiting St Lucia and was initially trapped as the condition of the sea prevented boats from reaching St Vincent. The following day Llewelyn reported to the Colonial Office that the estimate for fatalities on St Vincent was already at five hundred, but this estimate would more than triple to 1,600 when he finally landed on the island on 12 May. The injuries inflicted upon those who survived were as Llewelyn put it 'too harrowing to describe', worse than those typically caused by hurricanes. The island did not have the medical expertise to treat burns victims and he estimated that, of a group of 160 people brought to the hospital in Georgetown, only 6 would survive.

The government's initial response was comparatively generous. A steamship was sent to the Leeward coast, the most affected area of the island. At the cost of £50 per day, it provided around 3,000 people with indiscriminate aid in the form of food. Medical aid was later forthcoming from Barbados and by 16 May, Llewelyn reported that the immediate needs of the colony were being met with this assistance. Toward the end of May, Llewelyn turned his attention to resettling those whose homes and livelihoods had been destroyed in the eruption. Communicating with the Colonial Office he estimated it would cost £50,000 to keep the current relief measures going for six months and for the government to aid in the process of rehousing the labouring class.

As shown in greater detail in chapter 5, much of this relief was possible because of the rapid outpouring of charitable aid not only from Britain but from other Dominion nations such as Canada. I would also argue that the very nature of the disaster played a significant role in bringing forth not only charitable donations but, at least initially, a more caring response from the authorities. Unlike hurricanes, which, as shown in chapter 2, the colonial authorities were effectively content to live with, eruptions did not happen every year. Llewellyn himself made a point about the exceptional nature of the eruption when writing to Chamberlain in late May: 'A hurricane lasts a few hours … a volcanic eruption may continue for years. In this instance, it has now been active for 16 to 17 days, and still continues'.[53]

Though Llewelyn may have seen the eruption as exceptional, magistrates on the island were quick to express their frustration when the African-Caribbean population did immediately submit to labour.[54] On 9 May, only two days after the eruption, and with lava still flowing from the volcano, administrator Edward Cameron found that, much to his chagrin, the labouring population was reticent to engage with the work of burying the dead. Other administrators report people being too panic-stricken to engage with the work they were trying to press them into. Quite reasonably, many of the African-Caribbean population, even beside their shock and trauma, may have judged this work to be unsafe. There were still large amounts of scoria firing from the volcano, which was causing serious head wounds to those unlucky enough to be caught outside.[55]

The situation on the island seemed to worsen over the course of May with the number being provided with government relief increasing from 3,000 to 7,000. The nature of the disaster also created a number of problems that challenged the typical colonial response. Unlike with hurricanes, the governor could not simply ask people to return to their dwellings as they were utterly incinerated not just broken apart. As we have seen, the colonial authorities often liked to obviate urban crowding, and this was not possible either. People could not return to the land their homes had once occupied because it was covered in more than a foot of ash and lava.

In this intractable situation, the government took that most characteristic approach to 'relief': it began closing the aperture of eligibility. As of early June, relief works were enacted involving a general clean-up of debris and the restoration of an irrigation canal buried by ash. There was simply not enough work, however, and as a result, many passed June and July packed into crowded camps surrounding the island's capital, Kingstown.[56] Anger with the colonial response began in August when the free distribution of rations to those in these camps was stopped. Almost immediately, colonial administrators found themselves facing rising discontent. One reported several hundred people engaged in a demonstration outside his office with tents pulled down and general demand for resettlement elsewhere on the island.[57] Behind the scenes, however, a far longer-running saga was beginning to embroil Llewelyn.

As a means to potentially head off what he considered egregious relief costs, he had begun discussions with Chamberlain as early as the second week of May, on a plan to resettle at least five hundred refugees off the island in Jamaica. An offer had been extended by the United Fruit Company, which proposed, under an indenture for three years, offering accommodation and waged labour for Vincentian families. Similar offers also came in from Rowntree and Company who offered to take between fifty and one hundred families to Dominica. These companies were no doubt opportunistically looking to use the crisis to capture labour on islands where they had difficulty procuring their own constant supply. As of 15 May, these preliminary discussions had already made their way into the press. A member of the island's clergy, the Rev. J.H. Darrell, in a public letter printed in one of the island's newspapers, made it clear that he was strongly of the opinion that the emigration schemes were a means for the government to avoid its responsibilities to the peasantry of the country.[58]

The criticism, while public, did not gain much traction, perhaps because, in that third week of May, La Soufrière's eruption was still very much underway. Things changed, however, when Llewelyn actually began to try and implement the Jamaica scheme. He targeted the people of Owia and Fancy specifically, two villages located close to La Soufrière that were firmly within what was considered 'Carib country'. By the crude colonial racial descriptors of the era, the villagers were considered to be descended from a mix of Carib and African-Caribbean people.

In September, on a tour of the island, Llewelyn visited the villages and encountered the inhabitants with, as he put it, 'imaginary grievances' trying to get more money from the relief fund. Llewelyn's report implicitly suggests that they considered themselves unsafe if there was a future eruption. Primarily, they wanted the governor to provide them with new land on the island but indicated, because of the fear they had for the future, that some of them were prepared to go to Jamaica. Llewelyn did not trust their word and also feared that 'mischief makers' – no doubt referring to the critical May letter from Darrell – would still oppose their emigration.[59] As a result, he was keen to get them to sign contracts so he could compel them to board transport to Jamaica and even went as far to say that a 'forced' emigration could take place if the Colonial Office permitted it.

Despite this, Llewelyn was not quite as eager as Chamberlain for the migration plan. He disagreed with it because it involved many 'far-spreading' difficulties but also struggled with what to do with the people if they remained on the island. He actually agreed with the villagers and felt that plantation owners should disburse small parcels of land for them. Fearing that this would lead to a reduction in the overall pool of labour on the island, planters rejected this idea. Thus, in the absence of an alternative, he did come to support the emigration scheme.[60]

In September 1902, the Colonial Office began to put its weight behind the emigration scheme, with Chamberlain agreeing that, if the villagers refused, they should have the right to relief stripped from them.[61] Tensions around the resettlement programme rose with fresh eruptions on 3 September and then on 15 October 1902. Neither caused fatalities, but both rained more ash down on Owia and Fancy and increased the villagers' desire to be moved elsewhere on the island. Llewelyn steadfastly refused, arguing that the southern side of the island, where the villagers were asking to be resettled, had no demand for labour and thus any new development would descend into poverty and squalor. The villagers wanted to preserve a degree of self-sufficiency, but Llewelyn, espousing a clearly paternalistic and racialised view, did not think them capable of doing so. With this impasse, Llewelyn's administrators began preparing for a fight, with one suggesting that if resettlement was to be carried out, a 'strongly enforced staff' would be required.[62]

That fight did not take place, at least not physically. A public meeting was called on 17 October. In attendance were numerous 'caribs and other sufferers from the late eruption'.[63] The meeting was chaired by members of the island's clergy, ostensibly there to mediate, but it proved to be one-sided. Neither Llewelyn, nor any members of the colonial authorities were present and those who spoke were of one mind. The speaker, a Mr J.E. Sprott called Llewelyn 'obstinate, cruel and arbitrary'.[64] He also accused him of neglect. He called it a matter of public notoriety that money previously sent to the island for the establishment of industry had been squandered and that provisions sent from America for the relief of the people lay rotting in a storeroom. Furthermore, Sprott was of the opinion that there was land available at good prices to resettle people on the island. Ultimately, he argued that all Llewelyn's actions had been taken in the interest of depriving people of their right to relief. Sprott's argument was supported by the fact that as early as 20 May 1902, other people who had been made refugees on the island had been resettled and Llewelyn had ordered lumber to build five hundred more houses. In this respect, Llewelyn seemed to be taking a particularly punitive approach targeted specifically at these villagers.

The second speaker at the meeting was the same Rev. J.H. Darrell who had published the first criticism of Llewelyn's response in May. This time his criticism went beyond the emigration scheme, and he suggested that despite receiving abundant supplies, sufferers from around the affected area were still wandering about starving, half-naked and without houses or land on which to provide for themselves. Darrell would later go on to meet with the Legislative Council in December. His anger with the government had not subsided. In fact, his additional criticisms at this meeting reveal a further cruelty of Llewelyn's approach to the villagers of Owia and Fancy: at some point in September, in an effort to move them, the government had made continued relief conditional on the villagers selling their land. He was also angry that the relief, received in the form of food and clothes from America, was being sold off with no clarity about how the proceeds of the money raised from the sale were spent.[65]

The final speaker at the October meeting was a labourer simply addressed as Ragguett. He too was extremely critical of Llewelyn and the government but more than the others; in his interactions with other labourers in the crowd made clear that nearly all were extremely unwilling to emigrate. The meeting ended with a striking call to Chamberlain to send someone more capable than Llewelyn to restore the island. What they did not know was that Chamberlain not only supported the emigration scheme but also agreed with Llewelyn that relief needed to be further curtailed.

By November, Chamberlain was of the opinion that the relief situation was untenable in St Vincent and thus suggested the implementation of a labour test. All able-bodied applicants over sixteen were to be denied aid unless they agreed to provide one day of 'bona fide' labour reconstructing the colony's roads or in some form of cultivation. Furthermore, aged persons living with other able-bodied people were to be denied, as were mothers who were unwilling to leave their children for the day.[66]

Despite agreement in their broad approach to relief, Llewelyn clearly wanted to pre-empt the criticisms emerging in the colony. He sent Chamberlain an article from *The Sentry*, which detailed the meeting of October. Ignoring that Ragguett had made very clear the position of much of the labouring class concerned, he again expressed frustration at the 'unscrupulous agitators' who were upsetting the villagers and leading them astray.[67]

In the face of such pointed criticism, he clearly felt the need to defend himself and in doing so, he reveals the guiding principles of his disaster response. He denied anyone was starving and argued that the stores had been sold for a number of reasons, including paying the wages of the officers guarding them, to help shopkeepers and to encourage the circulation of money in the colony so that people would spend their dole on something.[68] Furthermore, he presented the fact that other administrators agreed with him that overall it would have been better had monetary relief arrived first, as food relief just 'demoralized and pauperized' the labouring classes.[69] He also further recorded the belief amongst some of the administrators that, as he had suggested when he met the villagers of Owia and Fancy, some people were trying to take advantage of the situation to gain land from the government without having to pay rent to a landlord, which, in turn, would have stopped them needing to sell their labour.

The matter seemed to be resolved when, in December 1902, it was suggested that the villagers be allowed to return to Owia and Fancy but also with the offer of emigration. Administrator Arthur Young, having observed that fifty-six of the villagers of Owia had died in the May eruption, recorded that the rest survived by sheltering in a cellar. As a result, he suggested that the confidence of the villagers might be improved if the government financed the building of three masonry boxes so that people could shelter from future hurricanes or eruptions. Apparently seeking seemingly to resolve the issue, in mid-December Llewelyn enacted a policy of refusing all males between sixteen and sixty relief, and ended relief work in St Vincent. Evidently frustrated not only by the villagers but also 'mischievous interferers', he no doubt saw this coercion as his only recourse to try and bend them to his will. It did not work.[70]

The villagers finally had their say on 22 December when they wrote to the governor stating, amongst many things, that they could not leave the island of their forefathers, and asking, 'why should we be asked to risk our lives in places where government officials and landowners would not risk theirs?' They further stated that they had been homeless for seven months in 'conditions most injurious to our health and to the moral life of our children'. They argued that they could be settled in the south of the island because there was sufficient water and great want of labour.[71]

The issue dragged on into 1903, when an exasperated Llewellyn finally made his motives for the whole debacle more explicit. In a communication to Chamberlain, he stated his opinion that the people of Owia and Fancy had no wish to go anywhere that they had to work, as they were happy to eke out an existence on St Vincent instead of improving their conditions through labour. As a result, he argued, charitable assistance was 'thrown away' on such characters.[72] There was also some intimation from his critics that Llewelyn had fallen particularly hard on these villagers compared to other who were resettled because of their 'aboriginal' blood. This criticism, while recorded in the colonial records, was not responded to by Llewelyn, or at least not within the printed record.[73]

Here, one can also draw a clear thread of continuity with how the Carib population of St Vincent was treated in 1812, at the time of the last eruption. There is remarkable similarity in the way in which, at both times, they were subjected to pointed attempts to remove a significant proportion of their population from the island. I would argue that this, in part, reflects how little the economic imperatives of Caribbean life had changed. Llewelyn considered the Carib population economically unproductive and, like the authorities in 1812, was simultaneously mulling over another use for their land. In a letter to Chamberlain, Llewelyn reflected on the schemes that been considered for using the fertile land for a centralised sugar factory. He was unsure whether, given the recent eruption, there would be an appetite for investment but considered that the land was best left to the government, and the Caribs disincentivised from resettling there. From his perspective, it seemed self-defeating on the part of the government to encourage the continuation of such 'antiquated' methods of cultivation on the land.[74]

In January, the matter was finally settled. With £30,000 still held in the relief fund, and the Colonial Office unwilling to engage in a potentially violent emigration effort, it was recommended that Llewelyn afford the villagers special treatment and settle them anywhere on the island.[75] By May, this had been accomplished. It is worth noting that both Chamberlain's and the Colonial Office's thinking may have also been shaped by a reminder of the outcomes of previous post disaster schemes. In January 1903, the acting Governor of Trinidad reminded Chamberlain that after the 1898 hurricane, 263 East Indians and African-Caribbean people were sent from St Vincent to Trinidad. By 1902 only thirteen remained and the whole exercise was deemed a failure in Trinidad and Tobago.[76]

Judging by Llewelyn's admission of his motives in January, the whole debacle appears to have been driven by those most persistent of white frustrations: the financial cost of maintaining the colonies and the desire to keep the African-Caribbean population in their place as labourers, constantly subjected to the disciplining force of labour. However, the fact that the people of Owia and Fancy were able to resist Llewelyn tells us that even with the state having replaced the planters as the main source of authority, those outside of the white elite were still shaping the relief effort: even though non-white people were not invited to the table, it was still a negotiation.

Race and fear in the urban environment

In 1902, as charitable donations poured into St Vincent in the wake of the 1902 eruption, Alexander Swettenham, Governor of British Guiana, stood alone amongst British Caribbean governors when he turned down requests to vote for a grant in aid for the sufferers of the St Vincent eruption drawn from the his colony's coffers.[77] Instead, not viewing it an appropriate reason for government expenditure, he allowed the opening of a public subscription despite, even by his own account, public opinion being at odds with his view.

Having just arrived in the colony the previous year, Swettenham appears to have been ignorant of the affinity between British Guiana and St Vincent, which stretched all the way back to when British Guiana provided aid in the wake of the 1812 eruption of La Soufrière. In the weeks that followed Swettenham's decision, the backlash appears to have been significant enough to cause him to soften his position, but he was still unwilling to back down entirely. He agreed to consider a grant of aid for St Vincent but only if the citizens of British Guiana made up the money with extra taxes.

This was a minor disagreement but one that already marked Swettenham as an unaccommodating governor, insensitive to public opinion and lacking in sympathy for those stricken by disaster. This moment does not appear to have harmed his governorship of British Guiana in the long run and he was effectively promoted from British Guiana to Governor of Jamaica in 1904. It was there, however, that he would face his greatest challenge and where his abrasive character would end his career.

On 14 January 1907, at around three o'clock in the afternoon, Jamaica was struck by an earthquake of around 6.5 magnitude. Parts of the southeastern coast were affected but the damage primarily occurred in Kingston, the entire city being all but reduced to rubble. The earthquake itself was devastating to life and property, but fires soon sprang up in its wake, which caused further damage and loss of life. The final death toll was estimated at 1,200 and damage to property was in the region of £2,000,000.

Unlike other disasters, the severity of the earthquake, combined with Kingston's importance within the Caribbean, meant that the disaster quickly filled international papers. Such was its significance that it also loomed large in Jamaican culture in the decades that followed, so much so that in 1957 the *Daily Gleaner*, Jamaica's largest newspaper, ran a special commemorative edition to honour the fifty-year anniversary of the quake.[78] This was then followed in 1959 by a call from the paper for survivors to submit their memories to be published in the paper. Even with a distance of fifty-two years, the indelible shock of what some experienced can still tell us much about how ordinary people experienced the quake.

Charles Taylor, a mechanic who had been working in Spanish Town, eleven miles to the east of Kingston, felt some small quakes but only downed tools when he noticed the shocking glow of Kingston burning on the horizon. He decided to walk back to the capital on account of having family there and, on the way, encountered streams of vehicles piled high with personal belongings as well as men, women and children. Upon arrival in Kingston, Taylor recalled the heat of the city and the sound of explosions all around him as he walked through the streets, and saw the horror of countless animals and people crushed and burnt beyond recognition.[79] Taylor's experiences are mirrored in many letters sent into the *Daily Gleaner*.

Fears of a tidal wave and – one of many strange rumours – lions escaping from a visiting circus sent some people running in all directions. Others stood in disbelief or desperately searched for loved ones amongst the rubble. The first response from the government was one that typically sought to control this chaos and protect private property. However, in contrast to the disasters considered so far, this one unfolded in a primarily urban environment and, as a result, presented a unique challenge for white elites.

Immediately after the earthquake, Jamaica's colonial government deployed four hundred members of the West India Regiment (WIR) who were then augmented by police officers from nearby towns. They patrolled the streets with bayoneted rifles and live ammunition and were given orders to protect property and prevent looting and other disruptions to the 'social order'. These vaguely defined orders were effectively a blank cheque to violently intervene in any transgressions against the pre-disaster hierarchy. Despite white concerns, there were no serious interventions recorded.

The danger they felt from crowded bustling urban spaces where, by virtue of demographics, the African-Caribbean population were nearly always in a majority, meant African-Caribbean mobility continued to be a cause for white concern long after emancipation. Indeed, parts of the state apparatus deployed in 1907 to keep order had come into being as a response to emancipation; Jamaica's force has its origins in an act passed in 1832, following a rebellion in 1831 and in anticipation of emancipation.

The ending of slavery and later the end of apprenticeship, gradually offered the African-Caribbean population the opportunity for greater mobility. Urban centres were attractive, not just because they were not plantations but also because, through trade and shipping, they offered a whole range of economic opportunities otherwise not existent in the country. Unlike the plantation, which had hierarchy built into its very layout with white and black dwellings separated by space and size, urban centres had less distinct separations. Urban space dissolved and elided such separations and as a result whites felt their power threatened. They felt an intensified need to maintain the ontological separation between themselves and the black population. Policing emerged as one of the central means to maintain it.

When seeking to understand the government response in 1907, we cannot overlook the fact that in 1865 the island witnessed the largest rebellion in the post-emancipation era.[80] The Morant Bay Rebellion, as it came to be known, plunged the country into chaos and ended with particularly violent reprisals from the then-Governor Eyre, who oversaw the execution of hundreds of free Jamaicans. To many whites, the Rebellion was a reminder of just how tenuous their grasp on power was in the Caribbean. These long-standing fears can only have been compounded by far more recent events. Four years prior to the earthquake, a riot in the capital of Trinidad, Port of Spain, had escalated to such a degree that the authorities were unable to prevent the burning of the colony's Parliament building.[81] The riot had only been eventually supressed by the arrival of British Naval reinforcements to the colony. For the authorities in 1907, such support would be out of reach because Britain had withdrawn the majority of its navy from the region in 1905 as it sought to focus on Europe.

Despite the insecurity felt by the government, implicit in its first actions, 'order' did not deteriorate in the wake of the earthquake. What looting did take place seems to have been confined to limited cases of citizens taking food where they could find it; one eyewitness saw 'large sacks of rice carried away on the heads of women'.[82] Despite this, not missing a chance to racially separate themselves from the African-Caribbean population, two naval officers reporting on the WIR deployment put the lack of looting down not to the unfounded nature of their prejudice but rather the 'extreme terror the natives were seized with'.[83] Nonetheless, even with little unrest, Kingston remained effectively under martial law and, as illustrated by the anecdote regarding the 'liberation' of sacks of rice, its citizens were effectively left to fend for themselves as colonial priorities lay elsewhere.

When government attention did eventually turn to the city's population it was primarily to enact further controls on their movement. Many survivors of the earthquake were trying to gain access to Kingston's wharves and hospitals in an effort to find and/or identify loved ones. Fearing that an influx of people might result in the destruction of private property or looting, the WIR began cordoning off both areas. We know from the account of Aulay Babington Macaulay, a senior officer on the *RMS Arno* docked in Kingston, that a system of passes was introduced to exclude the 'excitable' crowds gathering outside of these places. Through his account and his use of this descriptor, commonly deployed at the time to infantilise African-Caribbean people, it is clear that these crowds were primarily composed of African-Caribbean people whom the WIR later dispersed under threat of violence.[84]

Even with the WIR establishing a cordon and carrying out their orders as instructed, white insecurity about their control was not entirely tamped down. In fact, it actually extended to the WIR themselves. The Regiment comprised very few white troops, something which had been a long-standing cause for concern amongst whites in Jamaica. There was a fear that, in a time of crisis, WIR soldiers would refuse to follow orders and 'switch sides'. In 1907, this fear no doubt informed the composition of the forces keeping order on the street as the WIR was specifically augmented by white companies of Royal Artillery and Royal Engineers.[85] As with the worries around looting, no significant issues concerning discipline with the WIR occurred after the quake, but it did not stop whites passing comment. Charles Chenery, who would become editor of the *Barbados Advocate* in 1908, claimed some troops in the WIR were guilty of overlooking looting because there were not enough white commanding officers to manage the Regiment.[86]

Through the WIR, Governor Swettenham was able to take control of access to Kingston's wharves and its hospital, but he was not entirely able to control the population. Recognising that the city was still a very dangerous place to be – aftershocks and fires occurred in the hours and days that followed the earthquake – many people fled to open areas within the city, most notably to the racecourse just north of central Kingston. As people left the city, Swettenham and many in the colonial authorities were initially concerned with retaining at least the able-bodied men amongst them. In that most characteristic of British responses to disaster, they were looking to try and put parts of the African-Caribbean population back to work. The government organised work schemes to employ the African-Caribbean population in pulling down ruins and clearing the streets to enable movement through the wreckage. Owing to the difficulty they faced trying to find participants for these schemes, the government tried to incentivise participation by paying double the typical rates, around 4–5s a day.

Even with these raised rates, it was clearly hard for the authorities to procure enough labour. Just three days after the earthquake, Swettenham was already frustrated with the slow speed at which efforts to clear the city were proceeding. He made no allowances for the distress caused by the shock and instead put this reluctance down to the 'indisposition' of the African-Caribbean population to work.[87] Taking into account Charles Taylor's horrific descriptions of conditions in Kingston and of Macaulay's descriptions of crowds desperate to find and identify loved ones, Swettenham's words expose a complete lack of empathy for the African-Caribbean population.

Even if we set aside the physical and mental trauma that might have prevented many from engaging in these dangerous work schemes, the nature of these schemes might have discouraged people further. From two eyewitnesses who commented on labouring conditions in Kingston, we know that these schemes recreated something akin to the relationship between gang labourers and overseers on plantations. An American Rear Admiral, Charles Davis, following his involvement in a diplomatic crisis, which is discussed at length in chapter 5, wrote an extensive account of his experiences in Jamaica. In his account we get another perspective on these work schemes. Davis recalled seeing 'squads and gangs' of labourers working under white officers.[88]

Chenery, as per his comments on the makeup of the WIR, was clearly of the view that African-Caribbean people needed white guidance, and remarked that where there was 'efficient direction the ordinary labourers worked with a will'.[89] Disasters often became moments in which whites were able to reinstate and resurrect mechanisms of pre-emancipation controls, and 1907 was no exception. The plantation was based around gang or task work, but urban environments, where individual work proliferated, encouraged the inverse, and this had long stoked white fears of unrest.[90] The earthquake provided a state of exception that allowed the reinstatement of gang labour.

In addition to putting their energies into controlling African-Caribbean movement, white authorities spent much time criticising their behaviour. Major Chown, a British officer in Jamaica at the time, wrote that as the earthquake occurred 'the black and coloured population were stupefied with terror and amazement'.[91] By his account and many other white authored accounts, however, the white population was described as brave and otherwise stoic in the face of the danger; they helped whilst the African-Caribbean population instead fled from the city. As the earthquake passed, this terror miraculously gave way to an apathy as they were found 'lounging in the streets ... although labour [was] still in demand'.[92]

The African-Caribbean population was, of course, not alone in its terror and suffering but these infantilising racial stereotypes served, at least rhetorically, to maintain the ontological separation between white and black at a time when both were conspicuous in their distress. This is a concern we have already seen play out in 1898, but in 1907 it took on greater importance in an urban setting where it was harder to physically separate the populations.

It is also worth interrogating Chown's comments about the 'apathy' of the African-Caribbean population further. Those who participated in these work-for-relief schemes were paid in 'orders', which were effectively vouchers that limited the labourer to purchasing from specific government ordained stores or trusting that the government would transfer it into tender at a later date.

The government's initial response, continuing trends seen throughout the long nineteenth century, was not to provide relief but to respond to perceived threats to its authority. Work again was directed not just to the state's advantage – pulling down damaged buildings helped return the city to order – but was also a part of restoring the social hierarchy. In this case African-Caribbean people had to subordinate themselves to white authority to participate in the schemes. By limiting the distribution of relief but making food available for purchase with government orders, we can see that the early part of the government response was meant to discourage the use of charity and coerce the African-Caribbean population back to labouring. The African-Caribbean population remained beyond 'primary humanitarian concern'.[93] This was also reflected in death. In colonial records white casualties were listed with their names and as 'deaths of note', but most others were anonymised. Disasters often dragged the most regressive views on the question of entitlement to care out into the open. As one Barbadian newspaper put it at the turn of the century, 'if a negro's house is destroyed by fire or tempest, how long do you think it will take him to build another? Nature will give him food almost for the asking'.[94]

Once Kingston was secured and the governor seemingly content that no significant contestation of white authority was going to take place, a disaster relief effort did begin to unfold in Kingston. As it became apparent that the disaster was of such a scale that organised relief was going to be necessary to restore the town, on 16 January Swettenham commissioned the forming of a General Relief Committee with Archbishop Enos Nuttall as its head. It met on 17 January and began working to purchase the surviving food stores in the city and design a process for distributing them to the needy. That an organised relief effort emerged rapidly after the disaster marked a distinct development from the typical response of British authorities in the centuries prior.

Swettenham was not envisioning a mass distribution of free relief, however. On 18 January, he signalled to the Colonial Office his goal to limit the distribution of free food to the ordinary parochial system.[95] Despite reports of the earthquake filling newspapers and placing Swettenham and British governance more broadly under a spotlight, the rations being handed out were considered slim even for the time. A report from *Leslie's Weekly* described the rations as 'meagre', consisting of 'two potatoes, a piece of bread and some brown sugar and molasses'.[96]

The earthquake would have destroyed many of the food stores available in the city, so it is not necessarily the case that the slimness of these rations was intentional, but there seems to have been a lack of energy directed to improving the situation. Travelling around Kingston after the earthquake, Admiral Davis describes finding plenty of useable barrels of flour, rice and maize strewn across the Royal Mail Harbour. Having seen first-hand the hunger that many of Kingston's citizens were suffering from, he offered to take them and bake bread but was rebuffed.

Larger and more organised than previous British relief efforts it might have been, but the actions of Kingston's Relief Committee were not entirely free of characteristic British preoccupations around charity and dependence. Throughout February, the government funded the appointment of inspectors to examine every single relief claim, with the aim of reducing the cost at every possible turn. By 28 February, relief expenditure had been decreased drastically from a weekly cost of £748 16s 4d to £211 2s 3d. At the same point, the Relief Committee was selling back to commercial suppliers what it considered to be surplus stores, acknowledging that while much work had been done to procure the tools and machines needed to reemploy people, much of it was still languishing unused. In effect, the aperture for relief narrowed far more quickly than the opportunities for work supposed to replace it became available.

The majority of the people receiving aid were still, by the end of February, effectively homeless and living on the city's racecourse. The racecourse camp presented something of a problem for colonial authorities desirous of order and racial separation. In the first week following the earthquake, those on the racecourse were without any purposely designed shelter, instead taking what scraps of timber and metal they could find to build rudimentary shelters. Swettenham quickly tried to have it cleared, but such was the size of the grouping – around 3,000 people – that he found this impossible.

The camp became further entrenched when, on 22 January, tents arrived on the *HMS Indefatigable* from Trinidad and British Bermuda. These were distributed, in Archbishop Nuttall's words, 'indiscriminately' and as a result he had them recalled and redistributed to form a camp for a 'better class of people'.[97] This distinction was made even clearer by the fact that the reconstituted camp was later supplied with running water and even electricity. Furthermore, a small contingent of WIR troops was directed to guard it to maintain the privacy of its inhabitants. For everyone else on the racecourse, conditions resembled a shanty town with Admiral Davis observing that the population was encamped in the 'rudest and flimsiest improvised shelters, mere sheets and cloths' and with their only source of water contaminated. 'No effort ha[d] been made to build weatherproof shelters' … 'it seem[ed] to be nobody's business'.[98]

For Davis, the lack of care given to the majority suffering on the racecourse reflected a complete failure of leadership. 'The want of organisation and of organised effort was apparent. There seem to be no departments and distribution of duties and responsibilities under official heads.'⁹⁹ As shown in the following chapter, Davis was certainly at odds with Swettenham, but I would argue that we cannot entirely discount his comments as they resonate with many of the other tendencies in relief provision considered in this and the preceding chapter.

Despite emancipation, disaster relief remained an exercise in reinstating and reproducing the racial hierarchy that buttressed white, colonial rule. Controlling space and coercing the African-Caribbean population back to work remained the central goals of colonial governments. The insecurities they felt about their minoritarian rule were heightened severely by disasters, but they appear to have understood that they could not simply force the African-Caribbean population back to work. Even at the sharpest end of the spectrum, as in 1907 when men were put under guard as they worked to clear the streets, there was an unspoken negotiation taking place. The freedom of the African-Caribbean population could be curtailed in these circumstances and certain slavery era measures of control, like intense punishments and limiting movement, were resurrected, but these colonial governments knew they could only take them so far. Not only was it within their own self-interest to provide relief but they appear to have understood that they had little choice.

Notes

1 James Williams, *A Narrative of Events since the First of August, 1834*.
2 Lewis S. Ware, *The Sugar Beet: Including a History of the Beet Sugar Industry in Europe, Varieties of the Sugar Beet, Examination, Soils, Tillage, Seeds and Sowing, Yield and Cost of Cultivation, Harvesting, Transportation, Conservation, Feeding Qualities of the Beet and of the Pulp, Etc* (Philadelphia, PA: Henry Baird & Co, 1880), p. 28.
3 Patricia Ashman, 'Disraeli, Benjamin (Earl of Beaconsfield)', *Historical Dictionary of the British Empire*, Vol. II, ed. by James Stuart Olson and Robert Shadle (Santa Barbara, CA: Greenwood Press, 1996), p. 372.
4 Karen Fay O'Loughlin and James F. Lander, *Caribbean Tsunamis: A 500-Year History from 1498–1998* (Dordrecht: Springer, 2003), p. 59.
5 TNA, CO 7/74, Charles Fitzroy to Lord Stanley, 20 February 1843.
6 *Antigua Weekly Register*, 9 February 1843.
7 TNA, CO 7/74, Charles Fitzroy to Lord Stanley, 10 February 1843.
8 TNA, CO 7/74, The Governor in Chief to the Honourable the President and Board of Council and Honourable the Speaker and House of Assembly, 13 February 1843.
9 PP, HoC [441], p. 3, Fitzroy to Stanley, 10 February 1843.
10 HoC, Antigua. Papers Relative to the Earthquake in the West Indies [Antigua] [441], p. 3, Fitzroy to Stanley, 10 February 1843.

11 Ibid.
12 TNA, CO 7/74 (Antigua & Montserrat), Correspondence, Original – Secretary of State: Despatches, Charles Fitzroy to Lord Stanley, 13 February, 1843.
13 Sub enclosure no. 4 in W. Reid to Earl Grey, 23 October 1847, in Historical Documents of Trinidad and Tobago, No. 3.
14 Ibid.
15 Diana Paton, *No Bond but the Law: Punishment, Race, and Gender in Jamaican State Formation, 1780–1870* (Durham, NC: Duke University Press, 2004), pp. 6–7.
16 Ibid., p. 124.
17 In her study of pauper policies between 1750 and 1850, Samantha Shave provides many examples of workhouse boards using the terms 'idle and disorderly' to describe the inmates of which it was their duty to manage. Samantha A. Shave, *Pauper Policies: Poor Law and Practice, 1750–1850* (Manchester: Manchester University Press, 2017).
18 Michael Barnett, *Empire of Humanity: A History of Humanitarianism* (Ithaca, NY: Cornell University Press, 2011), p. 63.
19 Diana Paton, *No Bond but the Law*, p. 44.
20 Ibid., p. 27.
21 Rawson W. Rawson, *Report on the Bahamas' Hurricane of October 1866, with a description of the City of Nassau* (Nassau: E.C. Moseley, 1866), p. 8.
22 Ibid., p. 9.
23 Ibid., p. 13.
24 Ibid.
25 TNA, CO 23/185 (Bahamas) Correspondence, Original – Secretary of State: Despatches, Rawson Rawson to Earl of Carnarvon, 17 October 1866.
26 Rawson W. Rawson, *Report on the Bahamas' Hurricane of October 1866*, p. 17.
27 Ibid., p. 13.
28 Ibid., p. 25.
29 Ibid.
30 TNA, CO 23/185 (Bahamas) Correspondence, Original-Secretary of State: Despatches, Governor Rawson to Earl of Canarvon, 17 October 1866.
31 Ibid., pp. 20–21.
32 Ibid., p. 19.
33 Ibid., p. 29.
34 Dawn P. Harris, *Punishing the Black Body: Marking Social and Racial Structures in Barbados and Jamaica* (Athens, GA: University of Georgia Press, 2017), p. 93.
35 HoC [C 9205], Sir J.S. Hay to Mr Chamberlain, 14 September 1898.
36 HoC [C 9205], Sir C.A. Moloney to Mr Chamberlain, 16 September 1898.
37 HoC [C 9205], Mr Chamberlain to Sir C.A. Moloney, 16 September 1898.
38 Michael Barnett, *Empire of Humanity*, pp. 49–94.
39 HoC [C 9205], Sir J.S. Hay to Chamberlain, 29 September 1898.
40 HoC [C 9205], Enclosure 4 in Governor C.A. Moloney to Mr Chamberlain, 29 September 1898.

41 HoC [C 9205], Admiralty to the Colonial Office, 20 October 1898.
42 HoC [C 9205], Sir C.A. Moloney to Mr Chamberlain, 25 November 1898.
43 HoC [C 9205], Sir C.A. Moloney to Mr Chamberlain, 10 November 1898.
44 HoC [C 9205], Sir C.A. Moloney to Mr Chamberlain, 29 September 1898.
45 HoC [C 9205], Acting Governor Williams to Mr Chamberlain, 26 November 1898.
46 HoC [C 9205], Sir J.S. Hay to Mr Chamberlain, 10 November 1898.
47 HoC [C 9205], Sir J.S. Hay to Mr Chamberlain, 10 November 1898.
48 HoC [C 9205], Sir C.A. Moloney, to Mr Chamberlain, 10 November 1898.
49 HoC [C 9205], Sir C.A. Moloney to Mr Chamberlain, 25 November 1898.
50 PP (1899), House of Commons [C.9550], West Indies. Further Correspondence relating to the Hurricane on 10th–12th September, 1898, and the Relief of the Distress Caused Thereby, Enclosure in Moloney to Chamberlain, 31 January, 1899.
51 PP, HoC [C 9205], West Indies. Correspondence, Moloney to Chamberlain, 7 December 1898.
52 HoC [Cd 1201], Governor Sir F.M. Hodgson to Mr Chamberlain, West Indies. Correspondence relating to the volcanic eruptions in St Vincent and Martinique in May, 1902, with map and appendix.
53 HoC [Cd 1201], Governor Sir R.B. Llewelyn to Mr Chamberlain, 5 June 1902.
54 HoC [Cd 1201], Edward J. Cameron to Sir R.B. Llewellyn, 9 May 1902.
55 HoC [Cd 1201], Chief of Police to Colonial Secretary, 8 May 1902.
56 PP, HoC [Cd 1783], West Indies. Further correspondence relating to the volcanic eruptions in St Vincent & Martinique, in 1902 & 1903, Sir R.B. Llewellyn to Mr Chamberlain, 18 June 1902.
57 HoC [Cd 1783], Administrator Cameron to Sir R.B. Llewelyn, 18 August 1902.
58 HoC [Cd 1783], James H. Darrell, 'An open letter', 15 May 1902.
59 HoC [Cd 1783], Sir R.B. Llewellyn to Mr Chamberlain, 27 August 1902.
60 PP, HoC [Cd.1201], Llewelyn to Chamberlain, 27 August, 1902.
61 HoC [Cd 1783], Mr Chamberlain to Sir R.B. Llewelyn, 10 September 1902.
62 PP, HoC [Cd 1783], Enclosure in Llewelyn to Chamberlain, 23 October 1902.
63 *The Sentry*, 'A Protest and Appeal Unanimously Adopted', 17 October 1902.
64 Ibid.
65 HoC [Cd 1783], Unofficial Members of the Legislative Council to Administrator, 20 December 1902.
66 HoC [Cd 1783], Chamberlain to Llewelyn, 25 November 1902.
67 PP, HoC [Cd 1783], Enclosure in Llewelyn to Chamberlain, 23 October 1902.
68 HoC [Cd 1783], Llewelyn to Chamberlain, 4 December 1902.
69 HoC [Cd 1783], Enclosure no. 2 in Llewelyn to Chamberlain, 4 December 1902.
70 TNA, CO 321/218, Llewelyn to Chamberlain, 26 January 1903.
71 HoC [Cd 1783], Enclosure no. 5 in Report to the Colonial Office from Captain Arthur Young on the Subject of the emigration of the villagers of Owia and Fancy, 22 December 1902.
72 HoC [Cd 1783], Llewelyn to Chamberlain, 9 January 1903.

73 HoC [Cd 1783], Enclosure in Llewelyn to Chamberlain, 18 December 1902.
74 TNA, CO 28/258, Sir R.B. Llewelyn to Mr Chamberlain, 5 January 1903.
75 HoC [Cd 1783], The Earl of Onslow to Governor Sir R.B. Llewelyn, 17 February 1903.
76 HoC [Cd 1783], Enclosure in Acting Governor C.C. Knollys to Mr Chamberlain, 29 January 1903.
77 HoC [Cd 1201], Governor J.A. Swettenham to Mr Chamberlain, 21 May 1902.
78 *Daily Gleaner*, 'Kingston's Day of Death and Horror', 14 January 1957.
79 Jamaican National Library, 7/12/115, Charles Taylor, letter sent to *Daily Gleaner*, 28 November 1959.
80 Gad Heuman provides the definitive account of this rebellion in Gad Heuman, *The Killing Time: The Morant Bay Rebellion in Jamaica* (Knoxville, TN: University of Tennessee Press, 1995).
81 Bonham C. Richardson, *Igniting the Caribbean's Past: Fire in British West Indian History* (Chapel Hill, NC: University of North Carolina Press, 2004), p. 174.
82 Jamaica Archives Records Department, IB/5/76/4/56, E.A. Hodges, 'The Secret History of the Earthquake'.
83 PP, HoC [Cd 3560], Enclosure, *Report on Earthquake in Jamaica (Kingston and Port Royal) also Relief Measures, &c.* in Admiralty to Colonial Office, 4 May 1907.
84 DAR.1925.07, Box 4, Folder 60, Aulay Babington Macaulay, 'Account of Jamaican earthquake', 14 January 1907, pp. 6–7. Accessed online 24 May 2021, https://bit.ly/38ELYS0.
85 HoC [Cd 3560], Enclosure in Admiralty to Colonial Office, 26 February 1907.
86 C.L. Chenery, 'The Jamaican Earthquake', reprinted from the *Barbados Advocate*, 23, 24, 25 January 1907, p. 18.
87 HoC [Cd 3560], Swettenham to Grey, 17 January 1907.
88 TNA, CO 137/660 (Jamaica) Letters from the Foreign Office (March to December 1907) and 'miscellaneous offices', Mr Howard to Sir Edward Grey, 4 February 1907.
89 C.L. Chenery, 'The Jamaican Earthquake', p. 6.
90 Pedro L.V. Welch, 'Post-Emancipation Adjustments in the Urban Context: Views from Bridgetown, Barbados', in *In the Shadow of the Plantation: Caribbean History and Legacy*, ed. by Alvin O. Thompson (Kingston: Ian Randle, 2002), pp. 266–282.
91 PP, HoC [Cd 3560], Enclosure in Admiralty to Colonial Office, 23 February 1907.
92 HoC [Cd 3560], Enclosure in Admiralty to Colonial Office, 26 February 1907.
93 John Harrison, 'The Colonial Legacy and Social Policy in the British Caribbean', in *Colonialism and Welfare: Social Policy and the British Imperial Legacy*, ed. by James Midgley and David Piachaud (Cheltenham: Edward Elgar, 2011), p. 57.
94 Cited in Bonham C. Richardson, *Panama Money in Barbados, 1900–1920* (Knoxville, TN: University of Tennessee, 1986), p. 11.

95 HoC [Cd 3560], The Governor to the Secretary of State, 18 January 1907.
96 *Leslie's Weekly*, 'After the Fury of the Earthquake in Kingston: A Multitude of the Homeless and Destitute, Without Shelter and Scantily Supplied with Food, and Some Peculiar Effects of the Shocks', 21 February 1907.
97 PP, HoC [Cd 3560], Enclosure, *Report on Earthquake in Jamaica (Kingston and Port Royal) also Relief Measures, &c.* in Admiralty to Colonial Office, 4 May 1907.
98 Theodore Roosevelt Papers. Library of Congress Manuscript Division, Report from C.H. Davis to Victor Howard Metcalf, p. 14. Accessed online 21 March, https://bit.ly/3PFGsio.
99 Ibid.

5

Practical sympathy

In 1902, Joseph Chamberlain wrote to the Lord Mayor of London to request the opening of some form of charitable fund in aid of those suffering on St Vincent following the eruption of La Soufrière. It was all in the name of what he termed 'practical sympathy'. There was much contrition in his letter, and dismay at having to even ask the Mayor to open a fund, but he felt he could no longer refrain, and set out a short case for why it was justified, making clear that in the space of four years, the colony – 'among the most depressed' in the region – had been hit by two calamities, which it would be 'probably impossible to parallel in the history of a British colony'.[1] That Chamberlain, given his position and in such circumstances, felt the need to justify and make a case for charity, speaks volumes about the reticence that existed within the British Empire when it came to providing aid. That he made this request not for 'charity' or 'relief' but for *practical sympathy* is a pithy summation of how relief to the Caribbean was viewed: practical in that it was targeted toward reviving the economy but sympathetic to a degree, in that it showed British benevolence.

As we have seen, disasters plunged planters and colonial administrators into negotiating fraught and frenetic circumstances as they tried to uphold the rigid racist hierarchy while the material and psychological basis for their power lay shattered. The threats that whites felt to their authority in these circumstances rarely materialised or manifested a significant challenge to their rule, but the difficulties brought by disasters did not end there. With the material shortages stemming from the export-focused, plantation-centric economy, white authorities faced battles to rebuild and resume agricultural production, and with their capacity for self-sufficiency hamstrung, external aid was always required to resuscitate Caribbean colonies in the wake of disasters. However, the same planters and officials designing punitive relief programmes for colonial populations were themselves not able to escape the dictum that colonies were to contribute to Britain's wealth and not drain it. Thus they often found themselves drawn into a second round of protracted negotiations with the Colonial Office and Parliament.

These were lengthy discussions not just because planters, officials and those in London were often at odds, but also because prior to the extension of telegraph cables to the Caribbean in 1873, communication across the Atlantic was slow. Though in the nineteenth century, the Colonial Office was rarely willing to allow a colony to go entirely without aid, the scale and nature of aid remained a site of contestation. Whites in the Caribbean had to work hard to persuade the Colonial Office that a disaster had left them unable to rebuild without financial aid and petitions were the central vehicle through which they presented their case.

Though they found it difficult to ever secure financial relief even close to estimates they submitted, relief was nonetheless provided with a regularity that allowed the Caribbean colonies to survive. Given the vulnerability of the colonies, the costs attendant on importing supplies, and their declining revenues over the course of the nineteenth century, it is hard to see how the colonies could have survived without financial relief.

When a petition was successful, financial relief generally arrived in two forms: 'grants in aid' and loans. Grants were typically a large lump sum supplied with a loose stipulation – a stipulation rarely enforced – that they be spent on the poor and needy. Loans were often far larger sums that were supplied with a whole host of conditions that excluded small landowners and were thus primarily targeted at plantation owners. There was no set framework for judging what the scale of relief should be, and it changed on the whims of the Colonial Office and those in charge. Thus the importance of certain colonies and the influence of those with interests in them played a role in deciding the scale of relief. Over the course of the nineteenth century, as expanding print media and rapid communication technologies developed, the Colonial Office became increasingly subject to external pressures as its disaster response came under greater public scrutiny. This was particularly true in the case of disasters caused by phenomena such as volcanic eruptions and earthquakes, considered somewhat out of the norm for the region, unlike hurricanes.

These technological developments also fed the growth of an increasing concern from the general public for disaster-stricken colonies. The end of the nineteenth century saw the emergence of a growing global community, sometimes even materially unconnected to the Caribbean, who felt a keen need to provide genuine relief. This desire manifested in charitable subscriptions and collections for provisions, clothes and other post-disaster necessities. These schemes appear to have genuinely boosted the relief available to non-elite sufferers, but they did not come entirely without their own conditions. Nation states used disaster and relief as an opportunity for 'political game playing', often offering Caribbean colonies charity as a means to make and/or remake their relationship with Britain.

Though the nineteenth century saw the Caribbean fall from its previously high position in Britain's imperial designs, the frequency with which relief did arrive tells us that some still felt an obligation to the Caribbean colonies and held out hope for their revival. It was clear to many that this obligation was a begrudging one, however, and as such it was rarely well received. Some British politicians decried it as a waste of resources and the wealthy citizens of the Caribbean colonies often saw the reality of its half-hearted nature and increasingly looked elsewhere for support.

Rebuilding

Once the initial post-disaster need for food and order had at least partially been met, planters and colonial officials often looked toward rebuilding their homes, plantations and points of civic power such as barracks. Their concern then quickly became the availability of lumber. As we have seen, deforestation was rampant throughout the Caribbean colonies and thus timber was hard to come by, especially in the quantities needed to rebuild whole towns and multiple plantations. Distance meant these islands could not look to Britain for timber and the search was therefore directed to other British Caribbean colonies and sometimes the US. Despite the importance of timber and provisions to long-term recovery, the colonial state did not jump to using public money to fund bulk purchases for the islands. Instead, given the ever-present reticence toward public spending, managed adjustments in taxation were more readily pursued.

Planters, in particular, pressured governments to open the ports, meaning to suspend duties on specific items, making their importation cheaper. It was a strategy for feeding enslaved people and thus maintaining order that had been used throughout the eighteenth century and well into the nineteenth. This was a form of relief directed towards planters: in the era of slavery, especially, African-Caribbean people could not afford to buy these supplies, which ensured planters maintain control of the relief effort. The government removed duties but did not purchase these items itself, meaning the planters maintained the power to distribute them as they saw fit. For the enslaved or those subsisting on marginal incomes, importing at scale would have been impossible. Suspending import duties was a measure that therefore maintained the planter's favoured position as the nexus through which both punishment and aid was exercised.

For most of the nineteenth century, before the wholesale switch to free trade, the opening of ports after a disaster was very common, and was used after hurricanes in 1827, 1831, 1834, 1835, 1866 and after the earthquake of 1843. This frequency was borne not just from the fact that it suited planters but also because it was one of the options that governors appear to have had recourse to without permission from the Colonial Office. However, despite the readiness with which it was deployed, this strategy also often exposed the divides between planters and colonial officials. Ever conscious of their financial overheads, planters were often keen to try and take advantage of the reduction in duties and establish a permanent regime of lower duties.

On 27 August 1827, following a hurricane, the Governor of St Christopher removed import duties for a month on a range of provisions, including timber and shingles for roofs. Quickly, the island's planters sought to extend this suspension, arguing that a month was not sufficient to aid their recovery. The governor agreed but later retracted the suspension when it was found that members of the planter class had been taking advantage of the reduction, importing at a lower cost but then immediately selling the supplies to other colonies for a profit.[2] Others even sought to use disasters as a pretext to suspend tariffs when they themselves had not been affected. In 1835, after a hurricane, Governor Evan Macgregor issued a proclamation removing import tariffs on Antigua. Neighbouring Monserrat had been unaffected by the storm, but Governor Macgregor was later forced to travel there to stop attempts by its legislature to use his proclamation to suspend tariffs.[3]

The same group of politically active Barbadian planters who sought to use the 1831 hurricane as an opportunity to reduce the salaries of the Protector of Slaves and the Registrar of Slaves also applied pressure over duties in the wake of the disaster. In their meetings with colonial officials in September following the hurricane of early August, planters, conscious of the delays to the sugar harvest, pressed the governor to remove the 4.5 per cent export tax which had 'previous to this misfortune impoverished [them]'. Clearly, it had been a longstanding issue for them but within the context of the disaster they painted it as not just as something that would slow the island's recovery, but also, in a cynical attempt to connect with more liberal minds in Britain, attempted to make the removal of this tariff a moral issue. They argued that the export tax made both 'master and slave the victims of a misconceived and onerous policy'.[4]

The extent to which planters desired the removal of this tax is also reflected in the fact that a specific request for its removal was placed at the very top of the first petition received in London, ahead of a broader call for aid. There is also every indication that the planters of the island were planning ahead, using the hurricane to their long-term advantage. They called for blanket removal with no suggestion of it being a time-limited measure to help their immediate recovery. What is more, given the destruction of the plantations and the sugar crop in 1831, the planters themselves were at least another year away from wholly benefitting from the removal of the export tariff.

The planters of Barbados do not seem to have been successful in permanently suspending this tariff and pressure appears to have come from the Colonial Office to push the governor into considering other avenues for relief. It was eventually agreed that Barbados' ports would be opened with import duties – not export tariffs – on needed goods being suspended. Perhaps reflecting the frequency with which it had happened in the past, the Colonial Office was also keen to stress that under no circumstance were these imported goods to be resold at a profit. This point is a clear demonstration of the paucity of trust that often persisted between the Colonial Office and Caribbean planters.

While not only solely benefitting the wealthiest of the Caribbean's colonists, in the long run, suspending tariffs as a method of post-disaster recovery also created deficits neither the Colonial Office nor the planters were willing to cover. These would, predictably, fall on those at the other end of Caribbean society. After the hurricane of 1831, Barbados received a loan and a separate grant of £50,000 from Parliament. The grant was specifically for those without the means to access the loans, meaning those outside the circle of wealthy planters. However, with no oversight from Parliament, at least a fifth of the grant would be spent financing the £10,202 tax deficit left by the suspension of import duties. Planters succeeded in using the disaster for their short-term benefit and avoided the long-term cost by detracting from monies advanced to help those they were ostensibly so conscious of protecting.

As a purely economic strategy the suspension of import duties was not entirely successful because it did nothing to address the structural vulnerabilities baked into Caribbean society. In 1831, even with its ports open, Barbados struggled to obtain sufficient supplies of timber as neighbouring St Vincent, where it had imported from in the past, had also been hit by the hurricane and its already limited stock was further depleted.

It was a strategy that at its heart really benefitted planters; and, not uncoincidentally, as the centrality of the planters to colonial politics waned, so the recourse to opening the ports declined. It was used again in 1843, when Antigua was hit by an earthquake and the governor despatched boats to Puerto Rico (known then as Porto Rico) at public expense to try to rapidly alleviate a shortage of timber. It would not be until 1866, when Governor Rawson opened Bermuda's ports to import timber, provisions and cotton seed that it would be used again. By the end of the nineteenth century, aid from neighbouring islands seems to have been frequently donated without condition. In 1898, Trinidad and Grenada both supplied timber to Barbados and St Vincent. Later, in 1907, Bermuda donated tents for the shelter of Kingston's citizens. In both instances aid was supplied without condition.

Petitioning

In any case, the opening of ports alone was not enough to complete a colony's long-term recovery. That could only come with large sums of money, the primary source of which was Parliament. As already mentioned, from the outset of British colonisation in the region, planters and colonial officials could not rest assured that relief would arrive. That said, by the nineteenth century there was less risk of relief not arriving at all: though it did happen, the central debate became the scale of relief and its conditions.

For much of the nineteenth century, the lines between the planter class and colonial officials were blurred, with many planters serving in their respective governments. It was these overlapping groups that had to petition Parliament for their relief. In doing so they walked a tricky line, portraying their circumstances as dire enough to elicit sympathy but not so bad that they appeared to have lost control of the situation. They wanted to make it clear that they needed aid, but also that, once it was delivered, they would be the ideal agents to distribute it.

Centuries of these negotiations, starting with the very first hurricanes to affect colonists in the British Caribbean had established certain understandings on both sides. The Colonial Office typically assumed that the planters of the Caribbean were opportunistic and prone to exaggeration to try and increase the financial support they received. On their side, the planters rightly assumed that they would have to fight to get any money from Britain, let alone have their losses fully compensated, and they were right. Treasury papers relating to the hurricane of 1831 show just how firmly set the minds of Treasury officials were in this regard; one anonymous, private note written on the back of official documents stated that 'I do not intend [the planters] to have a complete compensation of their loss but only a sum of money'.[5]

Given how contentious estimates of losses were, petitioners were often at pains to position themselves as neutrally as possible. When sending estimates following the eruption of 1812, the planters of St Vincent tried to assure the Colonial Office that they were made by 'persons entirely disinterested in the … estates'.[6] Who exactly these people were, particularly given that planters dominated political power on the island, they did not elaborate on. Planters also often included accounts penned by people outside of their class. In 1834, after the hurricane on Dominica, planter James Matthews tried to bolster the credibility of his estimates by including descriptions of the damage printed in the Colonial Paper the *Dominica Colonist*.[7]

These steps may seem overly cautious, but the planters were clearly aware that, though financial relief was arriving with increased frequency by the nineteenth century, the Colonial Office could still be capricious. In 1817, it struck down a petition from the legislature of St Vincent, then supposedly struggling to recover from a hurricane, dismissing its claims of damage as 'absurd' and 'ridiculous'.[8] Incidents like this were also clearly instructive to other planters. Fourteen years later in 1831, the planters of Barbados felt the need to state that their own petition was free of 'those hyperbolic statements for which St Vincent was so deservedly celebrated'.[9]

Even if the Colonial Office considered that a petition had merit, its approval was only the first hurdle that planters had to clear. In these negotiations, the Colonial Office effectively acted as an intermediary between the planters and those with the ultimate authority over British expenditure – Parliament. In some cases, the Colonial Office, regardless of its own opinion on a petition, would stop it proceeding because of the scrutiny it would be subjected to in Parliament. In 1834, three planters were chosen by the Dominican Government to assess and record the extent of the damage on the island, only to find their report later refused by the then Secretary of State for the Colonies, Thomas Spring Rice. He felt that this report, authored by a group of three planters, without the oversight of a colonial official, 'lacked the necessary authenticity to go unchallenged in Parliament'.[10]

This desire for authenticity could also, on occasion, reveal distrust between some colonial authorities and the planter class, despite their many overlaps. In 1843, after the earthquake, the Governor of Antigua, Charles Fitzroy, wrote to the Colonial Office stating that he was unable to supply them with an estimation of the losses because he did not have enough officers to complete the job and he trusted no one from the planter community to supply accurate valuations. That said, there was a clear need for relief and so, were the Colonial Office to send any even without an estimate, he assured them that he personally would oversee its disbursement so that none of it would be used for 'speculative purposes'.[11]

From what is possible to discern from colonial records, when an assessment of losses was attempted, it was generally done with a very high degree of scrutiny. For example, in 1831, in response to some very small claims made by a planter on account of horses he lost during the hurricane, a man, clearly trusted by the governor, was despatched to the claimant's estate to investigate the corpses of these horses and to try and ascertain whether they were actually killed by the hurricane.[12]

Outside of trying to paint their estimates of losses in the most objective light, another key tactic deployed by planters was the use of hyperbolic predictions of what might happen were they not supplied with relief. Take for example a letter written by planter Robert Sutherland after the 1812 eruption of La Soufrière. In it he writes that 'if we do not get relief I fear we must abandon our estates, and our poor negroes must be divided into lots and sold for the benefit of our creditors, and the families torn from each other'.[13] Sutherland's appeal was unsubtle but he clearly understood his audience. He suggests that the failure to provide aid would first undermine the very purpose of British colonialism in the Caribbean – cultivation – and second, in a characteristically paternalistic manner, go against the interests of the enslaved population.

Petitions and letters from planters that came after Sutherland's also attempted to tap into this line of argument. In 1834, planters from Dominica stressed that if there was to be no parliamentary aid, 'sugar and coffee cultivation must be abandoned for ever'.[14] Similarly, another Dominican planter argued that unless the 'Mother country comes forward to offer help with a generous hand, the cultivation will cease forever'.[15] Underscoring these appeals was an economic claim that spoke directly to the heart of the colonial 'mission' in the Caribbean: the cultivation of wilderness and its conversion into profit for Britain. Indeed, as the aforementioned group of Dominican planters put it later in their petition, money from Parliament was needed to 'render the colony again a valuable possession of the British Empire'.[16]

The supposed near collapse of these colonies as conveyed in these planter's statements brings us back to the question discussed in chapter 2: why, if hurricanes, in particular, threatened to collapse entire colonies, did the planter class never work to make the colonies more resilient? One conclusion we can draw is that these colonies, while often devastated, were never close to collapse, and it appears that Parliament knew that, hence the process of negotiating and authenticating claims. The planters were doing what they thought necessary not just to elicit aid but also to remain at the centre of the evolving conversation about the future of British Caribbean colonies. This is particularly obvious in the conduct of the planters of Barbados in 1831, who, as discussed in chapter 3, sought to position themselves as deserving of aid because they were 'the class of persons upon whose support the wellbeing of the community rests'.[17]

As the British Caribbean began its transition toward the end of slavery, the injury the planters felt they had sustained as a result of this historic change gave them new terms on which to argue. Planters on Dominica in 1834 posited that they deserved relief more than ever, because they could not rely on the labour of the now apprenticed population despite, as they put it, still being compelled to feed and clothe not just those apprenticed on their estates but also their infant children too. Even on Antigua, which had not apprenticed the enslaved but instead proceeded to full freedom, planters tried to present this choice as a sacrifice that entitled them to relief after the hurricane of 1835. Implicit in their petitions was the suggestion that the economic misfortune they had experienced prior to the hurricane was, in part, the Colonial Office's fault and that relief would be an effective means to make them whole again.

Despite planters' waning power, toward the end of the nineteenth century, suspicion of planters and their claims remained a theme in parliamentary discussions around disaster and relief. In 1899, a debate began in Parliament about the calls for relief issued from Barbados following the 1898 hurricane. At the time of the debate a grant in aid had been promised to Barbados and discussions about a more sizeable loan had begun but not yet concluded. In these discussions, questions around the authenticity of the claims emerging from the island were quickly raised. Henry Labouchère, Liberal MP for Nottingham, called them 'very greatly exaggerated' but perhaps even more strikingly, he also went on to question whether, given the racial makeup of the Caribbean, the island even deserved aid regardless of the possibility of exaggeration:

> If you heard in England of 10,000 houses being destroyed by a hurricane you would stand aghast. But the honourable Gentleman who has just sat down will bear me out when I say that the houses in Barbados are simply bamboo huts ... no doubt a great deal of injury has been done, but it is only of a temporary character, because these huts which have been destroyed can be built again for £1 or £2, and when we talk of people being rendered homeless I have myself been homeless in the sense of sometimes sleeping under a tree, when I slept just as well as I could have done in a house.[18]

His arguments not only shows how mistrust of planters in the Caribbean persisted, but also how its racial composition could be instrumentalised against claims for relief. Evidently, even a stalwart Liberal such as Labouchère was of the paternalistic belief that non-whites were less deserving of aid on account of their living conditions – living conditions, it must be added, that colonial authorities had created.

Despite his protestations, Labouchère was obviously out of step with the Colonial Office and the government more broadly: they had, after all, already promised the island a grant. By the end of the nineteenth century, Britain's relief efforts were scrutinised on the world stage and those in charge of the colonies evidently wanted to project at least a limited image of benevolence. If they did not, particularly at this point in time, Britain would have been in danger of seeing charitable donations far exceed its own offerings of help.

The provision of charitable aid after Caribbean disasters was not entirely unknown before the end of the nineteenth century. Such was the scale of destruction of the 'Great Hurricane' of 1780 that charitable subscriptions – written or oral agreements to pay towards a certain charitable cause – were agreed upon in unprecedented numbers in Britain. This response reflected a broader explosion in subscription charities throughout the eighteenth century.[19] There were also examples of interregional charitable subscriptions:

in 1831, for example, members of the West Indian Regiment donated one to three days of wages to Barbados and, at the same time, $24,741 was subscribed in Jamaica for the same cause. These examples were exceptions though. For most of the nineteenth century, disaster relief was an insular negotiation that took place between planters, colonial officials and Parliament.

By the end of the nineteenth century, things were changing as trends in charitable giving and technology increasingly overlapped. It was the era of 'high charity' in Victorian society, where, in the absence of a fully interventionist state, charitable giving formed an essential part of life for many members of the middling and upper classes. It was also world in which technology more rapidly acquainted those at home in Britain with the terror of disasters even thousands of miles away. Rapid print media, telegrams and photographs brought home the horror and the suffering occasioned by disasters to an extent which people had previously been unaccustomed to. Together with events such as the truly unprecedented 1883 eruption of Krakatoa which, because of its scale, rewrote many people's understanding of disaster, these trends gave birth to a new culture of intra-imperial giving.[20]

Colonial officials stationed in the Caribbean were clearly aware of this trend. In an unprecedented step, reflecting the extent to which there had been changes in both the culture of charitable giving in Britain and in the Colonial Office's own attitude to disaster relief, when Barbados and St Vincent were hit by a particularly devastating hurricane in 1898, their respective governors still felt compelled to make a case for relief but from the outset took the step of borrowing from their island's public funds 'on reliance [of] ultimate assistance from charitable or imperial sources'.[21] One problem represented by this approach, however, was that they could not predict the scale or arrival window of charitable donations.

For governors so often concerned with limiting expenditure, and conscious that they would almost certainly have to repay these funds, this unpredictability alone may have circumscribed their spending on relief. As they would find out, the bonds between those at home and colonists could be fickle. Both the type of disaster and the perceived importance of a colony within the Empire had an impact not just on parliamentary decisions but also on the success of charitable collections. Events in 1898 proved to be a stark reminder of just how far the Caribbean, especially its periphery colonies, had fallen in the estimation of the British public.

Moloney, Governor of St Vincent, and Hay, Governor of Barbados, argued that both of their respective colonies were deserving of aid because of the economic depression already afflicting their islands, with Hay making clear that given the 'present financial situation' of the colony, it simply would not be able to 'bear the strain of [providing] relief' alone.[22] They also wrote of the suffering of their subjects, but the economic justification remained at the forefront of the arguments. Indeed, it was clearly considered the most convincing factor not just by the governors but also those in London. When he later decided to instigate a charitable collection in their aid, Lord Selbourne, Under Secretary of State for the colonies, used a very similar line about the economically depressed situation in the colonies to build sympathy. Selbourne turned to the Lord Mayor of London, who had, as one of his key powers, the ability to open the Mansion House fund.

The fund was effectively a form of nationally franchised charity collection in which the Lord Mayor decided upon a cause and civil leaders from across the country then collected money on his behalf.[23] By the 1870s, the Mansion House Fund had superseded other patrician fundraising committees and had effectively become the nexus for British charitable aid-giving both nationally and internationally. In 1898, Selbourne made representations on the behalf of the two colonies to the fund, claiming that they needed 'substantial and timely' aid because they were already 'struggling' and 'impoverished'.[24]

When covered in newspapers, the official line to support the fund was that the imposition of sugar bounties meant the islands lacked the funds to recover on their own. In the second half of the nineteenth century, European nations had increasingly sought to boost their own domestic sugar production through a system of bounties. This had a significant effect on the price of Caribbean sugar, with the value of British Caribbean sugar dropping by 6s per 100lb in 1884 alone.[25]

Despite press coverage and the appeals from Selbourne, embarrassingly, the Mansion House Fund did not deliver as hoped. It brought in just £38,000, enough to cover the estimated £25,000 for restoring peasant huts but with little left for anything else. In 1877 the fund had raised £250,000 for victims of famine in India and in 1897 it had raised an astounding £773,000 for the same cause.[26] In 1882, it had raised £108,000 for the relief of persecuted Jews in Russia, something which is notable as it was a cause concerning non-Britons and was outside of the Empire.[27] Charity for international causes, even where the recipients were not British subjects, was evidently not in short supply.

Why then did the fund raise so little for Barbados and St Vincent? The West India Committee (WIC), which represented British Caribbean interests in Britain and specifically in elite political circles, was convinced it was because the British Government had failed to challenge the bounty system and place countervailing tariffs on European beet sugar. At a meeting on 31 October 1898 members argued that because Britain had betrayed Caribbean planters there was little sympathy for a top-down charitable effort, and that the British state was perceived as having been responsible for the very economic circumstances it was arguing rendered aid essential.[28] A number of letters sent into the press suggest that, despite their obviously self-interested reason for critiquing the government, the WIC could have been right about sentiment amongst the public.

One man, Henry Blake, sent a letter to *The Times* in which he argued that Moloney and Hay had done what they could to help their respective colonies but that it was 'unfavourable' economic policies that prevented them doing more. Like the officials and planters who wrote from the Caribbean, he also made an appeal to precedent, stating that, as Britain had done in 1789 (it is possible he was erroneously referring to the hurricane of 1780), it should again provide these islands with the relief they needed to recover. He also noted that the Caribbean had generously given to Mauritius following a hurricane in 1892 and should now be rewarded for this past beneficence (Mauritius would itself make a charitable donation to Barbados and St Vincent in 1898). He did not note his occupation, but Blake's letter chimed remarkably well with the opinions of the WIC; his knowledge of such intricacies of Caribbean relief suggests someone with more than a passing interest in the region.

The point about precedent was something that also motivated other letters. Clearly many readers were of the opinion that Britain had a duty to help the Caribbean. One concerned reader, Colonel G.E. Boyle, wrote that if Britain had been able to supply the Caribbean with relief in 1780, at a time of war, then it should be more than capable of doing so in a time of peace.[29] The *Morning Post* ran an editorial arguing that because the government had neglected the Caribbean it bore an 'elevated responsibility' for helping Barbados and St Vincent recover, with the editor further writing that it would be a 'happy conclusion' if the hurricane 'stirred' the government to provide aid not just in the wake of the hurricane but in the longer term.[30]

Both islands would go on to receive substantial financial aid from Parliament, not necessarily from any sizeable public feeling – it remained a relatively niche issue – nor from the lobbying efforts of the WIC but because the Caribbean colonies, long forgotten, found a champion in Chamberlain. He was determined to redevelop what he had once described as the 'Empire's darkest slum'.[31] He would also go on to successfully lobby for the ending of the European bounty system in 1902.

Despite his championing of the Caribbean, Chamberlain did not have an entirely free hand when it came to expenditure on relief, and did have to make concessions. Barbados and St Vincent were not the only colonies to have sustained damage from the hurricane, they had just suffered the worst. Other nearby colonies, namely St Lucia, did put in claims for compensation. St Lucia did not have its own governor but fell under the jurisdiction of the Governor of the Windward Islands, which was Moloney of Barbados. As a result, it was left to a colonial administrator in charge of the island, Charles

King-Harman, to make representations as to the circumstances on the island following the hurricane. He put forward a case for relief, arguing it was essential because despite comparatively limited damage on the island, it was only four years since a hurricane had last hit the island, causing £4,000 of damage, and, he argued, St Lucia had not yet fully recovered and many were still suffering 'extreme poverty'.[32] Without aid, he suggested that the island would languish in poverty for the following decade.

Replying to King-Harman, Chamberlain made a comprehensive case as to why the island was not to receive aid. It had only suffered thirteen casualties and, perhaps more importantly, the majority of its cane crop and the requisite processing equipment had survived.[33] Furthermore, it had a large crop of cocoa that had survived the storm. The British Government, as per the Royal Commission's report, were convinced that diversifying from sugar was essential to a wider economic recovery in the region. Thus, from Chamberlain's view, the island had every chance to recover under its own steam, even if there was to be ongoing poverty: industry on the island was intact and, in true British fashion, the labour it could provide would be a source of amelioration for that poverty. Chamberlain made it clear to King-Harman that were he to grant St Lucia relief it would set a bad precedent and open up ground for more unreasonable requests. It was easy for Chamberlain to wave away the island's requests despite King-Harman's pleas, because to the outside observer the island looked prosperous. In the years prior to the hurricane, it seen an influx of money and construction activity as it had grown into an important military coaling station in the region. In reality, however, this influx of money primarily entered the hands of private business and not the government and labourers.[34]

Chamberlain was unlikely to face any damaging political ramifications from this course of action. The island's sugar industry had already entered terminal decline before the beet-induced economic depression of 1884 onwards and increasingly the island's African-Caribbean population had abandoned the estates in favour of becoming small-scale peasant proprietors. Thus King-Harman, unlike many before and after him, could not make the case that the money was essential to the restoration of the estates and thus 'order'. While the planters of Barbados and St Vincent were able to make themselves heard via the WIC, the WIC had little representation on St Lucia and had little leverage given that the island had never been a major contributor to British coffers.[35]

Other small islands, such as Anguilla, St Kitts and Nevis, had all suffered some form of damage in the hurricane but found their claims similarly challenged. St Kitts and Nevis were given the small sum of £300, but Anguilla, which had already been suffering an extended period of drought that had begun in 1897 and in the wake of the hurricane was said to resemble those in the most 'malarious [sic] countries', was offered no more than £20.[36]

For all his talk of reviving the Caribbean and developing the underdeveloped estates, these examples of meagre relief and rejected claims reveal the limitations of Chamberlain's reforming tendencies. His help appeared to extend only to those who would in turn be able to enrich Britain in the long run. His policy of developing the underdeveloped estates, while looking like a new approach, did not stray far from the long-sacrosanct Colonial Office policy of limiting expenditure. He was prepared to invest more than those before him but, in the long run, still expected a healthy return.[37]

The experience of the Windwards and the laxity of charitable relief in 1898 is not just explained by what was in many respects a patrician debate over bounties. I would argue that the very nature of the disaster shaped the scale of charitable donations. The frequency of hurricanes normalised them not only to planters but also to those in Britain. They came to be seen as an accepted part of life in the Caribbean. For politicians in Britain, particularly when the number of casualties was comparatively low, they could have looked less like moments of disaster and more like extreme weather. By comparison, volcanic eruptions, rarer as they were in the Caribbean and with all the more horrifying effects, appear to have inspired much more generosity from the public and a quicker response from the Colonial Office.

In 1902, when St Vincent's La Soufrière erupted, Chamberlain authorised Governor Llewelyn to immediately begin borrowing from the colony's public funds to meet the emergency. Following this, Chamberlain himself contacted the Lord Mayor of London to request the opening of the Mansion House Fund. It raised £10,000 in the first twenty-four hours and went on to raise £52,016 in total with a further £700 coming in from a separate appeal in the *Mirror*. Although not a huge amount more, this was nonetheless substantial, especially as this time the sum was to be donated to one island and not split between two.

Even with a clear need for relief, such was the colonial tendency toward limiting expenditure that much of the initial communication between Britain and St Vincent struck an almost apologetic tone. Llewelyn 'feared' that he would have to expend public funds to feed and house the labouring population. Similarly, Chamberlain wrote that he had initially not felt 'justified' in requesting the opening of the Mansion House Fund but eventually found he could 'no longer refrain' when he received a clearer picture of the distress in St Vincent.[38]

This same rhetoric and concerns with stringent financial prudence even in times of obvious emergency would continue when the British Caribbean faced its biggest crisis in centuries, the Jamaican earthquake of 1907. The colonial authorities still found themselves having to justify their requests for relief from Britain. It would be granted but only in June, five months after the disaster. As with previous disasters, the uncertainty over the scale of relief can only have hampered the amount of money that the Jamaican Government was willing to spend in the interim. The Mansion House Fund was opened but economic concerns formed the central justification for opening it; donations were needed to restore Kingston as a 'principal centre of trade'.[39]

The importance of Jamaica's long-term economic prospects was a common theme in the two main cases for aid that followed the opening of the Mansion House Fund. One was a petition made by Bishop Enos Nuttall, head of the Relief Committee, and the other was in communications made by Sir Edward Grey, Secretary of State for the Colonies. Both men were keen to stress that Jamaica, having begun to emerge from the regional economic depression before the earthquake, was beginning to experience prosperity, and that the earthquake would seriously check this progress if no help were provided. Both also made the point that this would have serious impacts on the social order of Jamaica. Nuttall, in particular, no doubt conscious of the authenticity provided by his first-hand experience of Jamaican life, painted a picture in which without aid targeted at the businesses and employers of Kingston, the mass of labouring Jamaicans would descend into a permanent spiral of charitable dependency. When he spoke of dependency, Nuttall, consciously or subconsciously, was speaking of the very condition that, as we have seen already, the British wanted to avoid at all costs. It was evidently a persuasive argument. Nuttall and Grey were no doubt making what they considered a humane argument because, like many of their patrician class, they clearly believed the surest way to safeguard the wellbeing of the labouring classes was not to help them directly but rather provide them with the opportunity for personal betterment through work. Within this framework, helping business was the key to an overall revival of Kingston for all classes. In the end, the Mansion House appeal raised a modest £54,053, certainly more than other appeals in recent years but relatively small given the scale of the disaster.

Businesses in Kingston also joined in the lobbying, but most of these petitions did not make it beyond local newspapers. However, one group, the WIC, as we might expect given its centuries-long connection to Westminster, was more successful than most at getting its case in front of Parliament. It of course made a case for aid based on economic considerations and, like Grey and Nuttall, argued that aid to business would be essential to preventing social collapse and civil unrest, but it also went further. The WIC made a case for aid based on geopolitical considerations particularly vis-à-vis the US which by then was already jostling with Britain for hegemony in the region. As the WIC saw it, relief paid to business in Kingston would allow the colony to stem the drain of labourers to the US-owned Panama Canal construction company. They did not hide from saying that this would be a positive outcome because it would disadvantage the American company. However, they knew that this alone would not stop the building of the canal and nor did they want it to. In fact, in the long term, it argued that relief to Kingston was essential to the colony benefitting from its proximity to the canal when it eventually opened.

These economic considerations formed a central part of the petitions put to Parliament and the monarchy throughout the nineteenth century and both were mostly receptive. When humanitarian considerations were mentioned, it was never as an end in themselves, but rather in the service of economic good. Those in the Caribbean and those in Parliament may have quibbled on the size and nature of relief but this they could agree on. So powerful was this framing logic that it continued to play a fundamental role in the contours of relief when it arrived in a colony.

Distributing relief

As mentioned, parliamentary relief could be given to a colony it two forms: grants and loans. Grants were not required to be paid back and were generally intended for the enslaved and, later, labouring classes. Loans came as a lump sum loaned to a colony, from which its colonists could take smaller individual loans. These required some form of property as a security, along with clauses detailing minimum loan sizes that de facto excluded all but the wealthiest whites. Due to the distrust between the planters and the Colonial Office, throughout the nineteenth century, the size of these relief packages rarely, if ever, matched the planters' requests. Planters were thus effectively incentivised to limit the expenditure on general suffering and instead to try to find ways in which to pocket the grants themselves. Given their centrality to colonial governance throughout much of the nineteenth century, they often found this easy to do.

In 1812, following the eruption of La Soufrière, the planters of the island estimated that their cumulative losses totalled £79,045. They received an initial £2,000 from Barbados' legislature to cover the immediate import of provisions but the next relief to be pledged to the island did not arrive until September, five months after the eruption. This relief, a number of monetary bills sent by Sir Alexander Cochrane, Governor of Guadeloupe and its dependencies, was to be expended for those in 'most need of immediate assistance'.[40] When they did arrive, the planters, who at this point still had no confirmation that relief would arrive from Britain, argued that the bills should not be passed through the public treasury and into the hands of colonial officials. Instead, they argued that they should go straight to the sufferers, or in other words, themselves.

Parliamentary relief did not arrive until over two years later when St Vincent's colonial agent, Frederick Nicolay, was permitted by Parliament to disburse £25,000. Interestingly, the money was a grant and not a loan. The parliamentary records that cover the process of how this figure and form of relief were arrived at do not survive but, given the value of the colony and the fear of an American attack, a grant at least guaranteed that planters would take up the money and use it to rebuild.

We do not have a secondary perspective on what happened as the relief effort unfolded in 1812, but in the years that followed it is clear that the planters did what they could to monopolise all available sources of relief. This was not unique to the planters of St Vincent, and the aftermath of the 1831 hurricane on Barbados provides us with an even clearer perspective on these dynamics. In addition to the shortages and racial strife that accompanied the hurricane in the short term, the island's financial picture was dire. Barbados' losses were estimated at £2,311,729 and St Vincent's at £500,000. Even if these were exaggerated to a degree, there was no getting away from the fact these islands were seriously suffering, and their future prospects looked poor. Three months after the hurricane, when Parliament had still not agreed upon relief, the General Assembly of Barbados felt it necessary, in a letter, to remind Parliament just how bad the situation was, writing that the 'privations of many were still increasing on a daily basis'.[41]

Parliament did eventually agree on a relief package for the two islands but not until a year after the hurricane, and the agreed amounts fell far short of the supposed losses. Barbados was allotted £50,000 and St Vincent £20,000 in non-repayable grant money. In apparent recognition of the seriousness of the situation on the two islands, a new commission, the West India Relief Commission, was set up to further assess the scale of the losses and went on to offer a further £91,450 in loans to planters on both islands. Crucially, however, these loans and the grant money were subject to a number of delays, not least because the colonies lacked the specie to honour even parts of the amount allotted without more cash being shipped in from Britain. Further to this, the planters were resistant to having £50,000 in money bills flood the market, fearing it would 'seriously embarrass' them.[42] Due to these delays, the majority of the money was not spent in any great quantities until 1834; life must have been hard indeed until then, for the enslaved population in particular, who did not receive any aid other than what the planters chose to provide them with.

The poor white population did receive some aid, with increments of money devised on the basis of a claimant's dependents and gender. Men, on average, received 2s 1d; women who had dependents received 3s 5d;

and single women received 1s 5d.[43] These amounts were roughly comparable to poor rates in Britain, but in Barbados the colonial authorities made every attempt to curtail the distribution of this cash as quickly as possible. The colonial government, as ever, put great emphasis on establishing the authenticity of people's claims. Commenting on the situation, Lionel Smith, a colonial agent involved with the distribution of the aid wrote 'the population of the island is immense, numerous poor families living together of the same all putting forward equal pretensions for losses, the labour of discrimination to prevent abuses required time, research and respectable testimony'.[44] Joseph Sturge, no friend of the planters, visited the island in 1836 and gives us a perspective which suggests that for all of the oversight Smith had talked up, those involved in the distribution were actually doing a lax job that led to much abuse of the money:

> The distribution of [the parliamentary grant] has been by no means satisfactory to many of the sufferers. It is complained that some persons of small property, who were entirely ruined by the hurricane, had no relief from it, while others of large fortune obtained considerable grants.[45]

Sturge also observed similar scenes of financial mismanagement on his travels to Dominica when, after the hurricane of 1834, he encountered planters who, two years on from that disaster, 'openly declare[d] their intention of never repaying' loans. He also noted that, unlike the planters, the African-Caribbean population were still in the process of rebuilding their homes and were doing so without any financial or physical assistance.[46] Sturge's primary mission was to evaluate the condition of the African-Caribbean population post-slavery; nonetheless the destitution must have been striking for the island to appear unrecovered two years after the hurricane.

The absence of aid for the non-white population is probably explained by the fact that Dugald Laidlaw, was the planter in charge of distributing relief on Dominica. He, as we saw in the previous chapter, was explicit in expressing his displeasure with the African-Caribbean population. In his role, he fixated on the need for 'evidence and verification' before he would begin the distribution of aid, but given the boasts recorded by Sturge, this stringency was something he clearly did not extend to his fellow planters.[47]

Disasters could have long tails that hastened or precipitated long-term decline for British colonies. The earthquake of 1843 appears to have done just that for a number of colonies in the Leeward Islands. Antigua, the main colony affected, was refused financial relief by Parliament in 1843 despite Governor Fitzroy offering all property on the island as security. This refusal was no doubt because, while infrastructure was destroyed in the quake, the sugarcane crop survived. Parliament did relent when, the following year, Antigua, Nevis and Montserrat were all hit by a hurricane. It offered loans to all three islands totalling £150,000, at an interest rate of 4 per cent between 1844 and 1846, with a sharp increase to 10 per cent after 1846. These conditions were onerous and seemingly disincentivised many, at least on Antigua, from applying. Travelling to the island in 1849, Robert Baird, an American, noted his and many other Antiguans' shock that Parliament did so little to help the island. Five years on from the hurricane of 1844, he observed that there was still evidence of its devastation all around the island.[48] On Montserrat, the twin shocks of the earthquake and then the hurricane effectively destroyed the sugar industry on the island, sending it spiralling into an economic depression which caused severe starvation, malnutrition and disease. Deplorable destitution was said to exist on the island for many years following.[49]

It was not just neglect that could worsen post-disaster recovery but the very conditions under which 'relief' was offered. Natasha Lightfoot has shown that on Antigua, the high interest rates on the loans accepted by the island after the hurricane of 1835 led to the raising of taxes on food and other essential goods. These rises caused widespread hunger and ended up being a driving cause of the wave of civil unrest that swept the island in 1838.[50] After the hurricane of 1831, there was much discontent amongst white colonists of Trinidad and St Lucia about the debt entailed by parliamentary relief. They had been partially affected by the hurricane but were not offered any grants, as Barbados and St Vincent had been. In his history of Tobago, Henry Woodcock provides perhaps the most directly damning assessment of this relief, stating that parliamentary loans 'generally speaking entail much suffering on a community, are not applied to the purposes intended and should not be resorted to but under pressure of the most urgent necessity'.[51] It is worth noting that Woodcock was not just a historian of Tobago but had been a member of its Legislative Council and, after the 1847 hurricane, had been opposed to the acceptance of a parliamentary loan and its debt burden. Of the £50,000 offered to the island, only £13,200 was drawn upon and the rest went unclaimed.

Providing relief through loans theoretically allowed Parliament not only to recoup the costs of relief but potentially to profit from them, but, by the midpoint of the nineteenth century even the act of providing relief to the Caribbean created contention among some MPs. William Molesworth, MP for Southwark, commenting in Parliament on the relief offered to Tobago stated: 'I utterly disbelieve that the West Indian colonies can ever be of the slightest value to the country ... they have been the most costly, the most worthless, and the worst managed of our colonies, a perpetual drain on the pockets of the people of England'.[52]

Blunt though it was, Molesworth's statement reflected what many in elite circles thought of the Caribbean by the mid-nineteenth century. It was an opinion that persisted right through the latter half of the nineteenth century and was of such strength that it played a fundamental role in shaping the relief that even the reforming Chamberlain was able to provide to Barbados and the Windwards in 1898. As already established, conditions on Barbados and St Vincent were dire after the hurricane and it also cannot have been far from Chamberlain's mind that the disaster was of the exact sort that the 1897 Royal Commission had warned could permanently set the region back. However, that same report had also warned the Colonial Office against large-scale loans to the planters of the two islands; they were so indebted and mortgaged by the end of the nineteenth century that they needed cash advances from creditors to even continue cultivation. Prior to Chamberlain taking office, the Colonial Office clearly felt similarly about the risks and in 1894 had turned down a petition from the planters of Barbados for a loan of £50,000.

Chamberlain, despite the aforementioned limitations to his development policies, did still represent a new more amenable direction for the Colonial Office. In addition to the £40,000 and £25,000 grants he secured for Barbados and St Vincent respectively, he also secured a package of £50,000 of loans strictly for the use of planters. This relief – reflecting both the Caribbean's low place in the colonial hierarchy and the trepidation of the government to lend to the region – was not only far less than the 1897 Commission's report had suggested would be necessary to restore Barbados and St Vincent to profitability even before the hurricane of 1898, but was also laden with strict conditions. Firstly, it was impossible to borrow less than £50 from the fund, which ensured it was for use by wealthy landowners only. Secondly, the hurricane relief could not be used to cover existing debt and/or repair any non-hurricane damage. Finally, and perhaps most strikingly given who the loan was aimed at, any misappropriation of the funds was punishable by six months of hard labour. This clause represented a change also in that it notionally subjected the planter class for the first time to a stringency otherwise only extended to the African-Caribbean population. There was no suggestion as to how these details might be enforced but, at the very least, they made clear the dominant power in this situation.

The grants Barbados and St Vincent elicited in 1898, though meagre in comparison to the estimated damage done to both colonies, were the largest the Colonial Office had extended to the region since 1831. This would change after the Jamaican earthquake of 1907. It became the first colony to end up with a grants and loans package that came far closer to actually meeting estimates of the damage caused. This was in part because Kingston was a richer, more densely packed urban centre and thus required more money to recover. It is also because for the first time, Britain had to use disaster relief to save face, as global attention focused its 'relief' efforts.

Disaster diplomacy

In the nineteenth century, foreign powers rarely factored in British disaster responses. By virtue of its proximity and the importance of trade links, the one exception to this was the US. As we have seen, in 1780 and 1812 the US influenced British thinking because the two states were at war. Britain feared an invasion of its weakened colonies, but the US did not take the opportunity; in fact, the US helped stricken British Caribbean colonies more than it ever directly hindered them. After the hurricane of 1831, Barbados' Governor, James Lyon, informed the Colonial Office that famine was initially averted 'only by American aid'. Whether this was aid that was delivered directly by American ships or collected by British ships we do not know, but the Colonial Office had no trouble with this intervention. In 1866, two US vessels of war aided Rawson W. Rawson's government in the Bahamas towing a beached steamship, and their crews also assisted with the repair of government buildings. The British later cordially thanked them for this assistance.[53]

As the largely insular process of disaster response was opened up by technology and public concern, the US was joined by more foreign nations in the act of charitable giving. The hurricane of 1898 had seen a number of US-based individuals donate money, alongside the Canadian Government, which donated £2,083 6s 8d.[54] It could be argued that given its status as a dominion colony, the Canadian donation did not represent a significant break from the insularity of the past but by 1902, when La Soufrière and Mount Pelée erupted simultaneously, it was clear that a wider range of nations were now donating to disaster victims. However, it should be emphasised that this moment did not represent a sudden explosion of global altruism. In fact, more countries than ever engaged in a form of conspicuous aid-giving closely resembling that which environmental sociologist, John Hannigan calls political 'game playing'.[55] In effect, relief is only given when it also stands to benefit the donor.

In 1902, the first foreign donations of aid arrived from the Netherlands and Germany, who pledged 1,000 florins and £500 respectively.[56] These donations were significant in that they came from the two countries that had worked with Britain to abolish European sugar bounties; this was perhaps an act that in part was born of a recognition of the damage the system had done to British Caribbean colonies. Belgium followed, with a substantial donation of 34,000 francs explicitly donated in recognition of British assistance during the Belgian Revolution and Britain's continually favourable attitude to the country.[57]

Where these nations were seemingly using aid to effectively strengthen their relations with Britain, others, Canada in particular, engaged in transparent attempts to use aid as a lever for influence directly in the Caribbean. Since the 1880s Canada had been trying to foster trade ties with the region and had even gone so far as to propose a union with Jamaica.[58] Despite that proposal being unsuccessful, Canada had continued to try and insert itself between Caribbean business and Britain, with some in the region wanting to sign trade deals with Canada but stopping short because they feared repercussions from Britain.

1898 saw a major Canadian overture to the Caribbean in the form of a unilateral 25 per cent preference, which it extended to British Caribbean sugar as part of what it called its 'imperial responsibilities'. This, however, provoked the ire of the British Government because, as they saw it, it allowed Germany to benefit from re-exports via a 'favoured nation' treaty that it had previously signed with Canada.[59] In this context we can see why Canada might have wanted to donate £2,083 to Barbados and St Vincent – an amount, it should be noted, that was four times that donated by other British colonies: it was determined to tamp down any tensions with Britain. Canada's overtures continued in 1902, when it donated a substantial sum – C$25,000 – and offered to cover the cost of provisions that were shipped to the island from Canada.

This donation can also be seen as part of a wider response to changes in economic conditions since 1898. Having annexed Cuba in 1898, from 1902 the US had extended a preferential tariff to Cuban sugar producers, which hit the already suffering producers in the British Caribbean hard. Up until 1902, British producers had survived the ongoing depression by the strength of their US export market. Thus, in 1902, Britain was having to turn to Canada to help support its Caribbean sugar producers. In this context, Canada's donation can be seen as a part of a wider pattern of cooperation between the countries regarding the region.

While Canada and other nations made donations at a distance, the US was the only foreign nation that delivered aid directly. In doing so, it walked a fine line between contributing to the rapprochement that President Roosevelt was aiming to build between the two nations and appearing to subvert British authority in the region. When the volcano erupted on St Vincent, the US communicated its desire to 'share' in relief efforts because it felt the disaster as if it 'had struck its own people'.[60] This offer was accepted and, perhaps gallingly for Britain, excepting the arrival of four doctors on a British Royal Mail steamer, via the *USS Potomac*, the US provided the first provisions to the island. For those concerned with the growth of US power in the region, this cannot have gone unnoticed, especially given that the punctuality of Britain's naval forces in the region was already a matter of ridicule.

Just two days after La Soufrière erupted, Mount Pelée on nearby Martinique erupted, triggering a far larger disaster, which killed in excess of 30,000 people. As a result, the US sent more supplies to the region and those brought by the *USS Potomac* were then supplemented by the *USS Dixie*, which brought with it 1,234 tons of food and clothing and then the *USS Sterling*, which delivered more foodstuffs as well as medical supplies. Cumulatively, the US delivered enough aid to St Vincent to feed its entire population for thirty-six days.[61] Given the reticence with which Governor Moloney actually distributed relief on the island, it would be interesting to know how Vincentians viewed the nation that had provided the relief when compared to the one that seemed to be doing what it could to prevent them from accessing it. Regrettably, no records were made or survive which capture this.

In private communications, the US offered even more support to Britain, suggesting that, in the absence of a British presence on Martinique, it could protect British 'vessels, interests and citizens' located there.[62] This offer did risk overstepping the line into subverting British authority, suggesting that Britain could not protect its interests in the region, and needed the help of the increasingly influential US to do so. However, Britain does not appear to have taken umbrage with this offer and instead apparently welcomed the support the US offered. One colonial official in St Vincent wrote that he would 'gladly receive and distribute any gifts sent to his care'.[63] That Britain was not offended by these bold offers, in part reflects a pragmatic response in a moment of crisis but also demonstrates that the US was increasingly willing to use its growing strength in the region.

Britain itself also took the simultaneous eruption of Mount Pelée as an opportunity to provide aid and strengthen ties between itself and France. Two days after the eruption on Martinique, the Colonial Office sent out a communiqué to British ships in the Caribbean, stating that, had the situation on St Vincent stabilised sufficiently, they should provide some aid to the French colony. A response came from Barbados which sent three nurses, a doctor and two members of the Royal Army Medical Corps alongside some medical supplies. These professionals tragically ended up with little work because the eruption had been so deadly that there were almost no survivors from the directly affected area, but the medical supplies were welcomed.[64]

Throughout this book, we have seen that the British in the Caribbean were reticent to provide comprehensive aid for their own colonies. Why then did the Colonial Office send out this request, even if it ended up being a relatively small donation of supplies and manpower? Here again we can return to the concept of relief as political 'game playing'. The gesture came at a moment in which Britain was actively trying to court friendship with the French as part of its wider concerns about the political stability of the European continent. For the second half of the nineteenth century, the two nations had largely regarded each other with oscillating suspicion and ambivalence. This eventually came to a head when, in 1898, following a number of territorial disputes regarding their respective African empires, two small military forces from the respective countries engaged in a stand-off over an Egyptian fort at Fashoda (now Kodok in South Sudan). With neither willing to risk a military conflict, the French conceded the fort. It was an embarrassing public climbdown, but it was motivated by a desire to try to forge closer ties with Britain because the French feared the Germans were exceeding their position as a 'status quo power' in Europe.

Britain was seeking friendship for the very same reason, and rapprochement began after the Fashoda incident, with its first fruits borne with the agreement to remove the sugar bounties system at the aforementioned Brussels conference in 1901. We can understand the Colonial Office order to aid Martinique as part of this thawing of tensions between the two nations. This generosity was added to when Governor of Mauritius, Charles Bruce, pledged 5,000 Mauritanian Rupees in an act of reciprocation for the fact that the French, probably moved by Mauritius' sizeable French population, had provided aid to the island when it had been struck by a devastating hurricane in 1892. These friendly overtures were well received and France's president, Émile Loubet, telegrammed the Foreign Office, stating that he was 'deeply touched by this new mark of sympathy'.[65]

While the Colonial Office could suspend norms about colonial expenditure when it suited wider objectives, it was not as easy for individual governors, particularly if they felt they were going to face a deficit as a result. Cornelius Moloney, who had been Governor of the Windward Islands at the time of the 1898 hurricane, was Governor of Trinidad and Tobago in 1902. After the eruption of Mount Pelée, many refugees had fled to Trinidad, which Moloney found troubling because while he 'appreciate[d] … their flight and their desire to get away' he worried that they would soon start to be a drain on the colony's finances as they had little opportunities on the island. There is no record of the number of refugees who arrived in Trinidad but given how few people survived the eruption on Martinique, it cannot have been many and, what is more, those that did arrive were, in Moloney's own words, 'old established French colonists … possessed of considerable property'.[66] So strong was Moloney's aversion to charitable dependence that it even transcended race in this instance. He subsequently requested that the Colonial Office petition the French Government for the permanent care of the refugees. This request was seemingly ignored, perhaps because it risked undermining the spirit of generosity that the British were keen to show the French. That said, the incident, however minor, shows us that while some could see the strategic advantage in dropping some dictums, others could not; the unwritten rules of British disaster response ran deep and could threaten even the wider goals of the Colonial Office. The expansive latitude of the governor did not hinder Anglo-French rapprochement in this case because Moloney contacted the Colonial Office first. In 1907, faced with far higher stakes, things went very differently for Jamaican Governor, Alexander Swettenham, when he did not work in concert with the Colonial and Foreign Offices.

Jamaica had long been the most important British colony in the Caribbean but, by the end of the nineteenth century, its primacy was even clearer. It had an economically diverse enough economy that it was able to weather the worst of the sugar beet depression of the 1890s and, since the Morant Bay Rebellion of 1865, had been ruled by Britain directly as a Crown colony. Though Jamaica was economically successful, with bigger financial prospects once the Panama Canal opened, some in the Colonial Office still had concerns about the colony. With the waning of the European sugar market Jamaica's continuing prosperity had been built on US export markets, so much so that some feared the colony was, by the twentieth century, fully dependent on its connection to America. As a result, some had doubts about the loyalty of its population – particularly that of its business community – to Britain. Direct US intervention in the relief efforts following the earthquake of 1907 brought these tensions to a head when Governor Swettenham appeared to reject US help very publicly over these very concerns. US intervention had never caused a diplomatic fracas before, but Americans' arrival in Jamaica would cost Swettenham his career as he triggered an incident that threatened a growing rapprochement between the two powers.

When the earthquake levelled Kingston on 14 January 1907, Swettenham sent a telegram to the British Minister in Havana requesting basic medical supplies such as bandages. In what would be a running theme throughout Swettenham's response to the quake, this request reflected a serious underestimation of just how dire the situation was in Kingston. *HMS Brilliant* and *HMS Indefatigable* were dispatched on 16 January 1907 but, just as in 1902, the Americans would reach the island first. The British Minister in Cuba knew that the British ships would not make it to Jamaica fast enough and so asked the US naval commander Admiral Evans for assistance. Evans ordered the dispatch of a wide range of medical supplies and foodstuffs under Rear Admiral Davis who arrived on 17 January. It should be noted that Swettenham was not informed of this change but the Foreign Office, which was informed, praised the minister's quick thinking.[67]

Davis brought the supplies but, upon landing in Kingston and assessing the chaotic situation, deemed it necessary to deploy a force of armed Navy bluejackets. Under his orders, their first task was to make their way to the

US consulate and protect it. Part way through this task, Davis encountered Kingston's chief of police who, in the absence of any British forces, implored Davis to send his men to the city's prison where it was said the prisoners were close to revolt. According to Davis, in the process of completing both of these objectives he encountered nothing but praise for his actions. Officials at the prison were extremely grateful and, in his own account of events, British naval officer on the *RMS Arno*, Aulay Macaulay, wrote of a pleasant meeting with Davis.[68] However, of all those officials Davis that met on the first day, the head of the US consulate was particularly effusive in his praise: he 'thanked god for [Davis'] arrival' and argued that this alone had stopped Kingston's white population from being 'murdered in their beds'.[69] While a hyperbolic statement implicitly based on racial prejudice, this quote also hints at one of the main complaints that many in Kingston would go on to have about Swettenham's response to the disaster: that he and an organised response were largely absent from most of the first week. An American doctor who landed Davis also remarked that upon their arrival at the city's hospital, some citizens thanked God that something would now be done about the situation.[70]

Two days after his arrival, Davis left. At great embarrassment to Britain, he had been personally asked to leave by Swettenham. As we have seen, never before had American intervention caused a diplomatic issue, even when they were as bold as they had been in 1902. What is more, America had already provided aid to Jamaica, albeit just financially, as recently as 1903 after a hurricane and at a time when the British Government refused to provide relief.[71] The particularly vexing part for Swettenham seems to have been what he considered an undermining of his authority, in that he was not aware of Davis' arrival and no permission was asked for him to land or send armed troops through Kingston. It must have stung all the more that many, not just from Kingston's American community, praised Davis' alacrity of action. There was a precedent for US forces landing without invitation to provide aid: in 1895, when fire threatened the Port of Spain, the capital of Trinidad, two hundred US sailors landed without a prior invitation and were thanked graciously by the governor. It was still generally considered protocol to ask permission to land, however, and the British had done this before sending medical personnel to Martinique in 1902.

Later explaining his actions to Davis in a letter, Swettenham, citing a recent event in New York where a mansion had been robbed by thieves, argued that had British vessels been in nearby waters they would not have been justified in intervening either.[72] Swettenham's argument is a weak one given that in this hypothetical situation New York was not in ruins and the robbery was an isolated incident in a city with functioning law enforcement.

He might have made mention of the fact that after the 1906 San Francisco earthquake, which was far more destructive than the 1907 Jamaican disaster, the US refused all British offers of aid.[73]

Swettenham's frustrations and the fallout from the incident reveal much about the state of the Caribbean, its relationship to Britain by the end of the long nineteenth century, and the motivations and anxieties that still underpinned British disaster response. Furthermore, with Britain providing an unprecedented amount of relief to Jamaica after the earthquake – a grant of £150,000 and a loan of £800,000 – understanding this event is also crucial to understanding that unprecedented relief package.

Swettenham's actions might seem an overreaction but, understood within the context of popular discussions about Jamaica and its relationship with the US they make more sense. Writing of his travels in the West Indies, James Froude noted that there were many Jamaicans who longed for America to annex the country. He also remarked on Jamaica's isolation from the rest of the Caribbean, noting that it was: 'farther off than Gibraltar from Southampton'.[74] The 1897 Royal Commission had also noted the colony's relative isolation, highlighting how little trade and contact there was between it and the other Caribbean colonies. Perhaps the clearest intimation of Jamaica's close relationship with the US came in the work of popular American travel writer, Frederick Ober. In his 1904 book, *Our West Indian Neighbours*, he suggested that had Cromwell not set down a flag in 1654, the US may have been the first to do so, as they simultaneously put one down on Puerto Rico. Speaking of the Jamaican population, he noted that while they were still loyal to Britain, they recognised the contiguity of the US market, 'as opposed to the inefficiency of … the little island 5000 miles away'.[75]

These lines of thinking are all present in the manner with which Swettenham defended his actions. Indeed, when communicating with the Colonial Office he revealed that it was Davis' desire to appear 'conspicuous in succouring Kingston' that particularly galled him.[76] Toward the end of his first day in Kingston, Davis did meet Swettenham at the tent in which he and his were camping outside the ruins of his governor's mansion. The meeting was cordial, but Davis noted in his report his opinion that all of Swettenham's advisors were essentially out of their depth, disorganised and unable to deal with the crisis at hand. Swettenham himself, he also noted, had been on horseback for the previous two days riding around Kingston and had had almost no sleep.

Later, Swettenham accompanied Davis back into Kingston by buggy. It was there, according to Davis, that Swettenham made clear that he did not need his assistance because he planned to make Kingston 'relieve itself and refuse outside aid'.[77] Davis would retrospectively argue that this case could only have been made because Swettenham did not understand just how bad the situation was in Kingston. For his part, Swettenham's argument to the Colonial Office reflected his desire to keep 'Jamaica dependent on the mother country'.[78] Clearly, Swettenham viewed the American landing as an implicit attempt to subvert British authority on the island, something his later more famous brother, Frank, would also argue when defending him.[79] While cordial with the high ranking Davis, Swettenham was, in the words of one American doctor who encountered him, utterly hostile to the extent he found himself at a loss as to how to explain or understand his attitude.[80]

In the eyes of Swettenham, Jamaica was British property, and the Americans therefore had no right to intervene without explicit permission. This was a difficult position to defend not least because of the exceptional circumstances but also because the British had withdrawn so much of their naval strength from the region. It is clear, however, that protocol took on a greater importance for Swettenham than stemming the loss of life in Kingston and providing continuing aid to its citizens.

Swettenham's actions reignited discussions about Jamaica's loyalty back in Britain that went on to have a significant impact on the relief provided to the island. The British press engaged in much grandstanding about the incident and tried to push Parliament to support significant relief for Jamaica. This passage from the *Globe* encapsulates the tone of the British press following the incident:

> we ought not to fritter away over the corrupt and lethargic officials of China and portion of our charity when our own kith and kin, who have stood by us for centuries, are wounded, homeless, and starving ... time and again Jamaica might have recovered her lost prosperity by seeking annexation to the United States ... against her own interests she has preferred the old flag: now it is time for us to show her that it is not for nothing that she is an integral part of the British Empire.[81]

Similarly, the *Westminster Gazette* argued that 'Jamaica is part of the British Empire, and it must be our pride to come to the rescue'.[82] More than ever before, providing disaster relief became a patriotic duty, not just an exercise in minimising expenditure at all costs.

The Americans embarrassed Swettenham because they had provided relief where he was doing everything he seemingly could to refuse aid and downplay the seriousness of the situation. In the week after the earthquake, uncertainty reigned over a potential relief package from Britain and thus, very typically, the initial relief effort was very constrained as the Relief Committee had no sense of how much money it could spend. This uncertainty and the scope of the initial effort could have been ameliorated by the considerable charitable aid that was being pledged to Jamaica. However, Swettenham turned down both C$50,000 raised by the Canadian Government and an even more impressive sum of £220,000 raised by subscription in Philadelphia and New York.[83] That these donations had been made at all, reflected an impressive desire to give to the people of Kingston. In the immediate wake of the earthquake, Swettenham had been a source of much misinformation about the earthquake, downplaying its scale, which meant that even five days after the disaster, British papers such as the *Daily Graphic* were reporting that only a 'sixteenth' of Kingston was damaged.[84] Such reports had a major impact on the speed with which relief arrived from Britain as the necessity of funds could not be established.[85] In a later report Davis noted this too, writing that 'the situation was far more grave, the calamity more sweeping, and the sanitary conditions in the city more menacing than I had been led to believe'.[86]

This also gets to the heart of the other key problem that Davis' arrival presented for Swettenham, it punctured his narrative and threatened his control of the situation. Davis had, on his arrival, also offered support to the city's struggling hospitals, not just in the form of the supplies he had brought with him but also his own medical staff. The offer was rebuffed by Swettenham.[87] Later writing that he was 'forced by the dictates of common humanity', Davis sidestepped Swettenham's refusal by constructing a makeshift hospital on the grounds of a Jesuit cottage and offering the services of his staff not to hospitals but to anyone in need. Swettenham would later callously refute Davis' justification for these actions, saying that it was 'no longer a question of any humanity: all the dead died days ago, and the work of giving them burial is merely of convenience'.[88] In response to a Sister of Mercy stationed at the Jesuit cottage who pleaded with Swettenham's wife to allow the Americans to stay, Lady Swettenham made it clear she was of the opinion that the Americans 'had behaved very badly and had violated the law, and orders'.[89] No doubt this was an opinion shared by Swettenham himself. In reality, people were desperate in Kingston. Its mayor, C.W. Tait, even risked Swettenham's ire by writing to Davis profusely apologising for the governor's conduct and asking him to reconsider his withdrawal. The account of a doctor who accompanied Davis remarks that as they withdrew through the city, they encountered at every turn, men and women of every class and race, all without food or shelter, begging for their aid.[90] The same doctor even recorded a meeting with a mounted officer, who was a personal member of the governor's staff, where the officer admitted, in relation to Swettenham's inaction 'unofficially I will say that I agree with you, it is an outrage'.[91]

Swettenham's own character seems to be much at fault throughout this incident; 1907 was not even the first time he had clashed with the Americans. In 1906, he had obstructed the recruitment of Jamaican labourers for the Panama Canal, much to the frustration of the American Isthmian Canal

Commission. His character and handling of the earthquake is also called into question in a confidential account by E.A. Hodges, a British intelligence officer stationed in Jamaica. The account was never made public because 'the facts contained [within it] are unpalatable to many and in some cases criticisms of are made expressing view and fact against persons and doctrines'.[92]

Hodges suggests that throughout his governorship Swettenham always stood aloof from the Jamaican community and that in many respects he was always a 'square peg in a round hole'.[93] Hodges further argues that this separation from the community not only carried through to Swettenham's response to the earthquake, but also led to him, in initial aftermath, avoiding many of his responsibilities as governor. Mr Browne, Swettenham's secretary, was actually the first official from the Government of Jamaica that Davis met, with the governor being absent. Hodges argued that Browne's indecision also partly sowed the seeds for the incident because he told Davis 'I think you may steam your ship up the harbour and lay off the prison and we shall see how matters stand'; in Hodges' words 'there was no definite decision'.[94] Davis, in Hodges' view, then took advantage of this quibbling, saying 'well these officials don't seem to be able to make up their minds'; an unnamed minor official replied 'well you had better act on your discretion'.[95] Those around him were clearly not prepared to decisively lead but they should not have had to: Swettenham was the governor, but he seems to have been keener to focus on protocol and underplay the damage of the earthquake at every turn.

Swettenham embodied all the worst aspects of British disaster responses in one, preoccupied with just about everything but providing relief to the people of Kingston. The Colonial Office would later reprimand him and all but force his resignation, tellingly not over his abject failure to help Kingston's population, but rather the tone of the written communications he exchanged with Davis during the crisis. The situation was an extreme embarrassment to Britain, which had been courting Roosevelt's friendship. This tells us much about how little importance was placed on relief: even into the twentieth century, it remained a secondary consideration.

In the aftermath of the earthquake and the incident between Swettenham and Davis, there were reports of small-scale Anglo-American tension through Kingston. Though disputed by Britons present at the time, a report in the *New York Tribune* suggested that US tourists were supposedly turned away from a makeshift hospital constructed on a docked ship at the Port of Kingston, and in other places refused help because of their nationality.[96]

In an irony that Swettenham himself cannot have been totally ignorant of, it was his handling of the disaster that sparked a pro-American backlash. As relayed by *The Times*, there was a gathering of Kingston's merchants on 30 January at which they made their disapproval of Swettenham's actions known and heaped praise on the prompt response of the US. They further criticised the British Colonial Government as 'out of touch with the community generally', 'remote' and 'unable to cope with the current situation'.[97]

On 24 January 1907 Swettenham requested his retirement; the request was accepted, with the official reason being 'old age'. Private Colonial Office documents detail an agreement, signed by Winston Churchill, to make this the official reason while making it clear that Swettenham was to be removed from post to save face with the US. Such must have been the stain on the Swettenham name that, following his death in obscurity in April 1933, his widow and brother wrote a joint note to the editor of *The Times* still seeking to justify his actions vis-à-vis Davis.[98]

Swettenham's response to Davis and the earthquake of 1907 were callous in the extreme: this much is clear. However, Swettenham and his actions did not occur in a vacuum, and his were simply at the far end of a continuum of British disaster response that rarely, if ever, put the relief of human suffering first. Negotiations over primarily expenditure but also social order and sovereignty played the most important roles in shaping British disaster responses. Relief, when it did arrive, was subject to little oversight and existed primarily to keep the otherwise unsustainable plantation system alive; African-Caribbean people were fed and housed on the basis that their labour was essential to its survival.

Notes

1 PP, HoC [Cd 1201], Joseph Chamberlain to Lord Mayor of London, 14 May 1902.
2 TNA, T1/4396 Long Papers, bundle 852, part 2: West Indies relief, Huskisson to Rautins, 6 November 1827.
3 TNA, CO 71/79, Macgregor to Glenelg, 22 August 1835; Macgregor to Glenelg, October (without dated day), 1835.
4 TNA, CO 31/51, Assembly, 23 August 1831.
5 TNA, T1/4395, undated note signed by 'A'.
6 HoC [182], Address to His Royal Highness the Prince Regent, from the Council and Assembly of St Vincent.
7 TNA, T1/4397, James Matthews to Colonial Office, 2 October 1834.
8 PP (1831), HoC [197], West Indies. Copies of despatches from Barbados, St Vincent and St Lucia, relating to the late hurricane in the West Indies, M.A. Boson to Viscount Goderich, 18 August 1831.
9 HoC [197], M.A. Boson to Viscount Goderich, 18 August 1831.
10 TNA, T1/4397, Schomberg to Governor in Chief Antigua, 29 September 1834.
11 TNA, CO 7/74, Charles Fitzroy to Lord Stanley, 20 February 1843.
12 TNA, T1/4397, Comptroller Office to Lords Council of HM Treasury, 20 January 1832.

13 HoC [182], Extract from a letter from Robert Sutherland (no date given).
14 TNA, T1/4397, Government House Roseau to the Governor in Chief Antigua, 2 October 1834.
15 TNA, T1/4397, Extract of letter from Peter Lesawy, 2 October 1834, enclosed in Colquhoun to Spring Rice, 14 November 1834.
16 TNA, T1/4397, Government House Roseau to Governor in Chief Antigua, 2 October 1834.
17 TNA, T1/4396, Petition signed by J. Woodhouse, Holquhoun, Haran, J.P Mayers, H.M. Paul, H. Bouverie, P. Cruickshanks, J. Mayal to Viscount Goderich, 20 November 1831.
18 HoC Deb 10 March 1899, vol. 68, cols 496–497.
19 Joanna Innes, 'The "Mixed Economy of Welfare" in Early Modern England: Assessments of the Options from Hale to Malthus (c. 1683–1803)', in *Charity, Self-Interest and Welfare in the English Past*, ed. by Martin Daunton (London: Taylor & Francis, 2005), p. 115.
20 Simon Winchester, *Krakatoa: The Day the World Exploded, August 27 1883* (London: Penguin Books, 2004), pp. 22–23.
21 HoC [C 9205], West Indies. Correspondence, Sir C.A. Moloney to Chamberlain, 15 September 1898.
22 Ibid.
23 Sarah Roddy, Julie-Marie Strange and Bertrand Taithe, *The Charity Market and Humanitarianism in Britain, 1870–1912* (London: Bloomsbury, 2019), pp. 131–135.
24 HoC [C 9205], West Indies. Correspondence, Colonial Office to the Lord Mayor of London, 16 September 1898.
25 Bonham C. Richardson, *The Caribbean in the Wider World, 1492–1992* (Cambridge: Cambridge University Press, 1992), p. 61.
26 Sarah Roddy, Julie-Marie Strange and Bertrand Taithe, *The Charity Market and Humanitarianism in Britain*, p. 140.
27 Shalom Goldman, *Zeal for Zion: Christians, Jews and the Idea of the Promised Land* (Chapel Hill, NC: University of North Carolina Press, 2010), p. 79.
28 TNA, CO 28/248, contains copy of pamphlet published by the Anti-Bounty league titled 'The Bitter Cry of the West Indies: Report of the Proceedings at the Conference at Bridgetown Sept. 3rd 1898 of Delegates Representing Jamaica, British Guiana, Trinidad, Barbados and Antigua to Consider the Attitude of H.M.'s Government in Regard to the Foreign State Sugar Bounties'.
29 *The Times*, G.E. Boyle, 'To the Editor of *The Times*', 6 October 1898.
30 *Morning Post*, 'The Accounts of the Hurricane which has Swept over the West Indies are Terrible in the Extreme, and Will Excite Universal Sympathy', 16 September, 1898, p. 4.
31 Bonham C. Richardson, *The Caribbean in the Wider World, 1492–1992*, p. 62.
32 PP, HoC [C 9205], West Indies. Correspondence, p. 86, Enclosure no. 1 in Moloney to Chamberlain, 7 December 1898; Ibid, p. 120, Enclosure no. 1 in Moloney to Chamberlain, 5 January, 1898.
33 HoC [C 9205], Sir C.A. Moloney to Chamberlain, 27 September 1898.

34 HoC [C 9205], West Indies. Correspondence, Enclosure no. 1 in Sir C.A. Moloney to Chamberlain, 5 January 1898.
35 Report of the West India Royal Commission published in *Bulletin of Miscellaneous Information* (Royal Botanic Gardens, Kew) 131 (1897), p. 376.
36 HoC [C 9205], West Indies. Correspondence, Enclosure no. 1 in Sir F. Fleming to Chamberlain, 25 November 1898.
37 Peter T. Marsh, *Joseph Chamberlain: Entrepreneur in Politics* (New Haven, CT: Yale University Press, 1994), pp. 408–409.
38 PP, HoC [Cd 1201], Joseph Chamberlain to Lord Mayor of London, 14 May 1902.
39 PP (1907), HoC [Cd 4586], Jamaica. Further Correspondence Relating to the Earthquake at Kingston, Jamaica, on 14 January 1907, p. 18. (Appendix II. Summaries of other Relief Assistance).
40 TNA, CO 263/4, Privy Council, 1 September 1812.
41 TNA, CO 31/51, Barbados, General Assembly, 15 November 1831.
42 TNA, T1/4397, Lyon to Goderich, 17 April 1832.
43 Frederick Purdy, 'The Statistics of the English Poor Rate before and since the Passage of the Poor Law Amendment Act', *Journal of the Statistical Society of London*, 23:3 (1860), p. 290.
44 TNA, T1/4395, Lionel Smith to Earl of Aberdeen, 7 May 1835.
45 Joseph Sturge, *The West Indies in 1837*, p. 144.
46 Ibid., p. 103.
47 TNA, T1/4397, Lockhart to Governor in Chief of Antigua, 29 January 1835.
48 Robert Baird, *Impressions and experiences of the West Indies and North America in 1849*, p. 54.
49 John F. Cherry and Krysta Ryzewski, *An Archaeological History of Montserrat in the West Indies* (Oxford: Oxbow Books, 2020), p. 135.
50 Natasha Lightfoot, 'Race, Class and Resistance: Emancipation and its Aftermath in Antigua, 1831–1858' (PhD thesis, New York University, 2007).
51 Henry Iles Woodcock, *A History of Tobago* (Ayr: Printed for the author, 1867), p. 112.
52 HoC Deb 25 July 1848, vol. 100, cols 835–836.
53 TNA, CO 23/185, Rawson to Earl of Carnarvon, 30 October 1866.
54 HoC [C 9205], Enclosure in Acting Governor Williams to Chamberlain, 21 December 1898.
55 John Hannigan, *Disasters Without Borders: The International Politics of Natural Disasters* (Cambridge: Polity Press, 2012), pp. 97–99.
56 Linda E. Emeruwa, 'The British West Indies, 1897–1902, with special reference to the implementation of the 1897 Royal Commission Report' (unpublished MPhil thesis, University of London, 1973), p. 98.
57 HoC [C 1786], Phipps to Marquess of Landsdowne, 13 August 1902.
58 Peter K. Newman, 'Canada's Role in the West Indian trade before 1912', in *Canada and the Commonwealth Caribbean*, ed. by Brian Douglas Tennyson (Lanham, MD: University Press of America, 1987), p. 112.
59 Ibid., p. 123.

60 HoC [Cd 1201], Enclosure no. 1 in Foreign Office to Colonial Office, 15 May 1902.
61 HoC [Cd 1201], Sanderson to the Marquess of Landsdowne, 2 June 1902.
62 PP, HoC [Cd 1201], p. 61, Enclosure no. 1 in Llewelyn to Chamberlain, telegram, 5 June 1902.
63 HoC [Cd 1201], Colonial Office to Foreign Office, 15 May 1902.
64 HoC [Cd 1201], Enclosure no. 3 in Hodgson to Chamberlain, 5 June 1902.
65 HoC [Cd 1201], Foreign Office to Colonial Office, 17 May 1902.
66 HoC [Cd 1201], Moloney to Chamberlain, telegram, 5 June 1902.
67 Williiam Tilchin, *Theodore Roosevelt and the British Empire: A Study in Presidential Statecraft* (New York: St. Martin's, 1997), p. 120.
68 Aulay Babington Macaulay, 'Account of Jamaican earthquake' 14 January 1907, p. 23.
69 Ibid.
70 Report of Howard E. Ames, Medical inspector sent to Rear Admiral C.H. Davis, 20 January 1907. Accessed online 21 March 2021, p. 2. https://bit.ly/3NAiTGa.
71 HoC [Cd 2238-15], No. 438. Jamaica. Report for 1903–4. Appendix VII, Supplement to the *Jamaica Gazette*. A Statement of the Receipts and Disbursements of the Jamaica Relief Fund; *Manchester Guardian*, 'The Cyclone in Jamaica: No Financial Assistance from the Imperial Government', 31 August 1903.
72 TNA, CO 884/9 (Jamaica) Colonial Office: Jamaica: Correspondence respecting Imperial aid to the West Indies, Alexander Swettenham to Sir Edward Grey, 14 February 1907.
73 TNA, FO 371/159, Political Departments: General Correspondence from 1906–1966, United States of America, Washington to Sir Edward Grey, 7 May 1906.
74 James Anthony Froude, *The English in the West Indies, or, the Bow of Ulysses*, p. 178.
75 Frederick Ober, *Our West Indian Neighbors; the Islands of the Caribbean Sea, 'America's Mediterranean': Their Picturesque Features, Fascinating History, and Attractions for the Traveler, Nature-Lover, Settler and Pleasure-Seeker* (New York: J. Pott & Company, 1904), p. 129.
76 TNA, CO 884/9, Swettenham to Grey, 14 February 1907.
77 TNA, CO 137/660, Enclosure no. 1 in Howard to Sir Edward Grey, 4 February 1907.
78 TNA, CO 884/9, Alexander Swettenham to Sir Edward Grey, 14 February 1907.
79 *The Times*, 'The Jamaica Incident', 10 July 1907.
80 Report of Howard E. Ames, Medical inspector sent to Rear Admiral C.H. Davis, p. 4.
81 *Globe*, 16 January 1907.
82 *Westminster Gazette*, 18 January 1907.
83 TNA, CO 137/662 (Jamaica) Colonial Office to Treasury, 22 April 1907.
84 *Daily Graphic*, 'The Cost of an Earthquake', 19 January 1907.
85 *Western Press*, 17 January 1907.
86 TNA, CO 137/660, Howard to Sir Edward Grey, 4 February 1907.

87 Ibid.
88 TNA, CO 137/660, Secretary of State to Governor, telegram, 22 January 1907.
89 Medical report, p. 8.
90 Report of Howard E. Ames, Medical Inspector, sent to Rear Admiral C.H. Davis, p. 4.
91 Ibid., p. 8.
92 Jamaica Archives and Records Department, E.A. Hodges, 'The Secret History of the Earthquake'.
93 Ibid.
94 Ibid.
95 Ibid.
96 *New York Tribune*, 'Refugees Indignant', 23 January 1907; Arthur J. Evans, 'Experiences During the Recent Earthquake in Jamaica', *British Medical Journal*, 1 (1907), p. 348.
97 *The Times*, 'The Colonial Government Condemned', 31 January 1907.
98 *The Times*, Frank Swettenham, 'The Jamaican Earthquake', 27 April 1933.

Conclusion

On 10 September 1934, the Belizean, Antonio Soberanis Gómez, and a number of other men and women who volunteered alongside him, did what the British colonial governments of the Caribbean had always been so reticent to do: they offered free and unconditional relief, providing food to their fellow citizens. They offered this aid ostensibly because of the economic depression and resulting unemployment that had engulfed British Honduras, but the date of their action also had a pointed multi-layered significance: 10 September was regarded by many in the colony, both citizens and colonial administrators, as the colony's 'birthday'. The date had been chosen in 1898 by a group of the colony's middle-class creole population looking to cement their claims to legislative rights by emphasising the role their white forefathers played in defending the colony from overwhelming numbers of Spanish forces on 10 September 1798. The battle of St George's Quay, as it became known, was said to be one in which all races worked together for the good of the British Empire and was thus marshalled by some as representing a longstanding legacy of racial harmony at the heart of the colony's history. This view would certainly go on to receive much direct criticism in the decades that followed its concoction but for Gómez and the others involved in the distribution of relief that day, 10 September had another more recent and painful resonance. Three years earlier, on 10 September the colony had been struck by a hurricane and storm surge that had almost entirely levelled its low-lying capital and, most devastatingly, killed an estimated 2,500 people in a single afternoon, which for a colony with a total population of 50,000, 15,000 of which lived in Belize City, was a devastating 16.6 per cent of the population. Indeed, many newspapers remarked on the fact that death had visited every family in the city.

The response from the colonial government showed that many of the characteristic aspects of British disaster response established in this book were still evident well into the twentieth century. In the wake of the devastation, colonial officials anticipated mass looting and civil unrest. As result, African-Caribbean movement was quickly controlled through the instigation of a curfew, and police officers and American soldiers from a recently arrived ship were deployed (this time in agreement with British officials), but besides some trifling incidents they were surprised by how little looting there was. This common instinct to control movement and heavily police the sufferers of the disaster was followed up by a similarly common attempt to coerce the local population back into labour. A proclamation issued by the governor, John Burdon, the week after the disaster made it illegal for able-bodied men to refuse to provide their labour to the government. Those who did refuse faced twelve months' imprisonment.[1] Owing to the Great Depression as well as a general lack of interest in the fate of British Honduras – long considered a peripheral colony in Britain – financial aid was meagre, and when it did arrive it was largely spent on instituting work-for-relief programmes. Again resonating with the disasters that preceded it, this one seems to have been exacerbated by colonial approaches to the management of land in Belize City. One of the areas where the storm surge that followed the hurricane reaped its highest number of casualties was Loyola Park, where, prior to the hurricane, miles and miles of swamp land had been cleared to build a Jesuit school, and where further deforestation and drainage efforts were still ongoing at the time of the storm.[2]

Perhaps where the actions of the British Honduran Government showed their greatest links with that which had gone before was in its approach to disaster preparedness or lack thereof. Despite being telegraphically connected to the US early-warning system, not only were very few Belizeans forewarned about the hurricane, but the government actively chose to go ahead with the celebrations planned for 10 September. Donald Fairweather, a local radio operator, first received warning of an approaching hurricane on 8 September. He informed the government and even stuck a written warning of the storm's approach on one of the main bridges in Belize City. Some minor adjustments were made to the day's celebrations on account of early morning rain but the majority of them went ahead. This would prove to be a tragic mistake. Much of the city's population was out in the open and enjoying themselves on the local beaches when a lull in the storm was broken by a storm surge estimated to be between fifteen and forty feet high, which swiftly drowned many. Perhaps most painfully, because many of the day's celebrations involved parades by children, they would overwhelmingly be the victims of the storm. We do not know exactly why, despite the early warning of the hurricane, the celebrations were still allowed to go ahead. Many, both in 1931 and in the years that followed, argued that it was because there was a general belief that the storm would not hit Belize: as with Jamaica in the seventeenth century, there was a belief, simply by virtue of there having been no hurricanes in the previous century, that the colony was immune to them. There had not been a hurricane in Belize in living memory and many thought the hurricane might come close but would simply head north up the Yucatan channel and never make landfall. Even when the hurricane did hit, this lack of generational memory almost certainly increased the number of casualties; eyewitness accounts detail that a large number of people headed even closer to the shoreline before the storm surge, intrigued by the retreat of the sea and seeing it as a novelty rather than a warning sign – which some of the colony's more well-travelled fishermen did.

There is also the question around the celebrations themselves: why were they not called off even as a precaution? According to Governor Burdon's own reflections, a discussion does appear to have taken place between him and the rest of the British Honduran Government, but we will never know the exact reason, even if it was written down, as many of the documents from that period were destroyed by the hurricane itself and later by a second hurricane in 1961. The fact that the colony had not experienced a hurricane for a century certainly played its part. However, I think it important that we also consider Governor Burdon's deeply personal links with the colony's 'birthday' celebrations. In his 1927 book, *A Brief Sketch of British Honduras*, as Anne Macpherson puts it, he 'spun a heroic Rule Britannia interpretation of 1798 that reinforced the myths of benign slavery and racial deference'.[3] Reflecting later on the hurricane of 1931, Burdon himself said that the celebrations were important because they represented 'very real, living and deep-seated loyalty to King and Empire'.[4]

Belize's economy, based primarily on logging and the export of logging-adjacent products such as chicle, had been in decline since the late 1920s, and with the advent of the Great Depression was bracing for a further drop. Prior to the celebrations of 1931, there were rumours that the festivities would have to be cancelled because merchants were unwilling to participate due to their deteriorating circumstances, and they were almost postponed. For a man who clearly placed such great stock in the celebrations and their role in engendering racial hierarchy, it is no great reach to imagine that in the economic circumstances, with the potential for unrest, Burdon was keener than ever that 10 September be honoured. This line of argument is further strengthened by the fact that the eyewitness account of Guy Pilling, British Honduras' Colonial Secretary, suggests that Burdon only informed 'officials and leading members of the community' at the ceremony that a hurricane warning had been received on 8 September.[5] In confidential correspondence, those working at the American consulate in Belize expressed their shock back to Washington D.C. that so little was done to prepare for the hurricane, and asking for future warnings to be sent directly to them as well as the colony, thus allowing them to make their own preparations.[6] In the long run, American support in the form of troops deployed to keep 'order' and supplies delivered via military ships and Pan American Airways kept the colony from starving. The domestic British response was far tougher, with Parliament offering an aid package only in return for complete control of the colony's finances and, when that offer was refused, reducing the overall amount offered to the colony. The aid itself excluded most of the working people of Belize City and offered money to the small middle class, which most would struggle to pay back, meaning that hardship in the colony spiralled. The hurricane and the 'relief' offered sent British Honduras into a precipitous decline.

These events offer an interesting, coda to this history of disasters in the British Caribbean, because while they are connected to those disasters considered above through many threads of continuity, they also represented a break from what had gone before. Organisations from outside the British colonial apparatus had aided in the wake of disaster previously; the Red Cross, for example, had helped in Jamaica before Swettenham had dismissed it along with the Americans. In 1931, Belize saw the deployment of the Vivian Seay's Black Cross Nurses, who, affiliated with the United Negro Improvement Association, were the first home-grown, black, political group aiding in a British relief effort. Those who fled from Belize City were also welcomed in the nearby Stann Creek district by the Carib International Society, which worked to provide the refugees with food, shelter, and clothing.[7] This, followed by the fact that Soberanis Gómez and the group that would become the Labourers and Unemployed Association would go on to feed many of those still struggling three years after the hurricane, shows us that a new form of response outside of British control was possible and started to emerge in tandem with the growth of a new political consciousness in the region. The British response and the counter-response of the Belizean people would spur political change that would later sweep the colony, and this is what makes the hurricane of 1931 stand out from what had gone before it.

One of the central debates in the study of disaster is about whether they produce states of exception, or do they produce circumstances in which power is challenged and society is permanently changed? While 1931 provides us with a clear, if gradual, example of permanent political change emerging from disaster, disasters between the years 1812 and 1907 provide examples that do not neatly conform to this binary. In some respects, the political change that could have emerged from these events was forestalled because governors, planters and colonial officials were all desperate to keep Caribbean society in stasis: they could not imagine it without plantations and its characteristically strict racial hierarchy. Even after slavery, disasters only seemed to create small pockets of exception where resistance briefly emerged but wholesale political challenge never took hold. Movement and freedoms were restricted but while never making it explicit, the British were limited in the actions they could take by the demographic imbalances they had created. As the minority, they were forced to negotiate their approach because they needed the African-Caribbean population and their labour to continue the entire enterprise of Caribbean colonisation and, at the very least, rebuild after disaster. So, while wanting to restrict relief and expenditure, they could not entirely do so, and had to provide something. They felt keenly that hardship could provoke a challenge to their authority. Thus they had to negotiate a balancing act of providing the bare necessities to allow for the survival of the African-Caribbean population, and staying committed to limiting expenditure, without giving the impression to the non-white population that the orientation of government had fundamentally changed. They certainly did not want to fuel the idea that the government was now going to provide extensive charitable aid, and we have seen that many governors worked hard not only to impress this upon the labouring population but also to curtail the free distribution of aid as quickly as possible.

This approach developed into a more codified form, particularly after the end of slavery, as we see the influence of British law reforms begin to transmit across the Atlantic. Multiple governors spoke of the 'able-bodied' and turned to labour tests as a means to control the distribution of aid. Like those involved with the provision of poor relief in Britain, they above all wanted to avoid inculcating what they saw as a 'culture of dependency'. These similarities reflect the fact that those in elite British circles had a broadly common notion of how to mediate the relationship between state and dependant. However, this understanding could not be entirely translated to the socio-political context of the Caribbean and especially not in the context of disaster. Governors had to work on a more ad-hoc basis, responding to the challenges of circumstance in a way that sets the process of relief in the Caribbean apart from both Britain and other notable cases of disaster relief such as that in India, where crises such as famines unfolded slowly, and officials were in part insulated from being directly affected.

Through the long nineteenth century, disaster and the responses that followed from the British colonial apparatus give us much insight into the tensions and continuities of Caribbean life. As we have seen, colonial elites and planters understood that being a minority population made their position weak, particularly in the flux and chaos created by disaster. There was some unspoken understanding about the level of force that could be used in such a delicate situation. Evidently, when big rebellions did break out, white elites did not hesitate to retaliate with overwhelming force – the response to the 1865 Morant Bay Rebellion in Jamaica provides us with a clear example of the violence they were prepared to use – but disasters seemed to give them pause. With the physical manifestations of their power typically in ruins, they often turned to coercion as opposed to outright violence. Ironically, for a regime obsessed with limiting dependence and the expansion of governmental responsibility, the circumstances presented by disaster allowed them to use increased dependency to their advantage. Though not always entirely successful, as some African-Caribbean people simply shunned public works programmes or found ways to game the relief being offered, conditional relief had a good track record of achieving both the racial and ideological goals of many colonial officials seeking to restore order.

In this period, we can also see how the centrality of the plantation worsened disaster outcomes throughout this period, and that the British practised a form of 'relief' which preserved this highly damaging form of agriculture above all. Even when there was some enthusiasm for tackling economic issues in the region, as with the 1897 Royal Commission and Chamberlain, there was never the imagination to develop the Caribbean beyond its role as a 'sugar bowl', nor to rethink how it could be made more resilient to the annual natural hazards it faced. I would argue that because of the racial demography of British Caribbean, disasters became accepted as a part of the danger of colonising the region. Had the region been more valuable to Britain or been home to larger white populations, things may have been different. Instead, disasters and the limited response to them only served to further the decline of the colonies.

Truly disaster-resistant colonies would have been antithetical to the dependency on which the colonial project was built. Disaster resilience would have made manifest a level of autonomy that would have weakened the ties between Britain and its colonies. That much is clear in loans being the primary means through which financial assistance was given. Disaster served to increase obligations from the colony to the metropole over lengthy periods of time, and this dynamic is most clearly expressed in the fumbling and strikingly callous response of Swettenham in 1907. In his buggy ride with Rear Admiral Davis, he made the implicit nature of British relief explicit; Kingston was to recover on its own and to that end he was refusing outside aid external to the British Empire. He wanted to keep the colony dependent on the mother country. Granted, Swettenham lost his job for his actions, but that was because he was a man out of time, not realising that the geopolitical situation had changed significantly around him and overtaken by technology that exposed his failings and the backlash publicly. Even though Britain sought to defuse the 'incident' by pushing Swettenham into early retirement, these facts do not change the underlying principle of British relief: Jamaica would go on to be saddled with thousands of pounds of British debt to pay for the earthquake and the rebuilding. For nations that remain some of the most indebted in the world, this dynamic is one that sadly still plays out, though to an even sharper degree in the modern world. As Naomi Klein showed in her book, *The Shock Doctrine*, post-disaster financial assistance from international financial institutions is often designed to allow the lender long-term budgetary control.

The decline of the British Caribbean continued well beyond 1907 and through to the unrest of the 1930s, and there remains much to be written about where disaster fits into the story of the Caribbean in the twentieth century and beyond. Avenues for fruitful exploration are both individual events and long-term trends. For example, lessons were learned in Belize in advance of and during Hurricane Hattie in 1961, as the casualty numbers were far lower, but the hurricane was said to be far stronger. In the longer term, I think there could be much work done on unearthing the legacy of British responses to disaster in the region. At the very least, the export-focused economy conditioned by British colonialism has left behind economies that remain import dependent, leaving the region at the mercy of price fluctuations and supply chains, both of which continue to cause pain in the region. During an assessment of future pandemic vulnerability conducted by the United Nations during the COVID-19 pandemic which began in 2019, import dependence was identified as one of the region's biggest vulnerabilities.

Going forward in a warming world, the Caribbean sadly is to be on the frontline of a rising number of extreme weather events, and import dependence coupled with historic deforestation and astronomical indebtedness look set to create a toxic mix that could create many more disasters. It seems to me that as questions around reparations for slavery continue to be raised, one dimension of that debate yet to be fully considered is the ecological damage caused by colonialism. In the Caribbean, the legacy of the plantation is plain to see not just in the tourist resorts that have replaced them but also in the ongoing frequency of soil erosion and landslides. Considering that the enterprise which wrought this damage was a catalyst for the fossil fuel revolution that continues to heat the planet and now threatens the Caribbean so extensively, it would seem that compensation for this ecological damage is not just an ethical necessity but also one to protect future generations of Caribbean people. Throughout the history contained within this book, informal and formal negotiations were the main way in which societies attempted to move beyond and build back from disaster. As the region looks toward the future, though freedom may thankfully be resolved as a permanent part of Caribbean life, disaster relief and development look likely to be continuing sites of negotiation as it grapples with the best way forward in the face of a hostile future.

Notes

1 TNA, CO 127/26 (British Honduras, later Belize) Government Gazettes, 'An Ordinance to Provide Emergency Power', 19 September 1931.

2 Ernest E. Cain, *Cyclone! Being an Illustrated Official Record of the Hurricane and Tidal Wave which Destroyed The City of Belize om the Colony's Birthday, 10th September 1931* (London: Arthur H. Stockwell, 1934), p. 14.
3 Anne Macpherson, *From Colony to Nation: Women Activists and the Gendering of Politics in Belize, 1912–82* (Lincoln: University of Nebraska Press, 2007), p. 85.
4 Sir John Burdon, 'Hurricane in British Honduras', *Blackwood's Magazine*, December 1931.
5 TNA, CO 123/335 (British Honduras) Original Correspondence. Hurricane relief fund.
6 National Archives and Records Administration, R8 84, Vol. 99, Confidential telegram from American Consulate Belize, British Honduras to Secretary of State, Washington D.C., 6 October 1931.
7 Ernest E. Cain, *Cyclone!*, pp. 125–128.

Bibliography

Primary sources

Printed manuscripts

A captain in the Royal Navy, *The Seaman's Practical Guide, for Barbadoes and the Leeward Islands; with observations on the islands from Blanco to the Rocas on the Coast of La Guayra* (London: Smith, Elder & Co. Cornhill, 1832)

A Report of a Committee of the Council of Barbadoes, appointed to inquire into the actual condition of the slaves in this island (London: W. Sior, 1824)

Agutter, William, *The Abolition of the Slave Trade Considered in a Religious Point of View. A Sermon Preached before the Corporation of the City of Oxford, at St. Martin's Church, On Sunday, February 3, 1788* (London: Printed for J.F. and C. Rivington, St. Paul's Church-yard; and G. Philips, George-yard, Lombard Street., 1788)

Baird, Robert, *Impressions and experiences of the West Indies and North America in 1849* (Philadelphia, PA: Lea & Blanchard, 1850)

Bayley, F.W.N., *Four years' residence in the West Indies* (London: W. Kidd, 1830)

Beckford, William, *A Descriptive Account of the Island of Jamaica: With remarks upon the Cultivation of the Sugar-Cane, throughout the different Seasons of the Year, and chiefly considered in Picturesque Point of View; Also Observations and Reflections upon what would probably be the Consequences of an Abolition of the Slave-Trade, and of the Emancipation of the Slaves*, Vol. I (London: T. and J. Egerton, 1790)

Brandreth, Henry Rowland, 'Memorandum relative to a System of Barracks for the West Indies, recommended by Colonel Sir C.F. Smith, C.B., R.E., and approved by the Master-General and Board of Ordnance', *Papers on Subjects Connected with the Duties of the Corps of the Royal Engineers*, Vol. II (1838) 239–246

Bruce, Sir Charles, *Milestones on my long journey: memories of a colonial governor* (Glasgow: Robert Maclehose, 1917)

Burdon, Sir John, 'Hurricane in British Honduras', *Blackwood's Magazine*, December 1931.

Cain, Ernest E., *Cyclone! Being an Illustrated Official Record of the Hurricane and Tidal Wave which Destroyed The City of Belize om the Colony's Birthday, 10th September 1931* (London: Arthur H. Stockwell, 1934)

Carmichael, A.C., *Tales of a Grandmother* (London: Richard Bentley, 1841)
Chenery, C.L., 'The Jamaican Earthquake', reprinted from the *Barbados Advocate*, 23, 24, 25 January 1907
Coleridge, Henry Nelson, *Six Months in the West Indies, in 1825* (London: J. Murray, 1826)
Colquhoun, Patrick, *A Treatise on the Wealth, Power, and Resources of the British Empire* (London: J. Mawman, 1814)
Corbin, William, *A Sermon Preached at Kings Town in Jamaica Upon the 7th of June, Being the Anniversary Fast for That Dreadful Earth-Quake Which Happened There in the Year 1692* (New York: William Bradford, 1703)
Cowper, William, *Poetical Works of William Cowper*, Vol. I (London, Boston: Little, Brown & Company, John W. Parker and Son, 1854)
Dessalles, Pierre, *Sugar and Slavery, Family and Race: The Letters and Diary of Pierre Dessalles, Planter in Martinique, 1808–1856*, ed. by Elborg Forster and Robert Forster (Baltimore, MD: Johns Hopkins University Press, 1996)
Doolittle, Samuel, *A Sermon Preached upon the Late Earthquake, Which Happen'd in London, And Other Places On the Eighth of September, 1692* (London: Printed by J.R. for J. Salusbury, at the Rising-Sun near the Royal Exchange in Cornhill, 1692)
Editor of *The West Indian*, *Account of the Fatal Hurricane by Which Barbados Suffered in August 1831* (Barbados: Printed for Samuel Hyde, 1831)
Edwards, Bryan, *The history, civil and commercial, of the British colonies in the West Indies*, Vol. II (London: John Stockdale, 1801)
Evans, Arthur J., 'Experiences During the Recent Earthquake in Jamaica', *British Medical Journal*, 1 (1907), p. 348
Froude, James Anthony, *English Seamen: In The Sixteenth Century: Lectures Delivered At Oxford Easter Terms 1893–4* (London: Longmans, Green and Co., 1896)
Froude, James Anthony, *The English in the West Indies, or, the Bow of Ulysses* (London: Longmans, Green and Co., 1888)
Gardner, William James, *A History of Jamaica from Its Discovery by Christopher Columbus to the Present Time* (London: Elliot Stock, 1873)
Gurney, Joseph John, *A winter in the West Indies, described in familiar letters to Henry Clay of Kentucky* (London: J. Murray, 1840)
Hughes, Griffith, *The Natural History of Barbados in Ten Books* (London: Printed for the author, 1750)
Ligon, Richard, *A True and Exact History of the Island of Barbados*, ed. by David Smith (e-text, 2014, 5th edition)
Madden, Richard Robert, *A Twelvemonth's Residence in the West Indies; During the Transition from Slavery to Apprenticeship; With Incidental Notices of the State of Society*, Vol. 1 (London: James Cochrane and Co., 1835)
Martin, Robert Montgomery, *History of the West Indies: Comprising Jamaica, Honduras, Trinidad, Tobago Grenada, The Bahamas, and the Virgin Isles* (London: Whittaker & Co., 1836)
McKinnen, Daniel, *A Tour Through the British West Indies, in the Years 1802 and 1803: Giving a Particular Account of the Bahama Islands* (London: J. White, 1084)

Nugent, Maria, *Lady Nugent's Journal of Her Residence in Jamaica from 1801 to 1805*, ed. by Philip Wright (Kingston: The University of the West Indies Press, 2002)

Ober, Frederick A., *Our West Indian Neighbours: The Islands of the Caribbean Sea, 'America's Mediterranean'* (New York: J. Pott & Company, 1904)

The Parliamentary History of England, from the Earliest Period to the year 1803, Vol. XV (London: T.C. Hansard, 1831)

Piddington, Henry, 'Researches on the Gale and Hurricane in the Bengal on the 3rd, 4th and 5th of June, 1839; being a first memoir with reference to the theory of the Law of Storms in India', *Asiatic Society of Bengal*, Vol. III (1838), pp. 631–650

Prince, Nancy, *The West Indies: Being a description of the islands, progress of Christianity, education and liberty among the colored population generally* (Boston: Dow & Jackson, 1841)

Purdy, Frederick, 'The Statistics of the English Poor Rate before and since the Passage of the Poor Law Amendment Act', *Journal of the Statistical Society of London*, 23:3 (1860) 286–329

Rawson, Rawson W., *Report on the Bahamas' Hurricane of October 1866, with a description of the City of Nassau* (Nassau: E.C. Moseley, 1866)

Reid, William, 'On Hurricanes', *Papers on Subjects Connected with the Duties of the Corps of the Royal Engineers*, Vol. 2 (1838), pp. 146–151

Report of the Mauritius Royal Commission, 1909: Presented to Both Houses of Parliaments by Command of His Majesty, June 1910, Vol. II (London: H.M. Stationery Office, 1920)

Report of the West India Royal Commission published in *Bulletin of Miscellaneous Information* (Royal Botanic Gardens, Kew) 131 (1897) pp. 339–402

Schomburgk, Sir Robert Hermann, *The History of Barbados: Comprising a Geographical and Statistical Description of the Island, a Sketch of the Historical Events Since the Settlement, and an Account of Its Geology and Natural Productions* (London: Frank Cass, 1848)

Shephard, Charles, *An Historical Account of the Island of Saint Vincent* (London: W. Nicol, 1831)

Sloane, Hans, 'A Letter from Hans Sloane, M.D. and S.R.S. with Several Accounts of the Earthquakes in Peru October the 20th 1687. And at Jamaica, February 19th. 1687/8 and June the 7th. 1692', *Philosophical Transactions*, 209 (1694), pp. 78–100

Sturge, Joseph, *The West Indies in 1837: Being the journal of a visit to Antigua, Montserrat, Dominica, St Lucia, Barbados, and Jamaica; undertaken for the purpose of ascertaining the actual condition of the negro population of those islands* (London: Hamilton, Adams & Co, 1838)

Thome, James Armstrong and Kimball, Joseph Horace, *Emancipation in the West Indies: A six months' tour in Antigua, Barbadoes, and Jamaica in the year 1837* (Philadelphia, PA: The American Anti-Slavery Society, 1838)

Tobago Hurricane of 1847: Papers relative to the Hurricane in Tobago Presented to Both Houses of Parliament by Command of Her Majesty Queen Victoria, on April 11, 1848. Historical Documents of Trinidad and Tobago No. 3 (Port of Spain: Government Printer, 1966)

Ward, Edward, *A Trip to Jamaica: With a True Character of the People and Island* (London: 1698)

Ware, Lewis S., *The Sugar Beet: Including a History of the Beet Sugar Industry in Europe, Varieties of the Sugar Beet, Examination, Soils, Tillage, Seeds and Sowing, Yield and Cost of Cultivation, Harvesting, Transportation, Conservation, Feeding Qualities of the Beet and of the Pulp, Etc* (Philadelphia, PA: Henry Baird & Co, 1880)

Williams, James, *A Narrative of Events since the First of August, 1834*, ed. by Diana Paton (Durham: Durham University Press, 2001)

Woodcock, Henry Iles, *A History of Tobago* (Ayr: Printed for the author, 1867)

Calendar of State Papers

Calendar of State Papers Colonial, America and West Indies, xiii, 1689–92, ed. by J.W. Fortescue (London: Eyre and Spottiswoode, 1901), British History Online. Accessed 21 January 2021, https://bit.ly/3acKAGp

Church Missionary Society

Letter by M. Jackson of the Barbados Bible Society to the British Bible Society, 15 August 1831, Accessed online 23 March 2021, Adam Matthew Digital, Church Missionary Society Archive

Hansard

HoC Deb 23 January 1781, vol. 1
HoC, Deb 16 March 1807, vol. 9 cols 114–140
HoC Deb 22 January 1812, vol. 21
HoC Deb 25 July 1848, vol. 100, cols 835–836
HoC Deb 10 March 1899, vol. 68, cols 496–497

Jamaican Archives and Records Department

IB/5/76/4/56, E.A. Hodges, 'The Secret History of the Earthquake'

Jamaican National Library

7/12/115, Charles Taylor, letter sent to the *Daily Gleaner*, 28 November 1959

National Archives Records Administration

R8 84, Vol. 99, Consular Posts, Belize British Honduras

The National Archives UK

FO 371/159, Political Departments: General Correspondence from 1906–66, United States of America

CO 884/9 (Jamaica) Colonial Office: Jamaica: Correspondence respecting Imperial aid to the West Indies
CO 71/79 (Dominica) Correspondence, Original – Secretary of State: Despatches; Offices and Individuals
CO 71/78 (Dominica) Correspondence, Original – Secretary of State: Despatches; Offices and Individuals
CO 7/74 (Antigua & Montserrat), Correspondence, Original – Secretary of State: Despatches
CO 7/42, Correspondence, Original – Secretary of State
CO 37/100 (Bermuda) Despatches from Sir Stephen Remnant Chapman (items 1–17) and Sir William Reid (35 onwards), successive governors of Bermuda
CO 31/51 (Barbados) Sessional Papers, Assembly
CO 28/251 (Barbados) Letters received from various government offices (departments), other organisations and individuals relating to Barbados
CO 28/248 (Barbados) Colonial Office: Letters received from various government offices
CO 28/107 (Barbados) Despatches from Sir James Lyon, Governor of Barbados
CO 263/4 (St Vincent) Legislative Council; Privy Council
CO 262/11 (St Vincent) MS. Nos. 206–253 Return of the population of the island of St Vincent
CO 260/3 (St Vincent) Correspondence, Original – Secretary of State
CO 260/29 (St Vincent) Correspondence, Original – Secretary of State
CO 23/185 (Bahamas) Correspondence, Original – Secretary of State: Despatches
CO 23/185 (Bahamas) Correspondence, Original – Secretary of State
CO 137/662 (Jamaica) Letters from individuals on matters relating Jamaica
CO 137/661 (Jamaica) Letters from the Foreign Office (March to December 1907) and 'miscellaneous offices' (Government departments and other organisations) relating to Jamaica
CO 137/660 (Jamaica) Letters from the Foreign Office (March to December 1907) and 'miscellaneous offices'
CO 127/26 (British Honduras, later Belize), Government Gazettes
CO 123/335 (British Honduras) Original Correspondence. Hurricane relief fund
T1 4395 Long Papers, bundle 852, part 1: West Indies Relief
T1 4396 Long Papers, bundle 852, part 2: West Indies Relief
T1 4397 Long Papers, bundle 852, part 3: West Indies Relief

The National Library of Scotland

Ms 6, 396, Stuart Rothsey Papers, Stuart Rothsey, 'Account of the Eruption at St Vincent in May 1812 [&] its effects on Barbadoes'

Newspapers

Antigua Weekly Register
Baptist Magazine

Barbados Advocate
Barbados Globe and Colonial Advocate
Caledonian Mercury
Daily Gleaner
Daily Graphic
Dominica Colonist
Lebanon Daily News
Leslie's Weekly
Manchester Guardian
New York Tribune
Royal St Vincent Gazette
The Sentry
St Lucia Gazette
The Times
Western Press

Parliamentary Papers

HoC [197], West Indies. Copies of despatches from Barbados, St Vincent and St Lucia, relating to the late hurricane in the West Indies. 1831

HoC [Cd 3560], Jamaica. Correspondence Relating to the Earthquake at Kingston, Jamaica, on 14th January 1907

HoC [182], St Vincent. Report from committee on petition of persons interested in estates in the island of St Vincent, p. 11, Memorial of several merchants in London, on behalf of several proprietors of Estates in the Charaib country, in the island of St Vincent. 1812–13

HoC [441], Antigua. Papers Relative to the Earthquake in the West Indies, Antigua. 1843

HoC [715], Lighthouse (Barbadoes). 1847

HoC [C 9205], West Indies. Correspondence relating to the hurricane on 10th–12th September, 1898, and the relief of the distress caused thereby

HoC [Cd 2238-15], No. 438. Jamaica. Report for 1903–4. Appendix VII, Supplement to the 'Jamaica Gazette'. A Statement of the Receipts and Disbursements of the Jamaica Relief Fund

HoC [Cd 1201], St Vincent. Correspondence relating to the Volcanic Eruptions in St Vincent and Martinique in May 1902

HoC [Cd 1783], West Indies. Further correspondence relating to the volcanic eruptions in St Vincent & Martinique, in 1902 & 1903

HoC [Cd 4586], Jamaica. Further Correspondence Relating to the Earthquake at Kingston, Jamaica, on 14th January 1907

Theodore Roosevelt Digital Library

Report of Howard E. Ames, Medical inspector sent to Rear Admiral C.H. Davis, 20 January 1907. Accessed online 21 March 2021, https://bit.ly/3NAiTGa

Theodore Roosevelt Papers. Library of Congress Manuscript Division, Report from C.H. Davis to Victor Howard Metcalf. Accessed online 21 March 2021, https://bit.ly/3PFGsio

University of Pittsburgh, Darlington Autograph Files

DAR.1925.07, Box 4, Folder 60, Aulay Babington Macaulay, 'Account of Jamaican earthquake' 14 January 1907, pp. 6–7, accessed on line 24 May 2021, https://bit.ly/38ELYS0

Virginia Historical Society

Virginia Historical Society, Keane Family Papers, Mss 1 K197 a23, Hugh Perry Keane, Diary, 2–4 May 1812

Secondary sources

Ashman, Patricia, 'Disraeli, Benjamin (Earl of Beaconsfield)', *Historical Dictionary of the British Empire*, Vol. II, ed. by James Stuart Olson and Robert Shadle (Santa Barbara: Greenwood Press, 1996) 371–373

Bankoff, Greg, 'Time is of the Essence: Disasters, Vulnerability and History', *International Journal of Mass Emergencies and Disasters*, 22:3 (2004) 23–42

Barker, David and McGregor, Duncan F.M., *Environment and Development in the Caribbean: Geographical Perspectives* (Kingston: The University of the West Indies Press, 1995)

Barnett, Michael, *Empire of Humanity: A History of Humanitarianism* (Ithaca, NY: Cornell University Press, 2011)

Bavel, Bas van et al., *Disasters and History: The Vulnerability and Resilience of Past Societies* (Cambridge: Cambridge University Press, 2020)

Beauchamp, Ken, *A History of Telegraphy* (London: The Institute of Engineering and Technology)

Beckles, Hilary, 'Social and Political Control in the Slave Society', in *General History of the Caribbean: The Slave Societies of the Caribbean*, ed. by Franklin W. Knight (London: UNESCO, 1997) 194–221

Blouet, Olwyn Mary, 'Sir William Reid, F.R.S., 1791–1858: Governor of Bermuda, Barbados and Malta', *Notes and Records of the Royal Society of London article*, 40:2 (1986) 169–191

Boerner, Peter, *Goethe* (London: Haus Publishing, 2005)

Boyd, Charles W. (ed.), *Mr Chamberlain's Speeches*, Vol. II (London: Constable and Company, 1914)

Brown, Vincent, *The Reaper's Garden: Death and Power in the World of Atlantic Slavery* (Cambridge, MA: Harvard University Press, 2008)

Blyth, C., 'Piddington, Henry (1797–1858), meteorologist', *Oxford Dictionary of National Biography*

Cherry, John F. and Ryzewski, Krysta, *An Archaeological History of Montserrat in the West Indies* (Oxford: Oxbow Books, 2020)

Clouard, Valérie, Roger, Jean and Moizan, Emmanuel, 'Tsunami Deposits in Martinique Related to the 1755 Lisbon Earthquake', *Natural Hazards and Earth System Sciences Discussions* (2017) 1–13

Coen, Deborah R., *The Earthquake Observers: Disaster Science from Lisbon to Richter* (Chicago, IL: University of Chicago Press, 2012)

Connors, Michael, *Caribbean Houses: History, Style, and Architecture* (New York: Rizzoli, 2009)

Craton, Michael, 'Proto-Peasant Revolts? The Late Slave Rebellions in the British West Indies 1816–1832', *Past & Present*, 85 (1979) 99–125

Craton, Michael, 'Reluctant Creoles: The Planters' World in the British West Indies', in *Strangers Within the Realm: Cultural Margins of the First British Empire*, ed. by Bernard Bailyn and Philip D. Morgan (Williamsburg: University of North Carolina Press, 1991) 314–362

Craton, Michael, *Testing the Chains: Resistance to Slavery in the British West Indies* (New York: Cornell University Press, 2009)

Davis, Mike, *Late Victorian Holocausts: El Nino, Famines and the Making of the Third World* (London: Verso, 2000)

Delle, James A., *The Colonial Caribbean: Landscapes of Power in Jamaica's Plantation System* (Cambridge: Cambridge University Press, 2014)

DeLoughrey, Elizabeth 'Yam, Roots, and Rot: Allegories of the Provision Grounds', *Small Axe*, 15:1 (2011) 58–75

Eastwood, David, *Government and Community in the English Provinces, 1700–1870* (New York: St. Martin's Press, 1997)

Emlen, Rob, 'The Great Gale of 1815: Artifactual Evidence of Rhode Island's First Hurricane', *Rhode Island History*, 48:2 (1990) 51–61

Ghosh, Tirthanker, 'Historicizing Earthquake and Cyclones: Evolution of Geology and Cyclonology in Colonial India', *Indian Historical Review*, 46:1 (2019) 22–40

Goldman, Shalom, *Zeal for Zion: Christians, Jews and the Idea of the Promised Land* (Chapel Hill, NC: University of North Carolina Press, 2010)

Gragg, Larry, *'Englishmen Transplanted': The English Colonization of Barbados 1627–1660* (Oxford, New York: Oxford University Press, 2003)

Grove, Richard, 'The British Empire and the Origins of Forest Conservation in the Eastern Caribbean 1700–1800', in *Islands, Forests and Gardens in the Caribbean: Conservation and Conflict in Environmental History*, ed. by Robert S. Anderson, Richard Grove and Karis Hiebert (Oxford: Macmillan Education, 2006) 132–173

Hall, Catherine, *Legacies of British Slave-Ownership* (Cambridge: Cambridge University Press, 2014)

Handler, Jerome S., 'Freedmen and Slaves in the Barbados Militia', *Journal of Caribbean History*, 19 (1984) 1–25

Hannigan, John, *Disasters Without Borders: The International Politics of Natural Disasters* (Cambridge: Polity Press, 2012)

Hardwick, Joseph and Williamson, Philip, 'Special Worship in the British Empire: From the Seventeenth to the Twentieth Centuries', *Studies in Church History*, 54 (2018) 260–280

Harris, Dawn P., *Punishing the Black Body: Marking Social and Racial Structures in Barbados and Jamaica* (Athens, GA: University of Georgia Press, 2017)

Harrison, John, 'The Colonial Legacy and Social Policy in the British Caribbean', in *Colonialism and Welfare: Social Policy and the British Imperial Legacy*, ed. by James Midgley and David Piachaud (Cheltenham: Edward Elgar, 2011) 55–70

Heuman, Gad, *The Killing Time: The Morant Bay Rebellion in Jamaica* (Knoxville, TN: University of Tennessee Press, 1995)

Higman, B.W., *Slave Populations of the British Caribbean, 1807–1834* (Kingston: The University of the West Indies Press, 1995)

Innes, Joanna, 'The "Mixed Economy of Welfare" in Early Modern England: Assessments of the Options from Hale to Malthus (c. 1683–1803)', in *Charity, Self-Interest and Welfare in the English Past*, ed. by Martin Daunton (London: Taylor & Francis, 2005) 104–134

Kant, Immanuel, *Kant: Natural Science* (Cambridge: Cambridge University Press, 2012)

Kierner, Cynthia, *Inventing Disaster: The Culture of Calamity from the Jamestown Colony to the Johnstown Flood* (Chapel Hill, NC: University of North Carolina Press, 2019)

Kiple, Kenneth F., *The Caribbean Slave: A Biological History* (Cambridge: Cambridge University Press, 2002)

Knight, Franklin C., *Working the Diaspora: The Impact of African Labor on the Anglo-American World, 1650–1850* (New York: New York University Press, 2012)

Longshore, David, *Encyclopedia of Hurricanes, Typhoons, and Cyclones* (New York: Infobase Publishing, 2010)

Macpherson, Anne, *From Colony to Nation: Women Activists and the Gendering of Politics in Belize, 1912–82* (Lincoln: University of Nebraska Press, 2007)

Marsh, Peter T., *Joseph Chamberlain: Entrepreneur in Politics* (New Haven: Yale University Press, 1994)

Molesky, Mark, *The Gulf of Fire: The Destruction of Lisbon, or Apocalypse in the Age of Science and Reason* (New York: Knopf, 2015)

Mulcahy, Matthew, *Hurricanes and Society in the British Greater Caribbean, 1624–1783* (Baltimore, MD: Johns Hopkins University Press, 2006)

Newman, Peter K., 'Canada's Role in the West Indian trade before 1912', in *Canada and the Commonwealth Caribbean*, ed. by Brian Douglas Tennyson (Lanham, MD: University Press of America, 1987) 105–125

O'Loughlin, Karen Fay and Lander, James F., *Caribbean Tsunamis: A 500-Year History from 1498–1998* (Dordrecht: Springer, 2003)

O'Shaughnessy, Andrew Jackson, *An Empire Divided: The American Revolution and the British Caribbean* (Philadelphia, PA: University of Pennsylvania Press, 2000)

Oliver-Smith, Anthony, 'Peru's Five-Hundred-Year Earthquake', in *Disasters, Development and Environment*, ed. by Ann Varley (Chichester: John Wiley & Sons, 1994) 74–88

Paton, Diana, *No Bond but the Law: Punishment, Race, and Gender in Jamaican State Formation, 1780–1870* (Durham, NC: Duke University Press, 2004)

Pattullo, Polly, *Your Time is Done Now: Slavery, Resistance, and Defeat: The Maroon Trials of Dominica (1813–1814)* (London: Papillote Press, 2015)

Pawson, Michael and Buisseret, David, *Port Royal, Jamaica* (Kingston: The University of the West Indies Press, 2000)

Petley, Christer, '"Home" and "This Country": Britishness and Creole Identity in the Letters of a Transatlantic Slaveholder', *Atlantic Studies*, 6:1 (2009) 43–61

Raffe, Alasdair, 'Nature's Scourges: The Natural World and Special Prayers, Fasts and Thanksgivings, 1541–1866', *Studies in Church History*, 46 (2010) 237–247

Richardson, Bonham C., *The Caribbean in the Wider World, 1492–1992* (Cambridge: Cambridge University Press, 1992)

Richardson, Bonham C., *Economy and Environment in the Caribbean: Barbados and the Windwards in the Late 1800s* (Kingston: The University of the West Indies Press, 1997)

Richardson, Bonham C., *Igniting the Caribbean's Past: Fire in British West Indian History* (Chapel Hill, NC: University of North Carolina Press, 2004)

Richardson, Bonham C., *Panama Money in Barbados, 1900–1920* (Knoxville, TN: University of Tennessee, 1986)

Roberts, Justin, 'The "Better Sort" and the "Poorer Sort": Wealth Inequalities, Family Formation and the Economy of Energy on British Caribbean Sugar Plantations, 1750–1800', *Slavery and Abolition*, 35:3 (2014) 458–473

Roddy, Sarah, Strange, Julie-Marie and Taithe, Bertrand, *The Charity Market and Humanitarianism in Britain, 1870–1912* (London: Bloomsbury, 2019)

Roy, Tirthanker, '"The Law of Storms": European and Indigenous Response to Natural Disasters in Colonial India, c. 1800–1850', *Australian Economic History Review*, 50:1 (2010) 6–22

Schwartz, Stuart B., *Sea of Storms: A History of Hurricanes in the Greater Caribbean from Columbus to Katrina* (Princeton, NJ: Princeton University Press, 2015)

Schwartz, Stuart B. and Mulcahy, Matthew, 'Natural Disasters in the Caribbean to 1850', in *Sea and Land: An Environmental History of the Caribbean*, ed. by Phillip D. Morgan (Oxford: Oxford University Press, 2022) 187–252

Sen, Amartya, *Poverty and Famines: An Essay on Entitlement and Deprivation* (Oxford: Oxford University Press, 1981)

Shave, Samantha A., *Pauper Policies: Poor Law and Practice, 1750–1850* (Manchester: Manchester University Press, 2017)

Simonow, Joanna, 'Understanding Humanitarian Action in South Asia: Responses to Famine and Displacement in Nineteenth and Twentieth Century India', working paper, *Humanitarian Policy Group* (2015)

Stanziani, Alessandro, 'The Impact of Cyclones on Nineteenth-Century Réunion', in *Bondage and the Environment in the Indian Ocean World*, ed. by Gwyn Campbell (Cham: Palgrave Macmillan, 2018) 143–162

Taylor, Christopher, *The Black Carib Wars: Freedom, Survival and the Making of the Garifuna* (Jackson: University of Mississippi Press, 2012)

Tilchin, Willaim, *Theodore Roosevelt and the British Empire: A Study in Presidential Statecraft* (New York: St. Martin's, 1997)

Voltaire, *Toleration and Other Essays*, trans. Joseph McCabe (New York: The Knickerbocker Press, 1912)

Waterhouse, Carlton, 'Failed Plans and Planned Failures: The Lower Ninth Ward, Hurricane Katrina and the Continuing Story of Environmental Injustice', in *Hurricane Katrina: America's Unnatural Disaster*, ed. by Jeremy I. Levitt and Matthew C. Whitaker (Lincoln, NE: University of Nebraska Press, 2009) 156–182

Welch, Pedro L.V., 'Post-Emancipation Adjustments in the Urban Context: Views from Bridgetown, Barbados', in *In the Shadow of the Plantation: Caribbean History and Legacy*, ed. by Alvin O. Thompson (Kingston: Ian Randle, 2002), pp. 266–282.

Williams, Eric, *Capitalism and Slavery* (Chapel Hill, NC: University of North Carolina Press, 1994)

Winchester, Simon, *Krakatoa: The Day the World Exploded, August 27 1883* (London: Penguin Books, 2004)

Wisner, Ben, Gaillard, J.C. and Kelman, Ilan, 'Introduction to Part I', in *The Routledge Handbook of Hazards and Disaster Risk Reduction*, ed. by Ben Wisner, J.C. Gaillard and Ilan Kelman (Abingdon: Routledge, 2011) 11–17

Worster, Donald, *Dust Bowl: The Southern Plains in the 1930s* (Oxford: Oxford University Press, 1979)

Zacek, Natalie A., *Settler Society in the English Leeward Islands, 1670–1776* (Cambridge: Cambridge University Press, 2010)

Unpublished theses

Crawford, Nicholas, 'Calamity's Empire: Slavery, Scarcity, and the Political Economy of Provisioning in the British Caribbean, c. 1775–1834' (unpublished PhD thesis, Harvard University, 2016)

Emeruwa, Linda E., 'The British West Indies, 1897–1902, with Special Reference to the Implementation of the 1897 Royal Commission Report' (unpublished MPhil thesis, University of London, 1973)

Lightfoot, Natasha, 'Race, Class and Resistance: Emancipation and its Aftermath in Antigua, 1831–1858' (PhD thesis, New York University, 2007)

Matlock, Julie Yates, 'The Process of Colonial Adaptation: English Responses to the 1692 Earthquake at Port Royal' (unpublished Master's thesis, Eastern Kentucky University, 2012)

Spinelli, Joseph, 'Land Use and Population in St Vincent, 1763–1960: A Contribution to the Study of the Patterns of Economic and Demographic Change in a Small West Indian Island' (unpublished PhD thesis, University of Florida, 1973)

Index

absenteeism 42, 52, 54
Act for the Abolition of the Slave Trade 28
African-Caribbean population 1, 2, 6, 13, 15, 29, 34, 49, 57, 62, 68, 93, 99, 101, 109, 149
  British attempts to control 3, 5, 7, 36, 50, 54, 76, 83, 90–91, 92, 100, 101, 103–105, 107–108, 112, 113, 118, 124, 128–129, 172–173
  'lack of' documents written by 15
  response to disaster 77–78, 80, 102, 103, 116, 119, 129–130, 154, 177
America
  aid to the British Caribbean 157–159, 162, 165, 173
  comparison with Caribbean 42, 55
  hurricane warning system 65–66
  imports from 48, 139, 157
  tension with Britain 88, 164, 166
  War of Independence 49
Anguilla 149
Antigua
  earthquake, 1843 51, 59, 102, 143, 154
  hurricane 93, 153
  financial aid 155
apprenticeship system 2, 18, 90–91, 93, 99

Bahamas
  hurricane 1866 51, 106–109
Baptist War 90
Barbados
  colonisation of 19
  environment 14, 45

financial aid
  1781 27–28
  1831 89–90, 141, 146, 153–154
  1898 112, 147, 156
hurricanes
  1780 26
  1831 1–2, 34, 47, 50, 51, 59, 74, 76–83, 142–143
  1898 48, 51, 57, 65, 110–116, 146
  perceived overpopulation 109
Bayley, Frederick 55, 56, 57, 59
Beckford, William 26, 35
Beeston, William 23
beet sugar *see* sugar beet
Belize
  hurricane
    1934 172
    1961 174
Bermuda 36, 63
British Caribbean
  colonisation of 4–5
  comparison with French Caribbean colonies 55, 58
  developments in the eighteenth century 42
  developments in the nineteenth century 7–8, 100, 144
  environment 8–9
  white perception of 52, 61
British Guiana 114, 125
Bruce (Sir), Charles 64, 160
Burdon, John 173–174
Bussa's Rebellion 80

Canada 157–158, 164
Chamberlain, Joseph 54, 114, 120–122, 137, 148–150, 156, 177
Cowper, William 32

Darrell (Rev), J.H. 120, 121, 122
Davis (Admiral), Charles 129, 131–132, 161–167, 177
days of humiliation and fast 23, 36, 37
Dominica
  colonisation of 48
  financial aid 154
  hurricanes
    1780 26
    1834 34, 47, 74, 91–92, 142–143
  labour strike 94

emancipation 5–7, 13, 90, 103, 109, 113, 126, 132
  Act of 52, 90
enslaved people 1, 2, 5, 7, 24, 35, 36, 44, 49, 76, 78, 79, 84
equalisation of sugar duties 18, 100, 109

famines in Ireland and India 6, 94, 114
Fitzroy (sir), Charles 102
food shortages 43, 49, 52, 84, 91–92, 108
France 55–56, 100
  foreign relations with 27, 159–160
freedom after apprenticeship 100
Froude, James 42, 57, 163

Garifuna people 84–89
Goethe, Johann Wolfgang von 30
Gómez, Antonio Soberanis 172, 175
Graeme, Laurence 36
Grey (Sir), Edward 151
Guadeloupe earthquake, 1843 102–103

Hay (Sir), J.S. 110–111, 114–115, 146
Hodges, E.A. 166
Hurricane Katrina 11
hurricane shelters 56

import duties, suspension of 139–141

Jamaica
  earthquakes
    1692 20–22, 24, 26
    1907 66–67, 125, 127–128, 130, 131, 150, 161

financial relief
  1781 27–28
  1907 151, 156
hurricanes
  1780 26
  1812 50
  1815 46
  1903 51
  Kingston 24, 57–58, 66, 67, 125–131, 151–152, 156, 161–166, 177
  Port Royal 21, 24

Kant, Immanuel 30
King-Harman, Charles 149
Krakatoa, eruption of 146

La Réunion 95
Labouchère, Henry 145
landslides 46
Lisbon Earthquake 29–31
Llewelyn (Sir), R.B. 118–125
Lyon, (Sir) James 34, 36, 77, 78, 80, 93, 157

Macgregor, Evan 36, 93, 140
Mansion House Fund 147, 150–151
Maroons 93
Martinique 55–56, 57–58, 160, 162
  volcanic eruption in 159
Moloney, Cornelius 110–113, 115–117, 146, 148, 160
Morant Bay Rebellion 127, 161

New Poor Law Amendment 6, 105–106
Nuttall, Enos 130–131, 151

Panama Canal 66, 152, 161
Petitioning for financial aid 138, 142
Piddington, Henry 64
plantations 43, 53, 76

Rawson W. 106–109, 157
Reid (Lieutenant Colonel), William 60, 63
resilience (technical concept) 10, 63
Reynold (Sir), Alleyne 78–80
Royal Commission of 1897 110, 117, 156, 163, 177

Slavery Abolition Act 1833
Sloane, Hans 21, 22, 25
St Kitts and Nevis 149
St Lucia
  Hurricane 1898 48, 65, 110
  financial aid 148
St Vincent
  financial aid *1812* 152–153 *1898*
    11, 147, 156
  hurricanes
    1780 26 1831, 34
    1898 48, 65, 110–117, 146
  volcanic eruptions
    1812 19, 33, 50, 83–84, 125,
      142–143, 152
    1902 50, 51, 118–120, 132, 137,
      150
Sturge, Joseph 49, 52, 99, 154

sugar beet 54, 100, 109, 147, 149,
  161
Swettenham, Alexander 125, 128, 130,
  161–167, 177

Tangshan earthquake 10–11
Taylor, Simon 53, 56
telegraph network in Caribbean 111
Tobago
  hurricane, 1847 50, 51, 103
  financial aid 155

Voltaire 30
vulnerability (technical concept) 10,
  52, 54

West India Committee 66, 148, 151
West India Regiment (WIR) 126–129

EU authorised representative for GPSR:
Easy Access System Europe, Mustamäe tee 50,
10621 Tallinn, Estonia
gpsr.requests@easproject.com